SOCIOLOGY AND SOCIAL WELFARE SERIES

edited by Paul Halmos

Social Science and Social Purpose

A Reader in Social Administration
edited by A. V. S. Lochhead

Exercises in Social Science
J. Liggett and R. Cochrane

Industrial Democracy
Paul Blumberg

Social Science
and Social Purpose

T. S. Simey

*Lord Simey of Toxteth, Professor of
Social Science, University of Liverpool*

Constable London

First published in 1968
by Constable and Co Ltd
10 Orange Street London WC2
Copyright © 1968 by Lord Simey of Toxteth
All rights reserved
Printed in Great Britain
by The Anchor Press Ltd, Tiptree, Essex
SBN 09 455960 0

Contents

Preface

The subject of this book relates to important issues concerning the formulation of public policies in the large societies that have come to dominate our lives in the twentieth century. These societies are both urban and industrial, and the quality of citizenship in them is making it more and more difficult to associate the ordinary man with the daily business of government and administration. The present-day machinery of representative government, national and local, was designed in the nineteenth century to overcome this problem, but the twentieth century has been forced to accept a tendency to decide public issues in ways which are necessarily more remote from the lives and interests of the ordinary man. Common sense is no longer adequate to cope with governmental problems, and the search for experts and an expertise that can take its place is becoming ever more urgent, and perhaps somewhat critical. In consequence, the formulation of the fundamental values that guide our lives is increasingly a concern of the state alone, with public bodies and the civil service acting as trustees of the nation's conscience, responsible in such matters to private citizens only indirectly and distantly.

The issue derives its urgency from the fact that the future of modern societies, and indeed their very survival, has come to depend on the solving of at least the more urgent of the ever more urgent difficulties of the modern world. The continued existence of a democratic way of life that is something more than a mere appearance, or the insubstantial outcome of beliefs and traditions inherited from past ages, depends on the way in which we set about such tasks in the social and political world which we know. Indeed, the quality of contemporary citizenship can be said to be determined by the methods local communities adopt to inform themselves about problems, concern themselves with the discovery of viable solutions to them, and carry them into effect. In a world of rapid and fundamental change, the intensity and complexity of which increases day by day, it is therefore doubly necessary to arrive at a clear understanding of the task now before us; it is high time that we approached it with all the wisdom we can command, and set about it with greater determination than we have displayed in the postwar period. This is even more evident at a time when things are so much more difficult for us than they ever have been in peacetime, and the necessity to get to grips with events has become increasingly urgent.

It is especially unfortunate, therefore, that the theories which underlie policy-making often assume that, in so far as the process must be guided in directions determined by values, evaluation is in the last analysis a matter only of self-interest, the outcome of a struggle to satisfy one's desires, and to secure as much as one can for oneself, one's family, class, trade or profession, or one's nation. The theories of the utilitarians have been presented to us again, in a new guise. Undoubtedly, the Hitlers, Mussolinis and Stalins of the world have had many successes to their credit in recent years when they have followed this line, but that is not to say that they have had right or truth on their side. We must look at the problems of mankind once again, from this point of view in particular. Is it really true that policy-making is just a sophisticated kind of self-seeking? Should the policy-maker merely allow himself to swim with the tide, using modern gadgets like opinion polls and computers to list what the issues are that are likely to call for decision, and discover what people's naïve thoughts are about the ways in which they should be decided? This seems to be about to become the most typical of the difficulties that the politician has to face in the twentieth century. And the effort to avoid it by asserting (despite the immediate past) that it must be handed over to other wiser, better informed, and more adequately equipped people than the ordinary citizen may be considered to be one of the most ultimate rationalisations of the twentieth century.

Pursued to its logical conclusion, this argument constitutes a challenge to the belief that the ordinary man is capable of taking a broad and dispassionate view of society and politics. So is the belief, now current, that his opinions on public issues are mere epiphenomena, derived from the impact on his life of the economic order, or the outcome of his experiences of family living, as so many social scientists would have us suppose. This kind of theorising leads to the conclusion that man is nothing more than a mere creature of his times. It is impossible for him, if this is so, to give adequate consideration to the real issues of our public life, immensely complex and difficult to grasp as they are today. It is equally hard even to begin to cope with them, for the mass society that is characteristic of the present century is unfitted to take the necessary action that this seems to demand.

This book has been written in the belief that the time has come to question whether these underlying assumptions are justified. More specifically, the task that has been attempted in the succeeding chapters has been to show what contribution the social scientist can make to the understanding and solving of social problems, and how he is concerned with the values implied in the very nature of the problems themselves. It is suggested that the most urgent step required of the social scientist is to turn away from the negative idea that, because we are all exposed to the influence of impersonal 'forces' in the social world, social science has no alternative but to observe the ways in which we are compelled to swim (or drift) with the current of our time rather than strike out in a direction of our own. Such a view implies an outdated conception of science, just as it does unduly narrow limits to the functioning of the human mind. The discussion of this issue leads to the conclusion that there is a more positive way of studying human endeavour which might well be adopted. As Lord Lindsay put it, science should be imaginative, original, and daring.[1] Reason is a purely creative activity; in Kant's language, it is practical and imperative, the source of moral ends and purposes, the creator of values.

As against the optimism which is the essence of these thoughts, however, we are confronted by the pessimism embodied in the intellectual struggles of so many social scientists today. Too often they seem to be driven by a fundamental hunger for the untroubled world of certainties, to assert that man is determined in his social behaviour by physical or social forces out of his control, and that the function of the social scientist is not to free him from this kind of slavery to events and influences so much as to prove that social conditioning does in fact operate. Yet surely, what the citizen of today needs to know is precisely how the opposite process can be brought to life; how man can escape from this kind of subjection. He can have little use for social sciences which exist to persuade us to submit ourselves to our several fates, without complaint. It is the purpose of this book to argue that the true objective of the social sciences is fundamentally different. Not only should they enable us to live our lives more intelligently and to greater purpose in the conditions of today, but they should also seek to spell out in some detail Shakespeare's remark that, if we are to some extent the playthings of fate,

> The fault, dear Brutus, is not in our stars,
> But in ourselves, that we are underlings.[2]

Before we can discuss how exactly the social sciences could play a more positive role in our lives and our affairs, as this would require, it is necessary to examine what it is that they do at present attempt to achieve. If it is 'facts', and facts alone, that interest them, then it is easy for a social scientist to devote himself to his study without getting himself involved in any kind of trouble, academic or political. But is it possible to do so, save in a world of dreams? He can, and he often does, seek refuge under the 'value-free' umbrella that Weber sometimes used, to shelter himself from attack, and attempt to stick closely to the 'facts' of historical analysis and contemporary observation. Yet if he does so, it is doubtful, to say the least, whether he can overcome the problems of relevance and significance and, lacking a standpoint of his own, the facts he collects become the contents of the 'ditty bag of an idiot', as Robert S. Lynd put it. They can hardly be said to be the data out of which anything like a genuine science can be constructed.

The issue that underlies this discussion is really quite simple, but social scientists have found it exceedingly hard to reach agreement about it, perhaps because of its very simplicity. The scientist, it is argued, must be 'objective', in the sense that his theories must be based solely on the subject matter to which they are intended to relate, to the exclusion of his own desires and emotions. This can be difficult enough in the natural sciences, but what of the social sciences, which deal with man's behaviour? Can the social scientist remain aloof from everyday concerns, and at the same time come to understand anything of the realities of social life? And can he do so without involving himself to some extent in the troubles and achievements of his times? If he really does understand how it is that the ways of life of the world in which he lives have come to exist, he must surely be prepared to help with solving some of the most urgent difficulties that confront it, and accept any request to collaborate in furthering the legitimate purposes of his fellow-citizens that may be made to him.

The problem of how to observe a situation without changing it confronts some scientists more acutely than others. It may be a matter of important concern to atomic physicists, but the social scientist, who is himself sometimes a part of the societies or situations which he investigates, necessarily finds it particularly hard to overcome. He has to accept the fact that his own life must be lived in the social world; if this is so, his theories must apply to his own conduct, and cannot but influence it. There is no escape from this, though some social scientists may regard themselves as exceptions to their own explanations of other people's behaviour; this sometimes leads them into situations which are either absurd, or involve them in reducing the status of their 'science' so low that it becomes a mere collection of glimpses of what would be the obvious, to a man of common sense.

It will be argued, therefore, that it is impossible for a social scientist to try to keep himself aloof from common concerns, in order to preserve his objectivity. It will also be argued, perhaps more cogently, that he must be ready despite all the difficulties 'to become involved in the search for moral and social solutions to the problems thrown up by the advance of science'.[3] To the assertion that the pursuit of science and the solving of problems on the relatively narrow front of scientific advancement are fundamentally different activities, the reply will be made that scientific knowledge is at least 'a great advantage' to this kind of problem-solving. The argument will, indeed, be taken further to support the claim that scientific knowledge 'sometimes is even essential' for the making of value judgments required as a basis for remedial action.[4] Here lies the underlying theme of the present book, which attempts to discover how far and in what sense the clarification and the formulation of values is a truly scientific activity, and whether this requires the widening of the concept of social science to incorporate some of the attributes of philosophical criticism. The social sciences in general, and sociology in particular, will be presented as life sciences with special characteristics of their own, and it is hoped that it will be possible to show that they can function as such, despite the multitude of difficulties and problems that they have to overcome.

My thanks must be given to Professor Feichin O'Doherty, of the National University of Ireland, for his encouragement and his suggestions over many years. They are also due to Professor Irving Louis Horowitz, of Washington University, St Louis, who has helped me to understand a growing body of opinion in the United States whose views are of vital importance to the argument which I have presented, and who has made unfamiliar material available to me. I must also express my most personal gratitude and thanks to my colleagues and students in the Social Science Department of the University of Liverpool, who have become and remained my friends despite (or because of) three years of intensive discussion, based on the manuscript of this book.

The assistance of Miss Lythgoe, Superintendent of the Arts Library of the University of Liverpool, and my secretaries, Miss Kerfoot and Mrs Webster, has been as welcome to me as it has been essential, in turning the illegible manuscript which I have presented to them into readable drafts.

Acknowledgments

I should like to thank the following authors, publishers and other bodies for permission to quote from their work: The London School of Economics and G. Bell & Sons Ltd for L. T. Hobhouse's *Sociology and Philosophy* including Morris Ginsberg's introduction; The Free Press of Glencoe and Collier-Macmillan Inc. for Daniel Bell's *The End of Ideology: On the Exhaustion of Political Ideas*, Edward Shils' *The Present State of American Sociology*, and Edward Shils' and Henry A. Finch's *Max Weber and the Methodology of the Social Sciences*; Associated Book Publishers Ltd for Maurice Merleau-Ponty's *The Structure of Behaviour* published by Methuen; The Passfield Trust for Sidney and Beatrice Webb's *Methods of Social Study* and *Our Partnership*; Oxford University Press for Lord Lindsay's *Religion, Science and Society*; Faber and Faber Ltd for J. P. Mayer's *Max Weber and German Politics*; Heinemann Educational Books Ltd for S. M. Lipset's *Political Man*; Stanford University Press for David Lerner's and Harold Lasswell's *The Policy Sciences*; Routledge and Kegan Paul Ltd for Gunnar Myrdal's *Value in Social Theory* and *Political Element in the Development of Economic Theory*, and Harold Lasswell's *The Analysis of Political Behaviour*; Edward Shils for 'The End of Ideology' which first appeared in *Encounter*; and Duncker und Humblot for Franz Boese's *Geschichte des Vereins für Sozialpolitik*.

1. Introduction

The age in which we are now living is 'scientific' in the sense that we have come to rely on technology (or applied science) to provide us with the means of satisfying our basic requirements for food, clothing, and shelter. But does that make it desirable for us to be social scientists, or to develop a natural science of society? It is true that, from the Industrial Revolution onwards, science has enabled us to meet our needs in Great Britain and other western countries much more abundantly than at any time in previous ages, or in countries which have not yet been industrialised and are still being 'developed'. The West has shown what the possibilities are, and, in consequence, citizens all over the world demand today, insistently and urgently, that heed be given to establishing or improving social welfare in the way that the application of sciences to the business of earning a livelihood, community living, and family life has made possible. Is this the concern of 'science' as such, or of 'social' rather than 'natural' science, or both, and, if so, what are the interests of each? Much has been achieved, at least in the countries of the western world, and in some others such as Japan and Israel; but even so still greater plenty, or the first fruits of plenty, can be made to come from the cornucopia of science, if we will. Can we, we must now ask ourselves, bring this about? Can the social scientist, as distinct from his colleagues the natural scientists, play a special part in this endeavour? Can he facilitate the organisation of society for the production and the distribution of goods, and thus increase productivity by showing how people can take part in processes of production to greater effect, and at the same time maximise social welfare by demonstating how it can best be distributed, and the productive energies of mankind be aroused? And can we go further than this, and conclude that a basic rather than an applied science of society can be developed which can settle the vexed questions of government and administration 'objectively', as is often said today, without raising insoluble issues of morality, individual purpose, and social justice?

We must, at the same time, be equally mindful of the possibilities for disaster with which the future is charged by somewhat lopsided developments in science and scientific technology. The achievements of the biochemist may have revolutionised nutrition, but preventive medicine has increased numbers so rapidly that there is now a so-called 'population explosion' in many parts of the world, and with the conquest of diseases we have raised for ourselves the menace of the starvation of millions in the East. The physicist has presented us with the infinite blessing of atomic energy, but this is overshadowed by the spectre of the Bomb, a consideration that is not trite because it is so terribly true. Is there any hope, we have to ask ourselves, that the social sciences may enable us to understand, and control, human nature and human societies, and thus make it possible to tame and domesticate the human animal? Is there any real prospect of outlawing conflict between peoples and nations and mastering human passions so that what used to be called man's 'better nature' will predominate over his tendencies towards the destructiveness and cruelty which so impoverish the world, both spiritually and materially? It is, as yet, impossible to be optimistic. What our Victorian ancestors called 'progress' presented us with a bill which we have been called upon to pay, too often, with a blank cheque. We now find ourselves wondering whether we have purchased even material security with it, let alone social or psychological security. Our fears that the mushroom cloud we associate with scientific 'progress' will destroy mankind can only be kept in check by faith, and faith alone. There is no strictly rational argument that is available to us to quieten disturbed minds today. Whether or not the social scientist will be able to produce anything of the kind is a mystery that lies hidden in the future.

The processes of rapid material advancement which have been seen at work in western countries have undeniably led to substantial improvements in social welfare in terms of the lengthening of the expectation of life, the enjoyment of leisure, both day by day and at the beginning and end of life. They have also been seen in the spread of formal education and the greater availability of medical services and better housing. All this is accompanied by rapid social changes in the intricate machinery of an increasingly urban and industrial civilisation. Levels of living rise, partly at the cost of rejecting tradition in matters of manufacture, commerce, communications, and indeed in everything else to do with the manipulation of the material and social world; we make more, buy and sell more, and we travel further, faster and more often as the days go by. But the process does not stop at this. Many of the consequences of the economic and social upheavals which are associated with the new ways of living are infinitely complex, unforeseen, and unwanted. The new 'continuous' industrial processes, that cannot be stopped to suit human convenience, disrupt social life, not only within the family; they are also of critical importance in its religious, cultural, and recreational phases as well. They may bring with them higher incomes for some, but also social disaster for others, including whole families and communities. The replacement of a synthetic for a natural material may spell ruin for manufacturing towns in Lancashire and Louisiana, and for farming communities in both the West and East Indies, as well as prosperity for chemical engineering industries elsewhere. A new method of carrying out office work may take a clerk's job away from him, and leave him so bereft that it is unlikely that he will ever get another. And conversely, of course, if the processes are properly managed, the whole world may advance into prosperity as one united brotherhood. Or so we may hope.

Today, we are perhaps more conscious of the problems and the menace of innovation than our forefathers were only half a century ago. We no longer rest content in the complacent belief that the manufacture of more tons of pig iron and yards of calico is irrefutable evidence of the onward march of human progress. The appalling destruction of two world wars, the unspeakable wickedness of the concentration camps in Germany, the tortures in Algeria, the oppression of the human spirit in Soviet Russia and South Africa and of the Negro generally, the failure all over the world to understand the true nature of the phenomenon of juvenile crime, and the neglect of it by the multitude of those who just do not or cannot care: all these things testify to the fact that the human struggle against hatred, misery, and vice has gone only a pitifully short way along the road to ultimate achievement. Today, few of us are confident about these things, and many of us seem to be content to live in the present, rather than to continue to struggle to keep our steadfastness of purpose alive, which has hitherto vitalised our community and religious life. How far are these things the concern of science, how far of morals? How far can

B

science be trusted as a secure guide to replace the uncertain foundation of faith and belief on which our society has relied hitherto? We are weary of responsibility, tired of trusting our own judgment. We are eager for science to shoulder part of our burdens at least; but can we, we must now ask, seek its aid in our present difficulties and dilemmas, and how, exactly, are we to do so?

This book is concerned with the fundamental problems which arise when an attempt is made to match the scientific thinking of the natural scientists of the twentieth century – particularly the physicists – with the understanding of social scientists. It must be asked now, how far this has advanced in our own lifetime, and whether the process can be made to go further. The member of the Royal Society of the eighteenth – even the late nineteenth – century would be utterly at a loss to understand the concepts now relied on in the investigation of the material universe, but in matters of government, education, crime, and the literary culture generally, ways of thinking are nothing like so different. The pioneers of the eighteenth century, Rousseau, Howard, Montesquieu, and the French *philosophes* generally, would not feel themselves in an entirely foreign society today. But our natural science, its achievements and potentialities, would both mystify and terrify them, and be incomprehensible to their colleagues who were learned in natural philosophy. How can the social sciences, therefore, be brought up to date?

II

Before we can answer this question, we need to know more about science itself. The scientific truth of our day has come to be concerned with the physical world of things, which now includes one aspect or another of human behaviour, regarded as a 'thing' rather than as a part of the world of objectives, purposes, and values. Science takes no direct part in the struggle to better the world; it does not seek to fortify the good or restrain the bad. 'Science', it has been argued, 'concerns itself with matters of fact. It excludes the determination of value. . . . Science is concerned with events; not with doings and what is done. Consequently, it permits of no explanation through intention or purpose. This is a consequence of the proper limitation of science.'[1] But what we are troubled with at the moment is not knowing more about the natural world; we are getting along pretty well with that endeavour. The kind of ignorance which most troubles us is about the world of purposes and intentions, of responsibilities and 'concerns', which is, it is thought, out of bounds to the natural scientist. Here it will be suggested that the social sciences, unlike the natural, do deal with human purposes, the ways in which they are formulated, and the means established for their achievement. That is their most primary task. It is of critical importance, because it is 'science' that is called on today to help us to solve so many specifically human problems, and if human purposes are beyond its reach, we are back in the seventeenth century, where the natural sciences split off from human knowledge on their own, and we have come to the end of the road of understanding. Lord Snow touched on our predicament in the seminal lecture he gave in 1959 on *The Two Cultures*, and the depth of the interest he aroused is evidence of the seriousness of the problem he touched on. We have come to recognise our intellectual confusion, with his help; it is now so great as to lead to despair on the part of many of our colleagues, and the time has undoubtedly come to endeavour to clarify our thinking, and find a new way ahead. Lord Snow has stated the view, with considerable clarity and emphasis, that 'the intellectual life of the whole of western society is increasingly being split into two polar groups'. On the one hand, there are the "literary intellectuals"; on the other, the scientists, especially the physical scientists:

> Between the two a gulf of mutual incomprehension – sometimes (particularly among the young) hostility and dislike, but most of all lack of understanding. . . . Their attitudes are so different that, even on the level of emotion, they can't find much common ground. Non-scientists tend to think of scientists as brash and boastful. . . . [They] have a rooted impression that the scientists are shallowly optimistic, unaware of man's condition. On the other hand, the scientists believe that the literary intellectuals are totally lacking in foresight, particularly unconcerned with their brother men, in a deep sense anti-intellectual, anxious to restrict both art and thought to the existential moment.[2]

The result is that scientists tend to be self-impoverished, in the sense that their imaginative understanding is less than it could be. On the other hand non-scientists tend to be, as it were, tone-deaf over an immense range of intellectual experience. The literary intellectual is only too often ignorant of the language of science, and it is becoming more and more difficult to build bridges between the cultures as the years go by.[3] We tend to rest more or less comfortably in the belief that Science deals with Things, existing in the external world, whilst values are the concern of the literary culture. As Professor Macmurray has pointed out:

> when we contrast fact and value, the conceptual opposition leads to the assumption that the contrasted elements are on the same level and existentially exclusive. In the same fashion we tend to think that these are entities in the same sense and at the same level.

There is, in fact, no way of making anything like an uncompromising separation of fact from value, so that they can be kept apart in two watertight compartments. Professor Macmurray continued his philosophical argument by stating: 'It is clear that any assertion of value presupposes what is matter of fact; and the experience of value includes and supervenes upon the apprehension of fact. It is always fact that is valued.'[4] Looking at the matter from the scientific point of view, Lord Snow emphasises very strongly the importance of the intellectual and moral values which are inherent in the very existence of a natural science. 'There is', he writes, 'a moral component right in the grain of science itself, and almost all scientists form their own judgments of the moral life.' The more profound the knowledge of an author of the processes of scientific discovery, the more he appears to be aware of this, and to be ready to 'demonstrate the intellectual, aesthetic, and moral values inherent in the pursuit of science'.[5] While Professor Macmurray writes:

> Scientific activity, just because it is a human activity, is involved in valuation. To do is to choose; and to choose is to determine, as between alternative courses of action, which is the better. To be a scientist, after all, is to assert and live by the value of knowledge, and the sort of knowledge which science provides.[6]

These statements may be compared with the even more forthright pronouncement by A. N. Whitehead that it was only after the seventeenth century that 'the famous mechanistic theory of nature . . . reigned supreme, [and became] the orthodox creed of physical science, [so that] physicists took no more interest in philosophy, and came to illustrate by their behaviour the anti-rationalism of the Historical Revolt'. Nevertheless, he added, 'the history of thought in the eighteenth and nineteenth centuries is governed by the fact that the world had got hold of a general idea which it could neither live with nor live without'.[7] To Max Planck 'the ordinary scientist, who does not believe in the positivist attitude, admits the validity of the aesthetic standpoint and the ethical standpoint; but he recognises them as belonging to *another way of looking at nature*. Such a way does not come within the province of physical science.'[8] There is nothing in what scientific writers say which attempts to undermine moral or aesthetic theory; it is positivism which is attacked by them, and their writings show a readiness to adopt a wide point of view which accepts that the truths discovered by the natural scientists are only part of a much wider concept of truth itself, in which several kinds of truth may be contained.

Physical science, then, may be one thing, but the literary culture another. We now see that this dichotomy leads us into a blind alley, from which there appears to be no escape, and we ask, yet again, whether there is any other alternative. Can it be that social science is a third way of looking at things which is both scientific in the sense that it tries to show how human affairs are interlocked with the material, and 'literary' in the sense that it shows the influence purposes have in social affairs? Can we now develop a form of science which deals dispassionately and objectively with the realisation of man's purposes in regard to social welfare, and social organisation as a means of promoting them? Can mankind at last redeem itself from the frustrations of social entanglements? How far, we must now ask, are these part and parcel of our unalterable human nature, or is this as malleable as physical nature has now shown herself to be in so many ways? How, then, can the sociologist be a scientist? Unless he becomes aware of the existence of material that is objective because it does not depend on his intuition, desires, or beliefs, the study can in no sense be a science. But unless he has a lively appreciation of the living processes of evaluation and of taking up a position in society and actually experiencing the joys and sorrows, the understanding and the ignorance, and the achievements and failures that are the lot of the human being on this earth today, here and now, the social scientist is likely to go badly wrong in his appraisal of the significance of the events he studies, however many public opinion polls he conducts, or however many schedules he completes that are based on interviews or observations of the social scene.

Values, then, are part of the life-blood of his enquiries. To study them is a collaborative task in which the social scientist will join with other scholars, and it is the fact that he is compelled to do so that makes his science different from that of his colleague in the natural sciences. The disentangling of the rational or intelligent element from the unconscious factor in social processes is the task of the social as contrasted with the natural scientist, and it is the fact that he brings science into relation with the arts in this way that has led Lord Snow to welcome a means of bringing together the 'polar extremes' of the scientific and the literary cultures. There is something in sociology, he feels, 'which speaks the language of science, and something in it which is available to persons in the literary culture. It is no better than a very frail and often a very dubious bridge, but I would have thought it could be taught here with advantage to our entire intellectual world.'[9] It is this position and status that would be lost to the social sciences if their special responsibility for the consideration of values were lost.

III

We may therefore conclude from the foregoing that mankind has benefited in no small measure from the application of the natural sciences; man's primary requirements for food, clothing, and shelter are now fully met in many (admittedly privileged) societies in ever-increasing abundance as the years go by. Social welfare is increased by the development of new sciences, such as bacteriology, biochemistry, and genetics; preventive medicine becomes increasingly efficient, for instance, and nutrition is greatly improved by the synthesis of vitamins, whilst the application of science to plant and livestock breeding (together with the discovery of new fertilisers and pesticides) greatly increases the productivity of agriculture. But at this point social development is found to lag a long way behind technological advance, and that is a theme to which attention must be paid. The rigidities of culture match the progressiveness of science. The population explosion revives the recurrent threat of starvation, which man has had to endure for so many ages; the complexities of the industrial system have made it difficult to deal with the problems of management on the one hand, and of strikes on the other, and the intricacies of urban and industrial societies have made the problems of crime and overcrowding well nigh insoluble. Plenty has produced its own problems, moreover. Above all, the menace of war is ever present, with the ultimate possibility that the use of newly developed weapons may soon extinguish the human race for ever.

Science, of itself, is neither bad nor good; all depends on the kinds of uses that are made of it. No well-informed person would wish to return to the squalor, the disease, and the oppression of the Middle Ages, and there is nothing to lead us to suppose, as some 'literary intellectuals' do, that the utilisation of science in the solving of man's everyday problems is to be regretted because it impoverishes the human spirit. So, let there be more rather than less science. But of what kind? It is for consideration whether the way ahead does not lie in the fashioning of a new kind of science to deal with specific difficulties that now beset us. The troubles of today are now seen to be social rather than physical. It is not the releasing of nuclear energy that concerns us, but the Bomb. It is not the processes or technologies of manufacture or transport, or of engineering or medicine, that hinder the improvement of the welfare of the masses of the people, but the instability of the economy, exemplified in Boom and Slump and the inefficient deployment of managerial skills, and ineffective incentives for the generation and employment of the energies of the workers. We know far too little about the efficient constitution and operation of large-scale economic agencies and administrative bodies. In so far as we can construct new kinds of machines and set them to work, we can produce vastly more goods than the world has ever seen before. Yet this is not the only way of tackling our problems. The balancing of demand with supply not only requires greater productivity. The distribution of the national dividend is the social scientist's responsibility rather than his 'material' colleague's, and it will probably be found at least as important in the future to restrict luxurious and extravagant expenditure, and to distribute wealth more equitably between the various classes and nations, as it is to produce material goods in more adequate quantities.

Although machine power has so largely replaced manpower, we are nevertheless still unable, for mainly social reasons, to build enough houses and roads, hospitals, harbours, and schools to serve our needs at all adequately. We know vastly more about how to use land, but archaic systems of land tenure inhibit the development of a truly modern system of agriculture, and the reconstruction of our cities. Our towns still remind us of the conditions of life that obtained before the industrial revolution, because we have, as yet, no clear vision of the way of life a community should adopt today, let alone in a future age. The motor car obstructs our streets, rather than facilitates rapid transit. The car itself is a product of twentieth-century technology; the streets are constructed to fulfil the purposes that emerged in the minds of our ancestors who rebuilt London after the Great Fire; they exist today as adapted to the uses of Victorian England. And so on. The most worrying problems that now trouble us are the social ones that have been with us for generations, problems of crime and family conflict, of the mental subnormality of the dull and backward and, for the teacher, the education of the minority of the exceptionally intelligent. We still have child neglect to deal with, on the one hand, together with the unofficial strike, crime, prostitution, drunkenness in its modern form of drug-taking and a multitude of similar worries, on the other. As Professor C. Wright Mills has said:

> Man's chief danger today lies in the unruly forces of contemporary society itself, with its alienating methods of production, its enveloping techniques of political domination, its international anarchy – in a word, its pervasive transformations of the very 'nature' of man and the conditions and aims of his life.[10]

Fortunately, there seems to be no evidence that the ideas, theories and concepts on which the physical sciences of today are based have any irremediable tendencies or implications, direct or indirect, which in any way run counter to the promotion of man's welfare, or demand the construction of societies which might be regarded as destructive of the kind of personality we would wish him to have. No scientist today seems to think that evolutionary processes, for instance, demand the existence of a degree of competitiveness in our social organisation, and that the promotion of a system of co-operation weakens individual self-reliance because, in the long run, it produces a pampered type of person who would be unable to play his part in the development, and even in the maintenance, of civilisation. Nature may still be regarded as 'red in tooth and claw' in the animal world, but there is no scientific reason why civilised man should live either a withdrawn or a ruthless life. So we conclude in favour of more science in general, and more social science in particular. But the existence of a social science alongside the natural variety implies the existence of a number of grave logical problems, and to these we must soon turn. Before we do so, we must understand that the emphasis in modern physical science on the creativity and the imaginative powers of man's mind opens up the way to a similar freedom of speculation on the part of the social scientist. That is a helpful beginning. From this point of view the emphasis is on the investigation of possibilities for the development of societies in the interest of greater wellbeing for their members, rather than on the formulation of the precise limits within which human freedom must be deemed to be confined. Man is not to be conceived of as being subject to 'Iron Laws' which are the products of the scientific understanding of his nature. It is for the social scientist to be as free in his speculation as the physicist, and as inventive in his attitude to generalisations as to the nature of the world in which he lives, as the engineer. The natural sciences, pure and applied, may arrive at an understanding of the law of gravitation as a law to which all material bodies are subject. But this is not to be considered to be a 'law' in the legal sense that the practitioner is called upon to apply it in his daily life and to take steps to prevent its breach. It may be universal, but at the same time that does not stop the flight of aircraft; in fact, gravity is only one of the forces to which consideration has to be given in the development of the science of aerodynamics. The engineer who designs an aeroplane in no sense offends the laws of the physical world: in fact, quite the contrary. The same holds good with man's emotional disposition; it is applicable to the oedipus complex, for instance, and to his relations with other members of a social group, and his disastrously xenophobic tendencies.

The social scientist confronted by the fate of man in past ages cannot but be held entranced by prospects for a better future for him. The scientist has gone far to abolish Adam's Curse – the necessity for man to earn his daily bread by the sweat of his brow – by making him the master of machines, and of physical, chemical, and biological processes. If theology clings to ideas about the fallen nature of man, then so much the worse for theology. We can look forward to a time when the Industrial Revolution has gone its full course, and when unskilled labour, with all its degradation, has been done away with altogether by automatically controlled machinery. The electric energy now at our disposal is cheap, convenient for use, and highly transportable. There is no need for the mills in which our descendants will be employed to be in any sense dark and Satanic. Social science has in the creation of the Welfare State done much for humanity; natural science has done as much and more for man's physical environment through modern technology.

Further advance on the social front will require, in the first instance, a considerable clarification of the purposes in man's mind when he plans for the future, and a much greater understanding of the steps he will have to take to attain the objectives which he sets before himself. A new world of this kind can only come into being if the social scientist can find some of the answers to these fundamental problems; although the scientific revolution is 'the only method by which most people can gain the primal things [years of life, freedom from hunger, survival for children]', it will be open to men in the future to 'try to improve the quality of their lives, through an extension of their responsibilities, a deepening of the affection and the spirit, in a fashion which, though we can aim at it for ourselves and our own societies, we can only dimly perceive'.[11] Real affluence in the future depends on social development, particularly in the matter of our onward growth to maturity in our social thinking, and the clarification and integration of our purposes.

IV

It would be foolish to embark on the task of improving social welfare without making oneself clearly aware of the difficulties that must be overcome before any substantial success can be achieved. When social scientists have been confronted with enterprises of this kind, and the spotlight has been turned on them with 'painful directness', they have, in the main, been found to be 'unprepared to assume the required responsibility'. American university administrations, it has been said, are concerned with the short-run 'welfare of an institution', rather than with the long-run welfare of the American (or any other) culture. 'To go ahead frankly into the enlarged opportunity confronting the social sciences invites trouble. Putting one's head into the lion's mouth to operate on a sore tooth has its manifest disadvantages.'[12] Professor Wright Mills came to the conclusion that 'this uneasiness . . . [is], I suppose, part of a general malaise of contemporary intellectual life. Yet perhaps the uneasiness is more acute among social scientists, if only because of the larger promise that has guided much of the earlier work in their fields, the nature of the subjects with which they deal, and the urgent need of significant work today'. In his view, an 'essential feature' of social analysis is its 'direct relevance to urgent public issues and insistent human troubles'. Yet it is only after much preliminary work and much heart-searching on the part of social scientists that he could hope that 'the moral problems of social study – the problem of social science as a public issue – will be recognised, and discussion will become possible.'[13]

A British sociologist, Professor Bottomore, writing on the relevance of the social sciences as bodies of theory and description for practical decisions that are connected with social problems, has come to the conclusion that it is only certain techniques of investigation, developed or relied on by social scientists, that do so. The social sciences themselves 'play little part' in the really important fields of endeavour. 'Sociological studies may encourage a more realistic approach to such problems, and in particular restrain those immoderate moral denunciations which often exacerbate the difficulties', but all the same 'the principal contribution of sociology is generally seen as consisting in skilled investigation'. There are many who would agree with this view. 'It is', writes Professor Edward A. Shils, the devising of 'procedures of convincing reliability' by the social sciences that has 'led to their marriage with policy to an extent that could have been conceived only in principle in Weber's time, and it is this that accounts for their success.'[14] Professor Bottomore's final opinion is that:

> The Sociologist may supply information, elucidate the context of problems, point to courses or conditions, indicate the advantages and costs of alternative courses of action; in the longer run, his studies may, and I believe do, influence social ideals themselves. . . . Decisions rest upon judgment, on political wisdom, and upon interests.

In other words, sociologists cannot be regarded as philosopher kings, or high priests, as Comte would have had them to be. It is the elusiveness of the value-component in the concept of a 'problem', or still more so, in 'welfare', that makes it so difficult to develop a sociology that is really relevant to the everyday affairs of social administration and political life. But until sociology possesses a breadth and depth of understanding as a truly scholarly study, rather than the shallow usefulness of a technology, it is not to sociology that people with serious social problems will go to seek ways of solving them. It is only in a very general and educational rather than a practical, or still worse, technological sense, that Professor Bottomore would assert the values of teaching sociology.[15] There is, of course, much truth in this. Nobody would wish to place social scientists in positions of total authority, deciding issues affecting the lives of their fellow-citizens in matters of importance. But whilst social scientists obviously cannot be given the final say in the political or social fields, they cannot be allowed to free themselves from all responsibility for public policy. What should be their main concern in this field, we are forced to ask, if this is so? Is it the statement of policy issues as matters of technical interest, and arriving at conclusions on them based on fundamental studies in sociology and the other social sciences? This would be an undertaking which would be parallel with engineering and the other technologies, dealing with such matters as the siting of a bridge or the operation of a manufacturing plant producing penicillin. Social work and social administration would then be undertaken as applied sciences, depending on sociology and other social sciences such as psychology and economics, as 'pure' sciences existing in their own right.

There can be no doubt that many would have it this way. On the one hand, there has been for many years a high degree of prestige which has attached to the 'applied' sciences;[16] on the other, although this might at first sight be unwelcome to the social worker, social work is still regarded in extreme cases as an endeavour in which well-intentioned people persuade or cajole the poor to do what is considered by those in positions of authority or social influence to be good for them. Although it is hard to see how there can be social administration without reliance on the concept of 'the good', there has been in the last fifty years a tendency on the part of social workers to flinch away from it, and to exchange an amoral technology for moral principles. In the event, the social worker's position at the moment is involved in such doubt that she might well be glad to know where she stands in the academic world, even if this means the jettisoning of moral principle altogether, particularly as this might put her alongside a number of professional colleagues occupying positions of authority in the scientific world. As an applied scientist she might well find herself 'handing down' judgments (as lawyers sometimes say), occupying a comfortable seat on a kind of legal bench, able to give authoritative opinions based on laws derived from one science or another. That would involve the acceptance of responsibility for them, but the nature of this responsibility would be limited, and the judgments would be protected from attack by reason of the strength they acquire from being based on scientific foundations.

This kind of conception of the relationships between social

science and social work has an element of topicality in it, in so far as proposals have recently been put forward in Britain for the transfer of powers and responsibilities from juvenile courts to family courts and councils, composed largely of social workers. The professional status of the social worker at the present time is however hardly sufficient as things are to make it possible for her to wield authority of this order unassisted by the lawyer or the politician, but if it was commonly accepted that social work is a scientifically based technology, the situation might be very different. Many grave intellectual problems, both logical and moral, arise here, however, which would have to be overcome before anything could be generally agreed of this order.

v

If, however, value is not regarded as part of the subject-matter of social science, except as evidence of a special form of man's behaviour, if all 'matters of evaluation' are to be regarded as 'scientifically undemonstrable' as Weber thought, and if we have to insist on 'the rigorous distinction between empirical knowledge and value-judgments', as he said, we cannot but involve ourselves in difficulties if we seek to participate in matters of practical social policy as sociologists or social scientists. This is the beginning rather than the end of this matter, because 'it is certainly not', as Weber wrote, 'that value-judgments are to be withdrawn from scientific discussion in general, simply because in the last analysis they rest on certain ideals and are therefore "subjective" in origin.... Criticism is not to be suspended in the presence of value-judgments. The problem is rather: what is the meaning and purpose of the scientific criticism of ideals and value-judgments?'[17]

What is it indeed? Controversy has raged about it from the original publication of these statements in 1904 to the present day. As will be explained at length in the relevant chapters, the dispute first came to a head as the result of a stormy meeting of the Association for Social Policy in Vienna in 1909; the outbreak of the first World War suspended it at a time when it was getting into its stride, and it is by no means over yet. The problems of fact and value disputed about as the subject of sociological analysis (*die Werturteilsdiscussion*) have been left to us in our own generation and age. It is therefore necessary, if sociology is to make a contribution to the solution of the social problems of our day, and to provide a meeting-place between the sciences and the arts, to complete the work of clarification which Weber started. Man cannot but be regarded as being motivated in large measure – even preponderately – by his reason. If that were not so, there could be no science. His nature is such that he is deeply influenced by the presumptions he makes as guides to his actions, which we call values; if these are written off as existing outside the bounds of science except as facts of unreasoning or emotional behaviour, then not only is sociology in a chronic state of logical confusion, but it also, thus defined and limited, stands on the side of Lord Snow's gulf which is occupied by the natural sciences. If it is to assist in the task of bridge-building, it must be able to express, and develop, an interest in values as a necessary part of human processes of action. Some sort of meaning has to be found for it which the mind can comprehend, together with some sort of significance which will make it worthwhile to devote time and energy to its study.

In what sense, then, can evaluation be regarded as being guided by reason? Are values to be properly subjected to any kind of scientific or other analysis as true or false? Can societies be so organised that they can be based on true rather than false values? Is this a matter of the survival of the fittest, or can this process be made part of a process of understanding? How, exactly, can the human mind be stimulated to produce new thoughts about values, or is this as mysterious a process as the formulation of new scientific hypotheses by the questing mind?[18]

How, indeed, do values change? Is this a social process to any large extent, or is it more or less a matter for the individual experience of thinking? Some changes may be found to be supported by reason more than others, and make their impact on the framework of society because the beliefs that come to be associated with them prove to be stronger and more enduring than those they supplant. Others, again, arise from group or mass influences, and may stem from fear, envy or frustration. Ultimately, of course, it would appear to be reasonable to suppose, as many of us do, that the final arbiter so far as the acceptance or rejection of any given value is concerned would be the individual judgment, as Professor Bottomore has suggested. But this does not go without saying, and it is only true in a very limited sense. It is much easier to understand rational processes than irrational beliefs or conflicts, such as those between the so-called races, bitter as these are, which lie behind them. It is much less difficult to accept a rational interpretation, however oblique and well argued, of, for instance, anti-semitism under the Nazis, or under Communist rule in Russia. Yet it is fundamentally cruel and wicked, as is also the attitude of mind of the anti-feminists, and those who wish to hang, flog, or otherwise torment the convicted criminal. It must be accepted, little as we like it, in fact, that there is an emotional, and often a sadistic, component in human conduct, but the problem is how to come to terms with it, how to deal with it in the interests of social welfare and progress, not how to understand it and accept it, as something that is inevitable, as part of man's nature.

It is the purpose of this book to introduce the discussion of these problems so as to show how the individual may be given greater freedom in the exercise of his judgment – for our faith must be that, in the long run, reason will prevail over unreason, and the truth be found to be stronger than falsehood. How can might, ignorance, sadism, and intolerance be so understood that what is right and reasonable can be given a chance to prevail against them? Those who are responsible for the shaping of social policy must face the alarming fact that, with things as they are, there is nothing to prevent mankind from destroying itself utterly, before we have sufficient knowledge to deal with the very real dangers that beset us. Our rulers and masters have, however, first of all to be made aware that these dangers do beset us, and that there are serious human problems to be encountered and dealt with before anything effective can be done about them. Moreover, the elder statesmen of the western world need to know that the wish alone to do what is right will not give movements for reform strength and understanding. Knowledge as well as desire are needed for this purpose. A general intention of this kind, however sincere it may be, may not be strong enough to deal with such critical dilemmas as the problems of 'race' – the most important social problem of our times, after the Bomb – the growing menace of crime, or more serious, the hitherto unsolved problems of international conflict and war between the nations. The assumption that the moral nature of man is creative enough to promote the necessary action to deal with these cannot be justified by the available evidence. The understanding of the problems concerned must be relied on to bring them under control; given this the damage done by their continued existence can, it is hoped, be brought within the limits of the tolerable, and the critically explosive situations of the moment reduced to the viable and the manageable.

VI

The issue of positivism, the attempt to provide in the social sciences
a basis for the 'value-free' study of social phenomena familiar in the
material sciences, therefore becomes acute in social science as soon as
authority is sought for its findings derived from scientific analysis and
experiment. So far as social work is concerned, it is obvious that it
cannot be divorced from the conclusions resulting from the study of
moral philosophy, and if its foundations may partly be found in the
facts of social organisation which are to a large extent the business of
sociology, these must also be examined in the light of the values which
it is the business of the moral philosopher to investigate. The need to
study the problems of social work, and perhaps all social problems,
from a broadly moral point of view is generally agreed today. Writing
of psychotherapy, Professor Paul Halmos has said:

> On the whole, the counsellors are frankly and humbly agnostic, and
> for this reason, their much restrained piety is plausible and acceptable
> in this sceptical age in which they have to work. But they use a language
> of reverence, and even a theological language and imagery, as if they
> could not do their job effectively without their evocative power.[19]

There are, in fact, few people today who would wish to persuade
the world that casework can be regarded as a technology pure and
simple, and that casework policies can be developed on the basis of the
facts, and the facts alone, about social organisation. There is relatively
little resistance against the idea that judgment has to be exercised on
the facts, which must be regarded as the rawest of material presented
to it, and that one of the most important ways in which judgment must
be exercised is in regard to whether the facts of social life are good or
bad, and whether it is possible to improve them. There is, of course, a
great deal to be done to teach moral philosophy really adequately to
social workers, but that is all the more an objective to be striven for,
rather than to be neglected, in the future.

These conclusions seem to be fairly obvious. They can be applied
with equal force to sociology itself, but there is much more controversy
about this. It is generally recognised that the present position in
sociology is even more unsatisfactory than that in social work, as all
that is known at the moment amounts to what has been called a mere
'pile-up in a chaos of unrelated monographs and articles'.[20] But only
too often efforts to put things right are not directed towards an

attempt to put the confusion in the logic of our thinking straight, but seek to create a 'systematic scientific theory' to replace the absence of practically any 'scientifically valid, generalised sociological knowledge on a high level of abstraction'. 'Well designed and essentially "pure" scientific research on the fundamentals of social behaviour will, in view of our present practical dilemmas', Professor Shils wrote twenty years ago, 'contribute greatly to the clarification, not of the ends, but of the alternatives of policy and their implications for our ends.' But this may have the result, not of clarification by research, but of still more logical confusion.

It is important to note that Professor Shils ended his examination of the state of American sociology with two points, which will make it possible to follow the argument of his analysis in this chapter more easily. In the first place, he says,

> To achieve the dignity of science involves not only an appreciation of and skill in the use of techniques of accurate observation, recording and codification, [but] it requires also a sense of what is important. It requires a moral and political philosophy as a guide in the selection of problems. This does not mean that directives for conduct in this sphere of morals or policy can be derived from a scientific sociology; it does mean that a scientific sociology will not develop unless it is motivated by that broad curiosity about human nature and its vicissitudes in the universe which grows on the national level from the sense of responsibility to a great civilisation, a concern for the clarification and improvement of its moral rules and the practical desire to perceive the conditions of their realisation or maintenance or improvement.[21]

Secondly, this positive need for a better understanding of values is balanced by the negative desirability of disburdening American sociology of 'the deadweight of the factual survey which provides the policy-maker with everything except what he needs to know'.[22] Instead of more information for its own sake, the American sociologist needs to strive to understand what are the compelling forces of society. 'A more realistic orientation of research to the everyday needs of policy is dependent on a more realistic and more responsible attitude towards political power' than American intellectuals showed at the time. In other words, a willingness to be helpful to those in positions of responsibility, and to involve oneself in their troubles, was insufficient of itself. 'The service of policy is no guarantee of this achievement of intellectual significance if other criteria are overlooked.' These criteria relate to good design of research projects from the scientific point of

C

view; 'the conflict is not between "pure" research and "practical" research', but between technically adequate research related to crucial problems, and research concerned with political prejudices and casual impressions.[23] As will be seen, these conclusions are echoed by the work of later authors.

This, however, does not go far enough, though it is on the right lines. What is required is to establish problems that are significant both from the point of view of sociological technique and from that of philosophical meaning. This would demand and justify the expenditure on research of adequate time and substantial resources in the interest of the maintenance and improvement of the good life of the society concerned. Sociology needs to stand on its own legs, as it were, and defend itself from the assaults of its enemies. It cannot do this as long as it has to be regarded as a mere pastime, without necessary relevance to the needs of the times. The service of policy is all very well, but there must be some means of determining ends and objectives that justify the service of the policy needs of the moment. Enemies of the people may be in control of a nation's policy, which may be directed to serve sectional interests rather than the common good. Professor Shils is well aware of this; his emphasis on the value of moral and political philosophy as a guide to what is important is evidence of it, but he is led astray by his overvaluation of the sciences of his day. What we want is both science to give us techniques, and morals to give us a grasp of values. They are equally important, for without both we cannot know any sociology that is relevant to needs and situations. Best of all, we want an amalgamation of the two.

VII

The dilemma with which we have become entangled is between the factual explanations of science and the moral concerns of philosophy. Neither is self-sufficient, but we have arrived at the illogical conclusion that we must choose either the one or the other. As the explanations of the physical sciences of the phenomena with which they deal have been so successful, we have endeavoured to build an apparatus of social science on the same model, and we have found that it is incapable of serving our social purposes. Our disillusionment is acute, and the chaos in our thinking boundless. The solution we adopt only too often is for more and more abstract theory of the 'pure' type that has no reference to purpose or to evaluation, and the more of it there is, the worse our muddles become. The way ahead for many people, in so far as there is one at all, lies in the direction of deciding to develop a form of 'pure' theorising, that has no reference to purpose and evaluation other than as mere forms of behaviour, possessing no characteristic justification or merit of their own; we concentrate our attention on forms of organisation as the products of tendencies and influences that can be regarded as abstract laws, leaving human intention and desire out of it altogether save, again, as mere forms of behaviour. Alternatively, sociology may be regarded as an 'applied' study, the determination of ends and purposes taken for granted, the energies of the sociologist being devoted to achieving somebody else's goals.

The first of these activities may be regarded as impossible of realisation, and the effort to attain it useless. But even if it is useless it is definitely harmless, though wasteful. The second, on the other hand, may be positively harmful and probably must be regarded as such. It is obviously a potential danger to society if it becomes an influential point of view, and well-equipped people allow themselves to be made tools of vested interests of one kind or another, and are prepared to take part in special pleading on a grand scale. Even if work of this kind may be on behalf of government agencies, the potential damage to the community is great if all the work done is in the interests of the realisation of one point of view. No opportunities may be presented for the expression of divergent opinions, and there is the suspicion, and sometimes the reality, that inconvenient information is being suppressed. The situation becomes critical when possible courses of action that are unpopular with the establishment are allowed to go by default or, at least, not given an adequate hearing.

It is understandable, of course, that there cannot but be a general unwillingness to allow public policy to be determined by mere whim or irrelevant preference of a personal kind. If this is taken to its logical conclusion it will not be allowed to influence the way public policy is shaped. It is the total situation that needs to be judged when an appraisal of alternative courses of action is made. How, we must find out, do you distil a policy from the facts of the case? How do you marshal relevant information so as to determine whether to do this and to refrain from doing that; how, in other words, do you move from fact to value? This applies in politics, industry, social work, and in planning generally, and in a multitude of other fields. It is in the determination of one's objectives and in showing that the specific facts of a situation can be brought within the ambit of a generalisation that the skill of the matter lies. This is not always thought to be so, and it may be asserted, surely mistakenly, that all that needs to be done is to find out what the facts really amount to. Yet it seems to be incontrovertible that one cannot move straight from fact to decision, and that some sort of value-judgment must lie between at an intermediate stage along the way.

One asks, for instance, how decisions are taken by industrial managers about, perhaps, personnel management, and one is told that these are largely determined by management's system of beliefs. That is unexceptional if it is allowed that beliefs must to a very large extent be made to depend on rational analysis and carefully sifted experiences. Yet if one is told that management 'must recognise that a system of beliefs becomes less necessary as factual knowledge is extended, and must be prepared to modify or relinquish their assumptions as soon as evidence is produced to show that they are no longer tenable',[24] one cannot but experience a severe intellectual shock. There is, of course, an intimate functional connection between belief and fact, research and evidence. But how can it be supposed that the need for belief and assumption can ever be done away with by improvements in our mere information? The positive conclusion that hard fact is all we need to know must surely be especially inadequate in a scientific age which has derived so much from speculation, and in a world which has gained so much from opening its mind to so many points of view and the loosening of so many orthodoxies.

The danger of 'value-free sociology' is that it leaves the individual sociologist free to participate in the activities of organisations, agencies, and industrial or commercial firms which have some special case or interest which they want to persuade the world to accept for their own advantage. The kind of freedom which is most to be feared in the modern world is freedom from responsibility; sectional interests are reasonably well looked after; on occasion, only too well. The interests of the nation as a whole and of local communities tend to be allowed to go by default in comparison. This is where the researches of sociologists in social structure and social change might play an even more important part in the life of the nation than is the case at present. This would be particularly so if the sociologists' concern with values as providing the driving forces or dynamic behind social affairs could be stimulated so that both an understanding of the social importance of values could be achieved, and a critique of values developed and thus the viability of a value-system could be made the subject of objective examination. One must also admit that values, freed from all restraints of this kind, may as easily produce distortions within a society as understanding.

The acceleration of the rate of social change in our own day and age will never be understood unless the social scientist studies values for what they are: as determining individual points of view, and social attitudes, and as governing the ways in which man's energies are awakened and employed. It is suggested that a study of this kind can assist in the building of the bridge between the Two Cultures; it will have its scientific as well as its literary aspect, but in some measure the latter will preponderate over the former in the new Third Culture; in the conditions of today it is the literary culture which is primarily concerned with values. If this is so, sociology can be developed so as to play an important role in this Third Culture, for in virtue of its dual quality it has the potential understanding and strength to mediate between the other cultures, the growth of which has preceded it. Sociology, then, can play a prominent part in the construction of a future society, and the reconstruction of our own. It can become, moreover, a decisive factor in the enlargement of our social welfare.

Mankind has experienced in increasing measure ever since the seventeenth century a steadily growing desire to establish a firmly 'scientific' basis for public policy, and to manage our political life in a commonsense and businesslike way. As Windwood Reade said in putting the rationalist point of view in the Victorian age, those like him expected that means would be developed to predict the future, to govern mankind 'with the quiet regularity of club committees', and to suppress evil forces 'that are within'.[25] This point of view is still alive. There is a strong streak of rationalism in the social sciences of our own time, and this has given rise to a great deal of muddled thinking. Though that may not be so troublesome today as it once was,[26] there is, all the same, an insistent and sometimes a rather shrill demand to strengthen the scientific element in the social sciences, without giving any really careful consideration to the manner in which these 'sciences' can be made 'scientific'. Much confusion has been occasioned by the fact that many social scientists seek to adopt the model of Victorian physics as their prototype of science, oblivious of the scientific revolutions of the early twentieth century which established a new mode of science, armed with new concepts and new aspirations, and exchanged the scientific uncertainty of today for the dogmatism of the nineteenth century.[27] The claims of 'science' to an understanding of universal truth, eternally valid in the objective facts of nature, are much more hesitant and much more qualified than they were a century ago. It is the purpose of this book to endeavour to demonstrate that the concept of 'science', if it is to be applied to social as well as physical phenomena, must be very substantially adapted and developed for the purpose. It will be argued that this can be done, but this will require very substantial modifications in our thinking. The result may be to bring the work of physical scientists much nearer that of social scientists, an outcome that, it will be generally agreed, is very much to be desired.

2. Sociological Empiricism[1] in Great Britain: Its Origins and Outcome

Prominent amongst the schools of thought that have developed during and since the last quarter of the nineteenth century has been that of so-called British sociological empiricism. The impact of the earlier effects of the Industrial Revolution on the public mind, especially on those persons concerned with the Poor Law and public health, had resulted in the publication of a large number of reports by newly created government agencies, commissions of enquiry and the census organisation, and the presentation of papers to the newly formed statistical societies, literary and philosophical societies, and the like. The origins of the new empirical school are thus to be found in the work of such administrators and researchers as William Farr, Edwin Chadwick, Sir John Simon, Charles Booth, and Sidney and Beatrice Webb, rather than in that of social philosophers such as Bentham (as distinct from his followers), Comte and Spencer.[2] A large mass of information became available concerning the true nature of the conditions under which life was led in our society, together with much evidence which threw light on the growth of industry and commerce, the system of education (or lack of it), the public health, the state of the poor, and social and cultural conditions generally. Much of it, as in the case of Chadwick's reporting on poverty and public health, was tendentious; but much also, as with Farr's work in the General Register Office, and Sir John Simon's on public health conditions and statistics, was accurate and highly influential. It became possible, by the end of the century, to give a reasoned account of one aspect or another of the nation's social or economic life, based on information that had been collected for routine purposes of administration; established methods could be relied on to gather supplementary information to fill out what was already available, if this was found to be insufficient.

The earliest event of importance in the development of empirical sociology in England was the publication of Charles Booth's first scientific paper in 1887, followed by his comprehensive Enquiry on the same subject, *The Labour and Life of the People of London*, in 1889–91.[3] As a practical man of business, Booth was much more anxious to understand how the industrial system of his time functioned, and to determine the nature of its impact on social conditions, than to propound all-embracing theories designed to explain why things had happened as they had, and what would therefore come to pass in the future. Was the nature of industrial and commercial enterprise the cause of poverty, he asked himself, or had the standard of living risen in recent years, and was it likely to go on rising in years to come? In other words, was capitalism a blessing or a curse? The questions he asked were even more specific than this. He had been made suspicious of *a priori* speculation by the theoretical economics of his day, and he tended to lean over backwards to avoid too tendentious argument or superficial speculation. He had no use for a 'big theory', and he clung fast to the idea that 'facts' could be organised within a 'large statistical framework', and this would then make it possible to formulate 'the theory and the law, and the basis of more intelligent action' in the world which was familiar to him. Over and over again, he asserted that he wished to 'let the facts speak for themselves', a remark that can only be compared with that of his successor, Seebohm Rowntree, who followed his example as an empirical sociologist, when he asserted that 'I did not set out upon my enquiry with the object of proving any preconceived theory, but to ascertain actual facts'.[4]

But this must not mislead us into a belief that Booth wished to display a narrow interest in forms of living rather than in the realities of social life. He was an empiricist only in the broad sense. His true position was midway between an interest in facts 'for their own sake', as the rather overworked phrase used too much today has it, and a concern for the welfare of individuals who could only be regarded by him as persons, and certainly not as social 'facts' in the more narrow statistical or sociological sense. He knew why he wanted to know more about the society in which he lived, and he knew what he wanted to study; his work was, as one would now say, problem-centred in high degree. His lack of interest in abstract theory has unfortunately led many people to undervalue his work, for it is too often by the complexity and extent of a man's theorising that his merit as a sociologist is judged today. His attitude to fine-spun philosophising was typically

British; remote as this must be from everyday affairs, he took no interest whatever in it, and he ignored it altogether. His complete Enquiry[5] has therefore been generally regarded as useful rather than as 'scientific', and his reputation has suffered accordingly. Beatrice Webb, for instance, credited him with the 'scientific impulse' but not with the practical capabilities of a working scientist, and he has usually been remembered as the author of the *Poverty Survey* which was so influential in the old age pensions campaign, rather than as a sociologist of understanding.

Booth has, however, been greatly misunderstood, and his importance as a sociologist underestimated. He pointed out the way which much of the sociological work of our own century has followed, and the course of the argument embodied in this book follows in its direction. However much he allowed himself to remain out of touch with the theoretical sociologists of his day, he carved out for himself his own territory in the world of ideas, and established his own framework of values, in which he felt himself at home; but he never displayed it to others, or even encouraged others to explore its extent or investigate its depths. Booth was an individualist who endeavoured to reconcile a faith in individualism with the fact of poverty; he imposed on himself the responsibility to find out whether the structure of his society needed reform, and to take steps to reform it if necessary, rather than to inspire others to ask questions of this kind themselves. His researches were designed to lead to action – not to question the need for it. Action was blended into research as a part of it; the acceptance of the values he held compelled him to examine relevant facts, and to change them when necessary and, for that matter, to transform his conceptions about values when the facts showed that their practical consequences would be untenable. He was, for instance, compelled to admit that the facts concerning poverty as he discovered them could not be reconciled with his values, and he was at length driven to refashion part of the social world around him in accordance with them, so as to diminish part of its misery. The interplay between fact and value, and the interaction of induction and deduction, was of fundamental importance in his system of thought, and the outcome profoundly influenced both his own life and that of the society in which he lived.

It was, in his own language, a 'way of looking at things', not a 'doctrine or argument' that he endeavoured to present to the world.

His struggle to achieve this highly individual point of view did not lead him to any final solution for the problems which he had sought to solve, for he saw his researches only as establishing the facts as to the 'character, extent, and symptoms' of the social ills he thought could and should be cured. 'May some great soul', he wrote, 'master of a subtler and nobler alchemy than mine, disentangle the confused issues, reconcile the apparent contradictions in aim [and] melt and commingle the various influences for good into one divine uniformity of effort.'[6]

The essential characteristics of Booth's work were, then, its timeliness, its practicality, and its accordance with the canons of the scientific enquiry of his age. It is not to be explained away as the 'working through' (as those addicted to psychoanalytic explanations of human conduct and experience might suppose it to have been) of the frustrations of an inhibited mind, or the compulsive behaviour of a man with a guilty conscience. It was, on the contrary, the result of the acceptance by an able man of affairs, with an aptitude for the rational analysis of situations and tendencies that amounted to genius, of a personal responsibility to understand the true nature of the society which he had done much himself to create, and to study the ways in which its harshnesses could be alleviated, and the level of living enjoyed by its members be raised to the highest point. The task which he set himself was at one and the same time of great practicality, a substantial contribution to learning, and of critical assistance to the cause of social welfare.

Booth's work was followed up and in some respects extended by his industrious apprentice, Beatrice Webb, especially during the early stages of her collaboration with her husband. The Webbs, like Booth, set out to be social scientists in the empirical school, but in perhaps a rather more self-conscious way. They attempted to bring fact and theory close enough together to set up a process whereby the hypotheses which emerged from their intellectual contemplation of the relationship between man and society might be validated in the light of the evidence they collected. Their understanding of this relationship led to practical improvements in the nation's institutional life; facts were selected for analysis according to their significance and importance in relation to one or another of their hypotheses. This method, as Beatrice described it, was very similar to Booth's; the Webbs' work undoubtedly derived much from his, but Beatrice also owed much to Spencer. In some important respects, however, the

Webbs' methods differed from Booth's. Not only were they more aware than he of the need to formulate hypotheses with care, but the partnership was greatly strengthened by Sidney's historical sense, and his practical abilities in historical research. They accepted the idea that their 'own speciality' lay in 'the analytical history of the evolution of particular forms of social organisation',[7] an endeavour which was so unlike Booth's apparatus of extensive statistical operations as to be quite foreign to his mind. His genius lay in the presentation of an 'instantaneous photograph' of things as they were, and in the testing of commonsense ideas which might explain the ways in which the several parts of the picture were connected with each other. His methods of analysis were relatively undeveloped, however, and he allowed himself to be deflected too easily from his chosen aim of criticising deductive theories.[8] It was, therefore, the task of the Webbs to take over from Spencer the idea and the method of institutional analysis; their indebtedness to him is obvious when they speak of 'the analytical history' of institutional forms.[8a] But they elaborated and refined the method of Spencer very greatly; instead of using facts for illustrative purposes, and assembling together material from all over the world and up and down the centuries, they concentrated, in the main, in their best and their earlier work, on dissecting individual institutions existing within the fixed social context of Great Britain; and they were thus able to discuss problems of growth and decay in a manner which had never been attempted before.

In sum, therefore, Beatrice learnt from Booth, and with Booth, that it was possible to incorporate large numbers of facts into a research, and to base a significant theory on them. This, coupled with a sceptical attitude to the *a priori*, and a preference for inductive rather than deductive methods, which she also learnt from Booth, became blended with Sidney's vision of a changing world. This new approach to social problems was given added force when Spencer's techniques of institutional analysis were incorporated in their methodology. The results became quickly evident in the early years of the Webbs' collaboration. *The History of Trade Unionism*, written and published in 1894 in the incredibly short span of two years after their marriage, is a classic of English social history; to the Webbs, however, it 'seemed little more than an historical introduction to the task we had set before us: the scientific analysis of the structure and function of British Trade Unions'.[9] The historical study of trade unionism was followed in 1897 by the publication of *Industrial Democracy*, constructed on a basis of differentiation between structure and function. The major assumptions of the Webbs' researches thus became plain at the outset of their work. Although interested in processes of change, they rejected so-called 'scientific theories as to the evolution of society'.[10] Their rejection of *a priori* ideas was, indeed, so absolute as to threaten their understanding of the fact that though the researcher should not begin his work with prejudices or preoccupations, he must start it with a distinct set of interests, a set of methods he is able to use efficiently, and, in general, an organised mind.[11] Their work, also Booth's, was intended to illuminate practical problems, and it was designed to be of assistance to those who were responsible for solving them.

What motivated the Webbs in the conduct of their investigations was not so much the alluring hazards of creative intellectual effort *per se*, and the 'joy of life' that is the by-product of sincere and successful scholarship[12] (still less the sordid pleasures of fact-finding), as the discharge of a basic obligation to solve some of the human problems of an industrial society. 'The very continuance of social science or sociology as a separate category of study', they thought, 'will depend on the world's experience of the practical utility of such a parcelling out of knowledge at the particular stage of the world's history that we may have attained'.[13] Social investigators had of course to be careful, in view of the limited value of their methods and the complexities of the phenomena with which they had to deal; the 'more modest' of them would not find themselves 'talking about the laws of nature', and would be cautious 'even about making sweeping generalisations'.[14] But the Webbs were confident that they had found 'a new method and a new theory' when they wrote their *Industrial Democracy*;[15] furthermore, they were convinced not only that it was 'possible to combine scientific research into social institutions with active participation in their operation', but that their duality was of 'reciprocal advantage' to them. They 'never got a satisfactory hold on the conditions and the expedients that determined success or failure', in the institutions that were studied, 'until we both had enjoyed brief and intermittent experiences of actual membership of these bodies'.[16] Beatrice describes her 'intellectual environment' when she first encountered Booth as one of 'politics and metropolitan philanthropy', adding that his impulse came from neither of them, but rather from 'scientific curiosity'.[17] The accuracy of this statement is doubtful, to say the least of it, but what she wrote in this way is of the greatest interest, for it is evident that it was to the marriage of politics and philanthropy with social science that she and Sidney devoted their lives.

It is therefore apparent that, when the Webbs sought to explain their motivations in carrying out their researches, and to describe the influences to which they felt they were subject, they expressed themselves as attempting something that was a blend of, or halfway between, the life of the natural scientist and that of the politician or public administrator aware of his responsibilities to his fellow citizens. The social scientist had, in other words, become something entirely different from the natural scientist, on the one hand, and the social worker or administrator, on the other. They seem to have thought of their own work as a kind of applied science, as the nearest occupation to theirs with which they were acquainted; they were modest enough, for they were well aware of its limitations when looked at from the scientific point of view, and they emphasised the quality of its 'duality', which made it plain that they valued it as an 'applied' rather than a 'pure' science. As will be seen later, however, this is a very unsatisfactory category of analysis when used in relation to the social sciences, and this becomes obvious when they discussed their objectives in the chapter on 'The Relation of Science to the Purpose of Life' in *Methods of Social Study*.

In this, they asked themselves the vital question how the mass of knowledge accumulated by the sociologist can be made useful; and whether, indeed, any applied science of sociology is possible.[18] Their answer was, that one is. Their reasons for arriving at this conclusion were not very convincing. Their view was that where somebody or some group had made up its mind about the desirability of getting something done, then the social scientist comes into his own to find out how it could be made possible; analytical studies had shown how the civil service, the audit system, professional organisation and trade unions had originated and developed, and had demonstrated how the relief of the poor by outdoor relief had been replaced by a framework of prevention, which had been substituted for repression and deterrence. These were examples of what the sociologist's future potentialities were; the successive improvement of the institutions concerned by 'Trial and Error' could be backed by researchers, 'contented to draw the specific inference from their studies that if such and such action were taken, such and such beneficial results would follow'. The steadily increasing knowledge of social facts had therefore led to one change after another in social structure during the previous century. 'This is, in fact, how sociology becomes increasingly an applied science.'[19]

This was surely a very superficial argument. It has no relevance to the problem why some people devoted their energies to researches of this kind, and why some men in public life were willing, and indeed anxious, to adopt the remedies they suggested to current ills (such as the prevention of destitution), whilst others opposed them. How had some people, they asked themselves, come to be influenced in this way, and others not? After much beating about the bush, the Webbs faced this issue briefly but directly at the end of their *Methods of Social Studies*. 'Is man's capacity for scientific discovery the only faculty required for the reorganisation of society according to an ideal? Or do we need religion as well as science, emotional faith as well as intellectual curiosity?' Their answer was a very indefinite one.

> Science has nothing to say of purpose. . . . No personal observation or statistical enquiry, or any amount of scientific knowledge, will tell us whether we *ought* to kill or cure. Our behaviour . . . is largely dictated to us by law or public opinion. Whenever the individual settles it for himself it seems to depend ultimately on intuition or impulse, on likes or dislikes, or to put it another way, on emotional outlook on life. . . . Individual men and women, all through the ages, have found in their minds indications, unknown to science, of what is the purpose of the universe, or, at least, what should be made the object of their own lives. . . . It is not to the intellectual outcome of science, but to some feeling in the individual consciousness, that we must look for guidance as to how to use the powers that we possess.[20]

It is on this very unsatisfactory note that the life work of the Webbs ended. It is plain that, according to them, it was to the emotions of man that we must look if we want any idea of the way in which societies were likely to develop, or how people decide on a course of action. The emotional life of man was, it appeared, paramount. [If so, then might was in this sense right, in so far as the emotions lend themselves so readily to manipulation.] The issue was soon to be tried in terms of our own lives. The book was published in 1932; Hitler seized power in Germany in the very next year, but though it appeared to be proven by the success of his system of government that intimidation and torture were the most effective political expedients, western man thought otherwise, and the great search began once more for a more solid and more rational basis to underpin social policy and social organisation. It was thus in a mood of rather hysterical frustration and of dire need, that the first phase gradually came to an end of what may be termed English Empiricism, administrative Trial and Error, or Political Experiment.

Although no ready solution had been found for philosophical and moral problems, nevertheless at the end of the first quarter of the twentieth century foundations had at least been laid for the study of social relationships, social institutions, and social problems alike. By the 1930s, the survey method developed by Booth had been used to good effect by others, notably Rowntree, Bowley, and Caradog Jones; the methods of social analysis had been employed for the public good, albeit on a rather narrow front, by Lord Beveridge, Sir Cyril Burt, and Sir Alexander Carr-Saunders. Substantial use had been made of all these newly-developed methods by Royal Commissions and Departmental Committees of Enquiry, from the Royal Commission on the Poor Laws of 1905–9 to the 'Hadow' Committee on education of 1927. The way seemed to be clear for the inauguration and development of sociological research by University Social Science departments collectively. Progress, however, proved to be much slower than the facts appeared to warrant, and the early hopes were largely falsified. The completion of Booth's Enquiry in 1903, and the development of the Webbs' work, might have been expected to have marked the beginning of a new era of sociological enquiry, in which empirical research would have assumed a leading, if not a dominant, place. But instead of the new era dawning, the spectacle that presented itself was that of a false dawn.

This is attributable to many causes, some of which appear to have been historical accidents, but all of them were part and parcel of the ethos prevailing at the end of the century. The age was undergoing a period of fundamental social change, and an era which was even more distressed and disturbed in this respect was about to open. What was called for, therefore, was not so much a technique of social enquiry, which Booth, Rowntree, and the Webbs had produced, but a far deeper understanding of the problems of society as a whole, and of the critical problems of motivation and change in particular. It was just this that the early academic sociologists were unable to provide. It was most unfortunate that 'academic' sociology, in the person of L. T. Hobhouse, parted company just at this moment from 'practical' sociology, in that of Patrick Geddes.[21] The doctrinaire thinking of

Bentham was restated as a conservative creed of a much more pedestrian kind by Charles Loch, and became the foundation of the anti-statism of the Charity Organisation Society, so that work that appeared at the outset to be promising, ended in a blind alley. It was only Hobhouse, who was the leading sociologist of his day (and was also a philosopher of much merit in his own right), who gave evidence of an ability to tackle the fundamental social and theoretical problems of the times, but he seems to have had no interest in Booth's work, which made no contribution to the understanding of the relationships between social life and the working of the human mind which was his predominant concern. The broad sweep of social and intellectual development, to the analysis of which Hobhouse's life was primarily devoted, and his deep philosophical thinking, remained widely separated from Booth's precise accounts of poverty and industrial organisation. Far from any marriage of the general with the particular in a contemporary social science being achieved, the century ended with something approaching an intellectual confusion and disaster, and a deadlock ensued. As Loch, the representative of the social workers, had advanced views on the necessity of relying on individual initiative (which he inherited from Bentham's social theory), and protecting society from being under-mined by the operations of publicly controlled social welfare agencies, he was bitterly critical of Booth, and no less intolerant of the Webbs.

This was something that inhibited them all. British empiricism sur-vived more as a by-product of government commissions of enquiry and of other bodies concerned with the application or formulation of social policy, than as a type of sociological theory. It thus came to be falsely identified with the 'useful' and the 'practical', and with the everyday operations of administrative agencies in the social welfare field. Only a small value was attached to it by the academic mind, which seemed unable to grasp the fact that a grave issue was involved in the assertion of contemporary philosophers of the 1930s that the individual was unable to make a rational choice between two courses of action, or that he was to be advised to avoid getting involved in meaningless disputes about political rights and social equality, which were mere superficialities. It was the era of the Spanish Civil War and Non-Intervention. Immediately ahead lay the searchings of the mind that the battles of France and Britain compelled; their outcomes, the Atlantic Charter and the Welfare State, still lay in the unforeseeable future. In particular, there was no reply at the time from British social and political philosophers to the weak pronouncements of the 'practical' politicians of their day.

In fact, things had to get much worse before they could take a turn for the better. The philosophers' own foundations were insecure enough, and were about to prove themselves insufficient to support the structure of British philosophy against the earthquakes that Wittgenstein's critical doubtings brought with them. At the time, therefore, the attitude of philosophers was one of noting where politicians had got, if they had any interest in them at all, rather than pointing out the way they might go. Their predominant position in regard to morals and values was at this time in agreement with the Webbs, for they held with them that ethical judgments were mere matters of preference, or whim, and were not to be regarded as subjects of rational argument. They were rather to be considered subjects of passing phases of fashion. The line that was followed was fundamentally that of Hume, and as social scientists were deeply influenced by it, it was no mere accident or matter of chance that made Hume's writings so frequently quoted by them, and the famous passage from his *Inquiry Concerning Human Understanding* became still more famous. Arguing from his conclusion that 'morals and criticism are not so properly objects of the understanding as of taste and sentiment', we can only ask ourselves, he thought,

> When we run over libraries, persuaded of these principles, what havoc must we make? If we take in our hand any volume, of divinity or school metaphysics, for instance, let us ask: *Does it contain any reasoning concerning quantity or number? Does it contain any experimental reasoning concerning matter of fact or existence?* No. Commit it then to the flames. For it can contain nothing but sophistry and illusion.[22]

This set the philosophers a problem which has only been satisfactorily dealt with in the last decade. In the intervening centuries, highly complicated *a priori* arguments were developed in reply to Hume, as by Kant; or abstruse metaphysical systems were constructed, as by Hegel. From the beginning of the last century down to the last World War, the work of the philosopher has been a matter of getting to understand something of what had been done in this way in preceding generations, rather than saying something which met the needs of the plain man in matters of responsibility, freedom, and obligation.

In the meantime, many homespun and familiar problems have tended

D

to go by the board, and be left to be settled according to the criteria of decency, good behaviour and common sense, that have always guided ordinary people in their daily lives down the ages. This left morals and values, social sciences and social work, exposed defenceless to any clever cynic who might wish to attack 'doing good' in order to excuse his own idleness, selfishness, or bad faith. Still more important, the treatment of the problem of public morals, social values, and national policy, particularly by the German political theorists, left the field wide open for exploitation and occupation by unscrupulous theorists and politicians, from Treitschke to Bismarck, and on to Hitler. Even so influential a social scientist as Max Weber found it impossible to formulate a clear or easily understood theory of value; not only did his thinking become contradictory and obscure, but the idea of 'value freedom' associated with his name, when studied in the background of Hume's teaching, led to very destructive ideas about the inability of social scientists to play their part in policy formation, which has greatly detracted from the public importance of the role of the sociologist even up to our own day.

For a long time, in fact, the situation has been difficult, if not perilous. Half a century ago, the doctrine had developed in the minds of Continental thinkers that the state, in contrast to its citizens, was everything. It was under virtually no restriction, and there was no philosophical justification for the placing of moral restraints on the way in which it might govern, especially in relation to other states internationally. The development of idealist philosophising was extreme and very one-sided; one of its tenets has been, as Professor Emmet has put it, that 'reality is the self-development of thought'.[23] This kind of thinking was never very congenial to the British frame of mind, but it might easily have become much more influential than it was. It was of the intrinsic attractiveness of this school of thought in general, and of the 'Greats' School at Oxford in particular, that R. G. Collingwood wrote:

> The Greats school was not meant as a training for professional scholars and philosophers; it was meant as a training for public life in the Church, at the Bar, in the Civil Service, and in Parliament. The school of T. H. Green sent out in public life a stream of ex-pupils who carried with them the conviction that philosophy, and in particular the philosophy they had learnt at Oxford, was an important thing, and that their vocation was to put it into practice. . . . Through this effect

on the minds of its pupils, the philosophy of Green's school might be found, from about 1880 to about 1910, penetrating and fertilising every part of the national life.[24]

Unfortunately the way in which these philosophical ideas was presented by German political thinkers immediately before the first World War, and also and more especially in England by Professor Bernard Bosanquet in his *Philosophical Theory of the State*,[25] appeared to recommend the idea that things could legitimately be done in the name of 'the state' or 'the people', that would be immoral if they were undertaken by individuals. To many scholars in England, this teaching was largely responsible for the first World War, and it was Hobhouse who became the mouthpiece of their opposition and deep disapproval of German theorising, expressed first and foremost in his *Metaphysical Theory of the State*.[26]

This book was written under the stress of knowing that his son was serving in the R.A.F. on the Western Front, and that his expectation of life was poor. His purpose in writing it was to express his detestation of the 'false and wicked doctrine' that had made the Hegelian theory of the 'god state' so influential. The consequence had been, he thought, a far-reaching sapping of the 'rational humanitarianism of the eighteenth and nineteenth centuries', and it had led to the first (and ultimately the second) World War.[27] Hobhouse, therefore, devoted his energies with much success to proving that 'when the state is set up as an entity superior and indifferent to component individuals it becomes a false god, and its worship the abomination of desolation, as seen at Ypres and on the Somme'.[28] Yet this line of argument was purely negative; Hobhouse himself knew how necessary it was for the ideal to grow out of the real, and for the 'ethically right' to be so constituted that it is by nature 'sociologically possible'. But he was only too well aware that it was nonsense, and dangerous nonsense, to attempt to show that 'nothing succeeds like success', because it was only one step from this to assert that 'might was right', and it was exactly this kind of assertion that he devoted his life to disprove. Any statement which attempts to show how a social change arises out of the events which precede it, whether we will it or not, is, from the point of view of his analysis, 'one of confusion'; morally, it is paralysing to the will:

> If there were nothing for us but to accept the trend of events as we find it, then our science would relapse into fatalism, and, as members of the

society we study we should be simply in the position of knowing the
course of the stream which carries us along without any increase in
the power to guide it. . . . When we allow Social Science then to persuade us of the inevitableness of things, we are reversing the normal
course of science. For, whatever else may be said of science, one of its
functions is to increase human power, and this applies to sciences
which deal with human life as well as to sciences which deal with inanimate objects.[29]

His final conclusion is, therefore, that Hegel leads us nowhere,
that far from the state having the task of shaping the life of the individual, the reverse gives a more accurate account of the facts, and it
would be better to say that the state exists to serve the interests of the
individual than the converse. The answer to the primary problem of
political philosophy 'must rest on this truth, that the higher ethics and
the deeper religion do not come to destroy the simplest rights and
duties of neighbour to neighbour, but to fulfil and extend them'. This,
however, is by no means a complete answer to the problem with which
Hobhouse was faced, since it provides in itself only the briefest outline
of an answer to the fundamental criticism of Hume on the one hand,
and Hegel on the other. These were most serious gaps in our knowledge that ultimately led to the logical positivism founded by Wittgenstein. But that lay ahead. The important thing at the moment was that
a philosophical reaction to idealism had come to contain within it a
sociological method of approach, and a nascent school of sociology,
that held great promise for the future of the social sciences.

What was wanted, of course, was a fundamental and essentially
realistic social philosophy or sociology which would provide an
explanatory account of the relationship of the individual with the
groups and societies of which he was a member. It was the absence of
this that was the fundamental reason why progress was so slow in the
development of sociology in England: as long as realism was at
loggerheads with idealism, there could be no realistic account of
society and social problems. If, as the chief spokesman in the last
phase of idealism emphasised, to the idealist the proposition that 'a
science of man must be a science of mind seems no longer disputable'[30]
thought was ultimately detached from events. In consequence, any
sociology that accepted this dictum in its undiluted form could only be
very partial and incomplete. It is, of course, equally true in our own
age from the opposite point of view, that the sociological works that

are based solely on a positive philosophy, are just as incomplete, or even more so.

The development of a school of sociology in Britain has had to wait, therefore, for the coming of the day when these philosophical extremes have given way to a more balanced view in which neither doctrinaire idealism nor doctrinaire realism monopolise the field, and the climate came to permit the development of a point of view which might take into account the truths latent in both idealism and in realism. This has begun to become possible only in very recent years. At the time we are speaking of, however, there were at best only the glimmerings that this might come to pass one day; these were plainly evident in the work of Hobhouse and other sociologists of the school of Booth and his successors, which has already been mentioned; it is true that their position was, both philosophically and sociologically speaking, somewhat naïve, but though this latter school has continued to exist and to do good work until the present day, it has never had the importance attached to it that it has, perhaps, deserved. Secondly, there were the ultimately fruitless attempts made by the idealists, paradoxically enough, to comprehend within the range of their work studies with an empirical basis underlying them. And thirdly, there was modern realism, but of that, more later.

These attempts were bold, but unavailing. 'Every "source" of sociological science', wrote Bosanquet, 'is at once a category, or point of view, and also a certain group of actual social conditions,' and he argued that special attention ought to be paid to the philosophical and sociological analysis of the ancient Greek City-State. 'Philosophy', he said, 'gives significance to sociology; sociology vitalises philosophy.'[31] In saying this, we now recognise, with half a century of hindsight to help us, that he was very much on the right lines, and both the general interest he shows in the work of the early sociologists, and his specific interest in the very down-to-earth researches of Geddes, are very significant indeed.[32] The other neo-idealists of the period that ended with the first World War also followed much the same line as his.[33] But, though this was a promising beginning, it was insufficient. The idealists, particularly Bosanquet, became far too much entangled with the narrow and moralistic doctrines of Sir Charles Loch and the Charity Organisation Society, and they never, as a matter of fact, got around to making, or encouraging, their sociological colleagues (such as they were) to undertake the practical investigations they said in their books were so important. Idealism somehow missed the flavour of reality, without which sociology is a sham. The work of the school as a whole, which had flourished so impressively and so usefully during its heyday at Oxford, fell under the blows of their University colleagues just before the first World War, and the hammer-stroke for which Hobhouse was responsible just before it ended.

It was Hobhouse, therefore, to whom the task fell of providing the philosophical justification for sociology after the first World War, rather than to Bosanquet or to any other idealist or neo-idealist. Hobhouse was much more suited to the task than Bosanquet, being far more in agreement with the scientific methods that were assuming increasing importance and significance, and he was at the same time in full sympathy with the ideas and struggles of the philosophers, whose outlook he shared.

He was, of course, a rationalist and a realist rather than an idealist, and his general line of advance was an analysis of the function of reason in man's daily life and affairs. In his *The Rational Good*,[34] he carried this argument a definite stage further, though he made the mistake of presenting reason as a separate and an over-riding faculty of the mind, which could be divorced from other aspects of living, such as the unreason which exists alongside reason, the quality and the quantity of daily and total experience, and the life of emotion. In consequence, *The Rational Good* came to be ignored by philosophers, who turned their attention away from reason as existing in a social context, which could best be studied by sociology, and towards another direction altogether, which led to the new departure of logical positivism. But his work was seminal, though its value was by no means recognised as such at the time, or in the period immediately following his death. It was based on a wider interpretation of the way reason functioned, and this ultimately proved to be the vehicle for the development of new philosophical ideas;[35] even though his own were loaded with out-of-date evolutionary theories, much more could have been done with them. Had not the school of English philosophy, as it then existed, been so devitalised and as remote as it was from the practical problems of the social scientist, the administrator, the politician, and the social worker, something of the kind could easily have happened. Hobhouse's notion of reason, therefore, for all that has been said against it, was one which could have been used to much greater effect. Reason, he said,

> is a principle of harmony pervading experience and working it into an
> organic whole. So understood, reason is supreme in the mind simply as
> that which embraces every element of experience, interconnects
> every feeling and thought, takes account impartially of every
> suggestion and every impulse, and weaves of them all a tissue which is
> never ossified but always plastic and recipient. It is the conscious
> expression of that impulse to harmony which dominates the entire
> evolution of Mind, and the rationality of the process is the best guaran-
> tee of its ultimate success.[36]

Hobhouse's thinking on sociological problems was broad, and his
sympathies wide; far broader and wider, in fact, than those of the
sociologists of more recent years, and it was both as a philosopher and
as a sociologist that he objected to Hegel, and sought to build his own
ideas on rational foundations. For him, sociology had to come to
terms both with social philosophy as a whole, and with the special
social sciences individually. Social philosophy was concerned primarily with the analysis and criticism

> of conceptions and categories, and with the problems of values; social
> science adheres to a description of facts as they are or have been, and to
> a determination of the agencies involved in social persistence and change.
> Yet the two studies are closely connected.[37]

His sociology, and his philosophy, were (as has been said) those of a
realist. And yet it makes allowances for both facts and values. He
recognises that

> ideals and values may and do themselves act as forces determining or
> conditioning changes, and to that extent they belong to the 'facts' of
> social life, and their mode or genesis and development may and
> indeed must be studied by the methods of social science. Neglect of this
> consideration has often led to an unduly fatalistic view of the nature of
> social process. In the second place, it is important for the philosopher
> engaged in the study of ethical ideals to keep in touch with historical
> fact. . . . But though the studies are closely related they must none the
> less be kept distinct. . . . A complete account of social life would
> involve a union of the two studies.[38]

On the one hand, there were the facts, which he considered could
be examined 'scientifically'; on the other, there were values, which
could be made the subject of valid philosophical analysis. Nevertheless,
the two had to be brought into some kind of constructive relationship

with each other, and 'in applying the notion of development to social change' he eventually found the means for effecting this union:

> For development may be studied as a question of historical fact and from the point of view of ethical valuation. The scientific problem is to correlate the several aspects of social change, and to measure the kind and amount of growth in the light of criteria not necessarily ethical but analogous to those that might be employed by the biologist in dealing with organic evolution. The ethical problem is to determine whether the development thus established, if it be established, satisfies ethical standards of value. The former type of investigation leads to a comparative study of culture deriving its data from anthropology and history, and seeks to discover whether there is a thread of continuity running through the tangle of the countless processes convergent and divergent which make up the life of man on earth. The other presupposes an ethical theory and a method of applying ethical criteria to the phases of historical development.[39]

The operation of the mind under social influence would produce both a scientific account of society's nature and possibilities, and an appreciation of the moral responsibilities and potentialities of the individual, from the point of view of social action. Mind would thus play a prominent part in shaping the social environment which surrounds it. He realised to the full that mind exists and functions in circumstances that hinder, condition, and limit it, as well as urge it on; if mind plays its part in shaping social conditions, it also has to be realised that it does so in the social context as existent at a moment in time. If it is true that 'mind makes for orderly growth and harmony', and that its life 'emerges eventually in conscious purpose' which is the dominant factor in social progress,[40] it is also true that mind is not omnipotent, and it must carefully study what it can try to do, and how best to do what it decides to attempt. Mind, in other words, must understand at least the salient facts of social life, in order to play its part in it. Sociology, he thought, was therefore a complex synthesis of philosophy and science: 'We may appropriately use the term "philosophy"', he said,

> for the discussion of value, whether it be the value of methods of attaining truth, or the value of modes of life and conduct, and the term 'science' for the investigation of facts and the interconnections of fact which we seek to exhibit as laws. As social life is the medium in which all that we most value has its being, it is clear that it falls within the purview of philosophy as here described, and, if we call the study of value ethics, it follows that any social philosophy is a branch or

application of ethics, as the Utilitarians justly conceived. But it is also clear that the application cannot usefully be attempted without knowledge of the facts of science. So far we have a justification for both the philosophic and the scientific treatment of our subject. A complete sociology would therefore embrace a social philosophy and a social science. But it would be a synthesis, not a fusion, of the two enquiries.

The whole field of society can and should be treated scientifically, and, when scientifically understood, can and should be reviewed philosophically. There is no objection to either method in itself, but only a confusion of the two. A complete sociology, indeed, aims at a synthesis in which the two parts, though always distinct, are brought into definite relation.[41]

As sociology has developed since Hobhouse's day, there has certainly been little reluctance to examine 'the facts'; there has only been a good deal of dispute as to whether the study of the facts must be preceded or assisted by some kind of theorising, or at least by the formulation of hypotheses with which the facts can be brought into some kind of relation. It is sometimes argued that the facts only need to be chosen for examination with reference to theory; otherwise, they should be studied 'for their own sake'. There have been sociologists who are concerned only with what has now been given the opprobrious name of 'fact collecting', but there are not many of them today. This semi-sociological (or pre-sociological) activity is, however, significant for the argument of this chapter, in so far as it has been supposed to clear the ground for the rejection of values as an integral part of sociology. This would compel the sociologist to be, to that extent, 'unscientific'. But this argument cannot be accepted in its entirety by any means. Men are actually influenced by values, and it is easy to discover that as a 'fact'. Hobhouse understood that well; his life was lived in the company of such men as R. H. Tawney, who understood to the full how men were motivated by their feelings of injustice derived from their experiences of subjection to social privilege or educational inequality, and what the outcome of this was in the political life of the country.[42] Hobhouse's close connections with the *Manchester Guardian* (and C. P. Scott in particular) was evidence of his lively realisation of the importance of understanding how men's moral outlook, and their values, were incorporated in their thinking and behaviour.[43]

It is much harder to estimate the extent to which a refusal to take values into consideration makes difficulties for those who do so. Those who attempt to make judgments on 'objective' grounds cannot but find it hard to remain within the world of reality. To assess the position of such people requires an analysis of the extent to which the influence of values really removes one from the world of realities, or makes it impossible to remain an essentially reasonable being.[44] It must suffice to say, on the contrary, that if one allows oneself to oversimplify what is essentially a complex problem, one then abandons the real world, and substitutes for what is real one's own version of reality; this is necessarily unreal, to some extent at least, and it is certainly not the real world to which people at large are compelled to make their own adjustments. Hobhouse gives a telling example of this, which applies to the best developed social science of his day – economics. This confined itself 'to one side of human nature, to motives and qualities which play a large part in life, but are not the whole of life, and if taken for the whole, transform man into a money-making machine'. The result was to prejudice the intelligent man against economics; from being a science which devoted itself to the study of a single and a narrow aspect of reality, it became the 'dismal science' that sought to explain the whole in terms of the part, and this 'attempted separatism' led to consequences which might serve as a warning to specialists in other departments'. Or, in other words,

> We cannot take any one single feature of [a society's] life and hope to understand it without reference to the rest. We cannot isolate one set of conditions and disregard the remainder of the life-history. If we follow up any enquiry far enough, we find ourselves branching off into other enquiries. How, for example, could we understand the basis and meaning of the law of any country if we knew nothing of its religion, of its religion if we knew nothing of its ethics ... or of any of them without some understanding of the social structure on which they rest, and the social life in which they issue?[45]

This argument applies specifically to the fact-and-value problem, but its significance is a wide one. Hobhouse saw as clearly as anybody else (for instance, Weber) that there was an acute danger of confusing the ideal and the actual, and that value had to be considered, not separately, but only from another point of view than that of fact; he never argued that fact and value had to be considered entirely apart. Neither did he argue that if something exists, and indeed prospers, is also to say (and Hobhouse never said it) that it is good. It is equally true that what is valuable is not necessarily real; that is one of the more telling criticisms of idealism:[46]

The foundation of true social method is to hold the ideal and the actual distinct, and use our knowledge of the one as a means of realising the other. We may pursue the two investigations, if we will, side by side, for we have seen how very closely they are interwoven. But every question that we ask and every statement that we make ought to be quite clearly a statement as to fact or an assertion as to what ought to be, and never a hybrid of the two.[47]

The general impression that Hobhouse's sociology makes is, however, too optimistic when it is looked at from the point of view of a later generation. It is too deeply influenced by the evolutionary theories of his age, and this may account, as has been said, for some of the neglect from which he now suffers. The basic idea underlying his theories was that there is a broad correlation between mental 'advance' and the growth of the social fabric,[48] which was displayed, for instance, in the way in which primitive science developed, in the organisation of animistic religion, and so on. The trouble about this theory was that it proved too much; it was typically Victorian in so far as it embodied an optimistic slant towards the world's affairs. The whole of early social development appeared, according to it, to be heading towards the grand climax of western civilisation in the nineteenth century. It was, in fact, based on the notion of progress, in a naïve form. As soon as doubts began to be felt after the outbreak of the first World War about the 'progress' that had become the object of such passionate belief to Victorian England, the whole of Hobhouse's system of thought began to come apart. Why, it was asked, had the check to development occurred? And if the wicked had begun to prosper, what was to be done about it? As Professor Ginsberg wrote in 1931,

It is true that recent history suggests the possibility that the humanitarian spirit was but a temporary product of the eighteenth and nineteenth centuries. It may further be that its triumph is not assured, but
it remains that so far on a review of the stages of ethical development
universalist humanitarianism is the highest yet achieved and the most
distinctive of the modern mind.[49]

The events of the last thirty-five years have justified these doubts and made us suspect that the 'universalist humanitarianism' that has been the glory of a self-conscious western civilisation for so long was not the peak of human achievement that it has been deemed to be. The truth is, that Hobhouse's work must be regarded as a most valuable approach to the understanding of the social realities that is a necessary prolegomenon to the gaining of a measure of control over our social environment. But no more. It was based too extensively on data drawn from our scanty knowledge of society as it existed at the beginning of human history, or among the 'simpler peoples' of today; again, he shared Weber's willingness to depend on the writings of colleagues, particularly historians. This was not what the world wanted from social scientists, however, though it might of course be a good beginning. It was absurd to believe, for instance, that very much light was shed on the troubles of religious bodies as they exist in our own society by a study of the religious beliefs of the 'lower hunters' rather than the analysis of the facts concerning the weakness of religious belief and practice as they were presented at the end of the Victorian age by Charles Booth. Hobhouse's findings were, in fact, only applicable in some measure to the 'simpler peoples' left undisturbed by civilised man, in so far as any of them still existed in his day; they were the work of a social philosopher rather than a social scientist. The facts about development in contemporary societies in general, and in urban and industrial Britain, were infinitely more complex and more subtle in their meaning than he seems to have realised. It is for this reason, perhaps, that Hobhouse's work has so regrettably little bearing on the sociology of the contemporary scene, with the result that only minimal attention is paid to it today, however great its importance may be from the philosophical or ethical point of view.

The curious thing about Hobhouse was that, whilst Hobhouse the philosopher overshadowed Hobhouse as a social scientist, he never followed up with any ease the influence mind exercised on social affairs through the medium of the formulation of values, or what passes for values. Here his analysis was weaker than Bosanquet's, though one likes to read into his work an ability to achieve the synthesis between idealism and realism that was so lacking at the time. He was much more ready to validate his thesis through a painstaking analysis of what he deemed to be the main outlines of the hidden and seemingly purposeless mechanism of social evolution, than to discuss the direct impact of mind on social change through the formulation and reformulation of values,[50] a line which would have led him much further. Philosophers such as Lord Lindsay came to attach much more importance to values than he did, within a decade of his death.

Writing of this disillusion, of the cynicism and indifference that many young Germans had suffered from during the 1930s, that had led some of them to welcome and support Hitler, Lindsay exclaimed: 'Had I not seen traces of the same disillusion and cynicism of minds as empty of faith and purpose and hope among students of our universities?' This might come, he thought, from a misconceived separation of science from evaluation, and therefore of fact from value. He went on to argue that this might be due to a belief that the teachings of scientific discovery were entirely mechanical, and to a wrongful application of these techniques to the social world in an attempt to show that human behaviour was entirely explicable in these terms. But, he argued,

> the achievement of physics had depended on the assumption that the object of science was quite different [from what should be the object of a social science. It was] determined, atomistic, uncreative, irrational, stuff for the physicist to master and manipulate, and mould to his purpose. . . . The new sciences were prevailingly mechanistic. They had taken all values out of the object to transfer them to the knower.[51]

The construction of this apparatus of thought was designed for the explanation of the behaviour of inanimate matter, and its application to the responsible and self-conscious behaviour of individuals in society was disastrous. According to physical science, he thought,

> Man in his internal constitution and his social relations must be regarded as if he were only a collocation of atoms and his society only a collocation of atoms. These methods cannot apprehend values and therefore in time we are told that there are no values; they cannot apprehend freedom and therefore we are told that there is no freedom; they cannot apprehend reason, and we are therefore told that man is through and through irrational.[52]

But this argument, he pointed out, is a strictly limited one, never applicable to the scientist (or the social scientist) as such. If there is one division between fact and value, it is often supposed, there is another between the rational world of science and the irrational world of common life. And it is obvious that it is no more possible to make the second, in practice, than the first can be made, in theory. If it were, 'the game would obviously be up'.

> The modern social investigator who believes in this method tells us that men are irrational, the victims of complexes or of economic forces, but in practice he means people other than himself. He does not say . . . 'Modern science has discovered that modern scientists are irrational, the victims of complexes and all the rest of it'. . . . Something more subtle and more sinister tends to happen. It is difficult to go on denying creativeness and spontaneity and to practise those virtues at the same time. The social scientist therefore tends to abandon

the real methods which have made possible the triumphs of the physical scientist, his imaginativeness and daring, and to become the passive recipient of impressions.[53]

That is, he becomes a positivist, and the whole sorry tangle which is so frustrating is on us again. But Lindsay brought his argument to an end just as it was becoming most profitable. He had not read his Hobhouse carefully enough. It was not sufficient to show that it was absurd to call on science and inductive philosophy to demonstrate that the creativeness of chance was a good way of explaining the social world around us, and that science could therefore discover 'whether or not spiritual things are real'.[54] In essence, this is a negative argument, and leaves the problem of the nature of sociological truth untouched. Its implication is not that the world of science is to be kept separate from the world of values, which leads to assumptions about the rationality of the one and the irrationality of the other, but that there is a need for the development of several kinds of science, adapted, *inter alia*, for the explanation of physical, biological and social problems respectively. Every science must be specially suited to the explanation of its own characteristic subject-matter, especially if an attribute of this is life in various forms and degrees. It must also have its own measure of responsiveness to its environment. The real distinction is, in fact, between individual kinds of science, rather than science and non-science. But Lindsay never recognised this; although Hobhouse had shown that reason was a far more complex thing than anybody had previously supposed, it was a conclusion that might easily have been arrived at in Lindsay's day.

The problem therefore has remained outstanding up to our own times whether 'scientific' techniques can in fact explain to any extent the essentially human problems of motive and value, or the conscious and self-conscious determination of value and goal-motivated conduct, and appraisals affecting the definition and determination of ends and objectives. It is a new conception of *social* science that we want, not a better understanding of the way in which 'science' at large can be used as a means of understanding man's social conduct. Hobhouse's awareness of the nature of contemporary society was much less vivid than his philosophical understanding of the concepts he used, and his ability to build a system of thought out of them.[55] His sociology, therefore, needed to be made more real than his philosophic realism permitted. If it appears to be Hobhouse to whom we turn most readily to find the foundations of the sociology of the future, it must be admitted that it will be his philosophical ideas that will play a larger part in this than his strictly sociological studies. It is his explanation of purposive action and his account of development which gave to his sociology something that is lacking today. His name occupies a correspondingly important place in the sociological history of our own times. It is now necessary for us to strengthen the scientific foundations that he laid by adding to them our own more adequate means of understanding the social nature of the affairs of the world in which we live.

It is the personal creativity, then, rather than the mechanistic processes underlying current affairs, that Hobhouse succeeded in understanding so much more clearly than his younger colleagues. To some extent he may be said to have accomplished that task by reconciling the idealism of his day with sociological realism, as is made evident in his very revealing article on 'The Philosophy of Development'.[56] If that is so, it is our own task to reconcile the superabundant realism of current social research with the need to make due allowance for the idealism of social policy and action, which are such prominent features of our age.

3. American Empiricism: A Sociological Dilemma

Unlike their English counterparts, the social sciences in the United States quickly assumed an independent academic existence, and took form and shape well before the end of the nineteenth century. The influences that led to this rapid development were much stronger in America than they were in England, but their similarities were striking. Both England and the United States had been through their own Industrial Revolution, and circumstances had forced the traditional way of life of the communities concerned to compromise with industrialisation and urbanism. Both countries ultimately endured the economic depressions of the interwar period, particularly the Great Depression of the 'thirties. But in addition, America had to come to terms with the existence of the immense Negro minority in the South and elsewhere, which made it so difficult to weld the nation together into closely-knit communities based on the American Way of Life, however strong this was.[1] Moreover Americans had to accustom themselves throughout the nineteenth century to the fact that another minority lived within their boundaries, the American Indians, and that they had to learn how to live with its members. Both socially and physically, many Americans lived even into the twentieth century on the frontiers of a great civilisation, in a manner which never confronted British citizens, despite the existence throughout this period of the Empire. And in addition to this, American legislators and civic authorities had to find ways of adjusting their society to the influx of hordes of immigrants, compelled to seek physical and social shelter in their midst, being driven to do so by Irish famine, Polish pogroms, and Italian poverty. Empiricism was even more a necessary expedient of government and a philosophical method in America than it was in Britain, and America's problems were perhaps even more social than they were moral. They were regarded as such more and more as the years went by.

American sociology, writes Professor Shils in his monograph on *The Present State of American Sociology*, developed at the time of the decay of classical and humanistic studies. Its original point of departure, evident in the work of Ward and Giddings, embodied the same principle of coherence and the same guiding standard which Continental sociology had obtained from its contacts with political philosophy. These were 'men of learning, large perspective, and synthetic disposition', but its second generation immersed itself in 'the first-hand experience of concrete situations'. The early American sociologists were therefore succeeded by the generation of Park, Cooley and Ross, who

> stood midway between the sociology of the library and learned meditation on the one hand, and increasingly circumspect techniques of the present day on the other; they had a profound influence, especially on the establishment of a precedent which requires sociologists to describe and explain the modern world.

Their task became to analyse social phenomena, rather than to criticise or appraise them, or to assess their moral implications for the development of civilisation. American sociology came of age with the achievements of the urban sociologists, particularly those of the Chicago School in general, and Park and Burgess in particular; they were evidenced by small community studies such as the classic *Middletown* (1929), *Middletown in Transition* (1937), and ultimately Lloyd Warner's *Social Life of a Modern Community* (1941). But a deep dissatisfaction with this kind of work developed amongst American sociologists. As a whole, sociology tended towards trivialities. 'Even under the direct inspiration of the living teacher', wrote Professor Shils, 'they were still not science':

> The numerous researches into the frequency of tax delinquencies in certain urban areas, into the residential distribution of persons applying for treatment for venereal diseases, and many others like them, never acquired the dignity of relevance or significance. From the point of view of their *direct* contribution to a systematic theory of human behaviour and social organisation, there was no value in them.[2]

The strength of American sociology was therefore its ability to study the contemporary social scene and its problems. Its weakness was due to the deficiency in American sociologists' training in wide historical knowledge, and the philosophical preparation which makes it possible to 'analyse the social conditions of the emergence, accept-

E

ance or rejection of different types of doctrines'. American sociology before the second World War was confined to the contemporary form which American society took from time to time, partly because of ignorance; this was also 'a result of the strong tendency – very praiseworthy from a strictly scientific standpoint – of seeking to come into first-hand contact with ones' materials'. A further explanation was 'the absence of the value-criteria' which would motivate the choice of some of the topics which had been left untouched, and this was due to the sociologists' lack of awareness of the philosophical significance of many of them. Professor Shils' final conclusion was, therefore, that the major vice of American sociology is the counterpart of its chief and distinguishing virtue; 'its hitherto predominant indifference to the formation of a general theory is closely connected with its eagerness for precision in first-hand observation'.[3]

This cleavage between the theorists and the empiricists left many American sociologists with a distrust of 'the deadweight of the factual survey', and a craving for a 'basic theoretical knowledge of social behaviour'. It accounted for the immense influence of Weber's ideas, particularly when his contributions to the dispute about the relations in logic between the social sciences and values began to become available in 1947 and 1949, in American translation.[4] As so much attention had been paid to factual investigations, particularly by the Chicago School of Urban Sociology and its offshoots, and so little by sociologists in general to theoretical or philosophical studies, Weber's ideas prevailed in their crudest form; the first blow was struck at the moral certainty of the new science of sociology through the diffusion of German sociological theory amongst American universities. Sociology came to embody the positivist ideas into which Weber's theories were transmuted in America, and sociologists began to think that they either had to be agnostics, so far as values were concerned, or values had to be regarded at best as unknowable, or at the worst, as nonsense.[5]

From this time on, sociology developed in two ways in America. In the first place, a strong interest in theory began to grow which, however, became increasingly abstract as the years went by. Although valuable investigations were carried out by Professor Talcott Parsons and his followers, which gained added impetus as the result of the examination of sociology generally in the wider context of the work of Durkheim and Weber, the total effect was that theory lost contact with empirical studies; the whole problem of values remained un-solved, especially so far as its practical manifestation in policy form-ation was concerned, and no secure links were forged between philo-sophy, particularly moral and political, and sociology. This was dis-astrous. As Professor Shils said, in the last sentences of his monograph:

> Political and moral philosophy is not the same as sociology, and it is no substitute for sociology. But sociology will not develop into a science unless these relations are rightly understood, and the role of moral and political criteria in the selection of problems worthy of study is adequately recognised.[6]

This was written in 1948, after the second World War, when it appeared that the social upheavals the war had occasioned might demand the development of a new sociology, capable of giving them adequate consideration. Robert S. Lynd, author of *Middletown*, had made this even more likely by writing a remarkable critique of American sociology as it existed at the end of the interwar period, which came to much the same conclusions, and had, no doubt, in-fluenced Shils to write as he did. His position for many years as Secretary of the Social Science Research Council had given him long experience of the execution of research projects, their significance from the point of view of scholarship, and their importance from that of public affairs. His book *Knowledge for What?*[7] was correspondingly influential. It was published at a critical time, when it appeared that social scientists had lost interest in most questions as to what current social developments really amounted to, having special regard to the overall quality of American civilisation; they thus gave an impression of excusing themselves from asking where their institutions were taking them, or where they wanted to go. Empiricism was conducive to realism, but it had also succumbed to a temptation to over-preoccupy itself with the affairs of the immediate moment. What, he asked, was the multitude of facts that had been accumulated for? He pointed out in his chapter on 'Values and the Social Sciences' that the latter had avoided having any commerce with philosophy, even though 'the out-standing characteristic of a well trained scientist is his ability to distin-guish "significant" from "insignificant" problems and data. . . . Re-search without an actively selected point of view becomes the ditty bag of an idiot, filled with . . . random hoardings.'

> The confusion that exists between the social scientists' professions to eschew all questions of value and what he so patently does is a confusion

on the point at which valuing is applied. Values may be and are
properly and necessarily applied in the preliminary selection of
'significant', 'important' problems for research. They may be but
should not be applied thereafter to bias one's analysis as the interpretation of the meanings inherent in one's data.[8]

Lynd's conclusion was therefore that sociological research should
be given a new direction. What was required was not more information, and still more information, so much as a keener awareness of
what were the significant problems, and painstaking enquiry into
them, with special reference to their significance. For instance, technicians in public administration 'are tending to over-reach themselves
in assuming that effective administration in the public interest can be
achieved by small administrative adjustments of the going system',
whereas what was lacking was not so much attention to details, as the
construction of 'a philosophy of Power in modern institutional life'.[9]
The 'old aloof ethics', he considered, had evaporated, and 'ethics today
is but a component of the cravings of persons going about the daily
round of living with each other', and if the sciences of human behaviour in culture could not 'escape dealing with man's deep values
and potential futures', it was necessary for them to ask what are in
fact 'the values and cravings of the human personality'. If man is but
sporadically rational,

> The task of social science becomes the discovery of what forms of
> culturally-structured learned behaviour can maximise opportunities for
> rational behaviour where it appears to be essential for human well-
> being, and at the same time provide opportunity for expression of his
> deep emotional *spontaneities* where those, too, are important.[10]

Above all, there was the desperate need to find some point of reference by which social science could get beyond the present paralysing
question: How are *we* to determine what *ought* to be? Lacking the
answer to that question, there is no firm basis for doing more than
merely to follow the determinisms of the moment. How, without it, is
social science to 'take up its work of appraising and reshaping our
culture'? How is it ever to ask how man's needs are to be met, how our
current institutions satisfy them, or 'what changes in the institutions
are required'? Above all, we find him asking in the concluding paragraphs of the book, what kind of culture would make it possible to
use intelligence 'freely and eagerly, constantly to rebuild man's
institutions'? 'What is it that we human beings want, and what things

have to be done, in what ways and in what sequence, in order to change the present so as to achieve it?' His peroration closes with the urgent, somewhat despairing assertion: 'With such research and planning, we may yet make real the claims of freedom and opportunity in America.'[11]

The generation of the 'thirties, given the climate of opinion prevailing in the conditions of the Great Depression and the New Deal, could be excused for devoting itself to practical studies and researches directed to finding solutions for the urgent and indeed catastrophic problems of the times. The social sciences had thus found themselves compelled to take on an austerely 'practical' attitude to their responsibilities. The Social Science Research Council and the Rockefeller-dominated Spelman Fund had underwritten President Hoover's Research Committee on Social Trends, the Report of which was a ragbag of miscellaneous information. Strong links came to be forged between university departments and governmental agencies. Roosevelt's Committee on Administrative Management pursued the same line as had been laid down by Hoover, and academic work came to be regarded as 'non-political' in the sense that it was devoted to the solution of everyday difficulties of government, rather than to the identification of its over-riding problems, and the propounding of any fundamental position or point of view in relation to them.[12] In these circumstances, the reception that Lynd's book received was by no means encouraging. What it said was true enough, but the tendencies which it criticised in the social sciences were too strongly entrenched in the times to allow any current of change to be set in motion; in any event, the wartime stresses which developed immediately after the publication of the book deflected interest from it, and it was never given the attention which it deserved. The predisposition of American sociology for 'scientific' certainties therefore continued.

The trends established in the 1930s may be said to have come to a head in the work of Harold D. Lasswell, undertaken for the most part in the 1930s and 1940s.[13] These works, particularly the second, made a great show of developing a 'scientific' understanding of politics and of the moral life:

> The significant advances of our time have not been in the discovery of new definitions of moral values, or even in the skilful derivation of old definitions from more universal propositions. The advances of our time have been in the technique of relating them to reality.

In the process, science has clarified morals. This, indeed, is the distinctive contribution of science to morality. With the best will in the world we cannot take the attitudes of our fellows into consideration unless we know what they are, and this depends upon an adequate staff of skilled observers. Lacking these instruments, good intentions cannot possibly be fulfilled in practice. . . . This much is clear: whether or not the methods of scientific observation contribute to the eventual completion of a systematic science of democracy, they are certain to contribute, here and now, to the practice of democratic morals. Without science, democracy is blind and weak. With science, democracy will not be blind and may be strong.[14]

This whets the appetite, as the passage professes to put morals on a scientific basis, which is what philosophers have been trying to do for hundreds of years; furthermore, it seeks to make the democratic way of life effective. However, all boils down in the end to the collection of facts, and yet more facts. The only problem is how 'data-gathers' are to proceed 'in determining the state of practice in a given situation'. 'Official records' are not enough, as they will not 'record the state of intimidation, or the degree of public confidence in the genuineness of democratic processes':

The needed facts can be obtained only by observers who possess skills appropriate to the observation of reality. Such observers must be equipped to establish themselves where they find out what is said and done. They must make reliable and consistent records of what they see. Then records must be properly analysed.[15]

So, in the end, everything turns on 'proper analysis'. Having regard to the extent to which Professor Lasswell's work is based on Freudian concepts, it appears that this will be a development of Freud's methods. In his chapter on 'The Criteria of Political Types' in his *Psychopathology and Politics*, for instance, he lays it down that:

The task of the hour is the development of a realistic analysis of the political in relation to the social process, and this depends upon the invention of abstract conceptions and upon the prosecution of empirical research.

But in the chapter on 'The Politics of Prevention', he states that we should abandon the assumption that the problem of politics is the problem of promoting discussion amongst the interests concerned; the accepted task is less to solve conflicts than to prevent them:

The achievement of the ideal of preventive politics depends less upon changes in social organisation than upon improving the methods and the education of the social administrators and the social scientists.[16]

The naked truth is that Professor Lasswell thought that he had discovered a method of dissecting the personalities of people involved in public life so that differences between 'administrators' and 'agitators' could be understood. The science of politics, then, rested in the development of an ability to give the administrators responsibility and to restrain the agitators, a popular task in America at periods of 'anti-liberal' practice, particularly in the years after the second World War, during the ascendancy of Senator McCarthy. But though the American liberal has had a continually troubled life throughout, the prestige of Freudian methods of enquiry, research, and action has fluctuated from the very high to the fairly low, and in recent years it has been on the decline. Consequently, not much has been heard in recent years of Professor Lasswell's specific proposals that were derived from his earlier Freudian studies. His somewhat undemocratic notions that the opponents of the American Way of Life (and big business) could be identified by psychopathology, and either dealt with by psychotherapy, or rendered harmless by restraint, also appear to have been forgotten.[17]

His work took a somewhat different direction when the war was over and the necessity for a more precise definition of the role of the social sciences in policy-formation became obvious. The problem then became to show how the main trends of the American social sciences could be continued in a situation which demanded that the social scientist should play his part in policy formation, even at a time when some were asserting that if he did so, his policy recommendations would have no more justification than personal preference, if not amount to mere whim or prejudice, and would certainly be 'unscientific'. Perhaps the statement most typical of his times was that of Professor G. H. Sabine, made in the 1950s. 'It is', he said,

> impossible for any logical operation to excogitate the truth of any allegation of fact, and neither logic nor fact implies a value. Consequently . . . the attempt to fuse these three operations, whether in Hegelian idealism or in its Marxian variant, merely perpetrated an intellectual confusion inherent in the system of natural law. . . . As for values, they appear to the author to be always the reaction of human preference to some state of social and physical fact; in the concrete they are too complicated to be generally described even with so loose a word as utility.[18]

The issue was plainly presented in *The Policy Sciences*[19] in 1951, which is today something of an historic text. This was a symposium, which appeared under the auspices of the Hoover Institute Studies, and Professor Lasswell was one of its joint editors. His own contributions to it were a somewhat modified version of the line he had taken in his own pre-war publications; they represented something of a retreat from the ambitious claims of his earlier books, and they now tended to be more in keeping with the claims which had become traditional amongst American social scientists. Their task was, namely, one of recording and exploration, rather than leadership and appraisal. In particular, he thought it to be only 'probable' that the policy sciences would 'be directed towards providing the knowledge needed to improve the practice of democracy'; his view thus expressed was much clearer than it had been previously, for he now held that the policy sciences would be responsible merely for *the creation* of 'instruments of social analysis'. He saw in this the need to cross the frontier between, for instance, statistical techniques and the criticism of existing institutions, but he was still confused in so far as he was unable to say how precisely this should be done. He was only willing to admit a very general commitment to the values of democracy 'in which the ultimate goal is the realisation of human dignity in theory and fact', but though he gave brief mention to Lynd's work, he showed no signs of being able to assimilate any of its criticisms of American social science in his own work. In his view 'it is to be foreseen that the emphasis will be upon the development of knowledge pertinent to the fuller realisation of human dignity', but no definite line of action followed from this.

His conclusion was that:

> The policy frame of reference makes it necessary to take into account the entire context of significant events . . . in which the scientist is living. This calls for the use of speculative models of the world revolutionary process of the epoch, and puts the techniques of quantification in a respected though subordinate place. Because of the instability of meaning of the indices available to give operational definition to key terms, it is particularly important to develop specialised institutions to observe and report world developments. This permits the pre-testing of possible changes in social practice before they are introduced on a vast scale.[20]

This is something of a comedown after the confident opinions expressed in the Introduction to the book that 'the sciences of society are essential to the formulation and application of policy at every stage':

Recent experience, particularly during and since the war, has demonstrated that reliance upon the techniques and substantive contribution of these sciences diminishes the policy makers' errors of judgment and gives greater assurance that the course of action decided upon will achieve the intended goals.[21]

The function of the social scientist, as seen by Professor Lasswell, thus boils down to the useful, but not very important, activity of 'observing and reporting' (for somebody else), and even this is not to evaluate objectives, but to see that the 'course of action decided upon' will achieve 'the intended goals', and that is at best only a very secondary function. But Professor R. K. Merton, who contributed a concluding paper on 'Social Scientists and Research Policy' to *The Policy Sciences*, went much further than this.

It had been taken for granted by the early British sociologists that it was their responsibility to criticise and recommend, so far as public services and public problems were concerned, rather than to assist with important details, as technicians. The danger that the life of the special pleader or laboratory technician might dominate the work of the social scientist did not, in fact, become anything like a living issue in Britain until advertising and market research discovered the value of the social sciences well after the second World War. But the greater influence of private business pursued by large and powerful corporations in America caused this to happen on the other side of the Atlantic very much earlier. Accordingly, Professor Merton deplored what was to him the familiar fact that American social scientists were often called on to solve 'problems' in a narrow frame of reference, by dealing with them as those who commissioned them saw the issues involved. That is, they allowed the values of their employers or patrons to dominate their work, rather than their own. It was, he maintained, to create a practical problem for policy-makers, for this 'represents a gap between aspiration and achievement', and he challenged his colleagues to close this gap rather than perpetuate it. 'A major function of research emanating from social science circles . . . may [therefore] be to establish new goals and bench marks of the attainable, [and] social scientists may seek to sensitise policy-makers to more effective means of reaching established goals.' This was harmless enough, but his argument quickly became more controversial. It can be assumed, he thought, that 'the policy-maker always has a set of values, tacit or explicit'; these limit the 'alternative lines of action to be investigated;

and the researcher must search them out 'in order to know in advance the limits set upon the investigation by the policy-makers' values. . . .

Thus, for example, policy oriented research may be requested on ways and means of improving the morale of Negro workers in an industrial plant.' The idea is obviously intolerable that research can be instituted on the assumption that Negro morale can be improved despite the fact that he may be subjected to segregation, evidenced in the use, for instance, of washroom accommodation. It is even more intolerable that research can be conducted that assumes that there are circumstances in which segregation should be promoted, or improved. It is therefore concluded that a 'socially oriented' scientist will only lend himself to carrying out schemes 'which do not violate his own values',[22] and the main task of social research therefore becomes the identification and the establishment of valid and viable values in any given community. So far as Professor Merton is concerned, therefore, what he is advocating here is that researchers should have their own value-systems, and regulate their professional lives in accordance with them; that is something quite different from Professor Lasswell's views, which regard the social scientist as little more than a technician, pure and simple. Professor Merton imposes a heavy burden of responsibilities on social scientists so far as participation in social planning and the evolution of underlying values is concerned; Professor Lasswell, on the other hand, restricts their functions to the 'clarification of objectives' and the creation of 'instruments of social analysis'. The general outcome of the argument was, indeed, that what was wanted was a 'guide to social action', and the guidance required must be securely based in the world of values and ends, as well as, or rather than, in the technical world of means.

It is therefore of great significance, in view of what happened later, that Professor Merton argued in *The Policy Sciences* that what was being advocated was not a new reconciliation between science and value, but the promulgation of a specifically American variant of the social sciences, which would exist to implement the values which might be deemed to be latent in the American Dream. 'The Social Scientist in America', he argued, 'has developed a tradition which emphasises empirical focus, reliable techniques, and precise data', or, in other words, precisely the same characteristics which were held in the last chapter to be typical of the British sociology of the nineteenth and early twentieth centuries, though he did not give British sociologists sufficient credit for assuming a measure of social responsibility. This American tradition, he added, 'contrasts strongly with the European tradition . . . which values theoretical outlook, speculative methods, and approximate insights', and that was correct, at least as far as German sociology was concerned. It remains to be seen how much of what is best in each tradition can be preserved, and made the basis of one common to all western civilisations.

Professor Merton's conclusion was, then, not so much that there should be a much more general agreement on the relative importance in the development of the social sciences of significant problem-solving and practical usefulness, but quite the reverse, that much more freedom should be accorded to the social scientist to carve out his destiny for himself in his own way. As things were:

> The scientist is called upon to contribute information useful to imple-ment a given policy, but the policy itself is 'given', not open to ques-tion. This often throws the scientist off the right track, for the data may indicate the need to devise a policy other than which is 'given'. Accept-ance of such conditions of research may become a threat to the functions of scientist *qua* scientist. So long as the scientist continues to accept a role in which he does not question policies, state problems, and formulate alternatives, the more does he become routinised in the role of bureaucratic technician.[23]

Here is the dilemma. If the 'scientist *qua* scientist' has his functions threatened when the conditions of a research are thrust upon him, to be accepted as 'given' and not to be questioned, and if he is thus prevented from devising policies which the conditions require, then it must be that the social scientist must, as such, demand to take part in the formulation of policy and this involves values. Otherwise he must accept the reduced importance and status of a 'bureaucratic tech-nician'. There is here a degree of ambiguity, in so far as it is left un-clear as to whether Professor Merton was assuming that one could speak of two sets of 'research' and 'value' conditions, not necessarily applying to both researcher and citizen; but this is cleared up in the concluding paragraphs of his chapter. For he takes the argument in them quite explicitly into the field of the moral, and applies it to the researcher. The American social scientist, the article continues,

> has seen too many examples in recent history of the intellectual com-mitting moral suicide by allowing himself to be routinised in the service of the directive-giving state. . . . It has become apparent that

the first condition which social scientists must observe if they are to make a contribution toward the attainment of a world commonwealth of human dignity, is to retain their own freedom of choice – among goals and values, among policies and decisions, among ways and means. If the social scientist is to contribute significantly to human welfare, he must be ready, willing and able to ask and seek answers for such questions as: can we get human welfare without the 'welfare state'? If so, how? If not, how can we get the welfare state without the total state?

Professor Merton's conclusion is, then, that the social scientist must explicitly demand the widest freedom, in matters of value, to determine the objects of social and political organisation (not in any sense to ignore values), and the methods whereby they are to be attained. This implies, firstly, that he possesses some means of distinguishing between the justification of one value and another, and the development of criteria whereby the success or failure of solutions to these problems can be judged. We shall not know, he says,

> just how much of a contribution applied social research can make until we have tried. And we probably shall not make very rewarding efforts until we have subjected the past achievements and failures of applied social research to rigorous self-evaluation.

But he ends on a more optimistic note:

> With the surer knowledge of present capabilities and limitations gained from such self-scrutiny, social scientists will better be able to plan the future of their science, by deciding who their clients shall be, and how to serve them. . . . The making of such decisions will put them further along the path of the developing policy sciences of democracy. And this path, we venture to suggest, may well be the most promising alternative to involuntary suicide.[24]

Hence the craving of American intellectuals for freedom regarding values, political and social. The crux of the matter is that interference in social science and university affairs generally, has gone much further in the United States than it has in Great Britain, and this has provoked a reaction that has taken two forms. First of all, there has been a turning away from the idea of 'pure' sociology; the idea of involvement in political life and in policy-making has been accepted and pursued. In a sense, the American intellectual is regarded as free only when he is involved. This has been the path followed by C. Wright Mills, and extended recently by many American sociologists who have been influenced by his ideas. A flourishing school of thought has been founded in this way after his death. In the past two decades, however, the American sociologist has tended to withdraw from the world of affairs and devote his time to the evolution of abstruse sociological theories with no direct, and only very indirect, bearing on the course of current affairs. This course, dubbed by C. Wright Mills 'grand theory', was denounced by him in *The Sociological Imagination*,[25] in which it occupied a prominent place only equalled by that devoted to the school he described as that of 'abstracted empiricism', which also enabled those sociologists who disliked the idea of joining in the discussion of current events and problems to withdraw into the valueless world of fact-gathering. This point of view has now been made explicit in 1964 in *The New Sociology*.[26]

In the first place, therefore, the reaction to the sociology of the immediate postwar period has been positive. The acceptance by sociologists of the constructive task of preserving and developing the true values of American (and other western) civilisation is now favourable, and it is agreed that it is necessary to assist in the solution of the problems that arise from threats to these in the daily life of the nation.[27] Secondly, however, the reaction has been a negative one in which the positivistic ideas on which so much sociological thinking has been based in the immediate past have been resisted and rejected. Under the first heading, an attempt has been made to construct a sociology in keeping with the intellectual and social needs of the times; under the second, a particularly bitter conflict has developed with those sociologists who have been led away from what have been the characteristically American (and British) methods of work towards more abstract and philosophical or speculative activities, based on classical sociology. In particular, the direction in which these activities have been pursued has been away from what have been supposed to be the intellectual hazards of value, and value-motivated action, and towards 'pure' theory theory. The pity of this has been that the attempt to protect themselves from the exploitation and undue influence of vested interests by escaping into the mists of 'pure' theory has been at the cost of losing contact with reality and actualities, and sociology has earned a bad name for itself amongst those who have accepted the responsibility for developing public policies and guiding, rather than suffering, events and situations.

Now the impression appears to be general amongst the English

sociologists of today that the development of the English tradition of
sociology is to be deplored[28] and should be replaced as soon as possible
by copying the ideas which came to be prominent in America twenty
years ago as to the importance of devoting one's time to 'pure sociological theory'. An American sociologist has reversed the argument by
seeking to defend Wright Mills' ideas (particularly those attacking
'grand theory' and remoteness from practical affairs) by asserting that
British social scientists, who have sought to determine the objectives
and to tackle the problems of the welfare state, have tended to give
them 'exceptionally close ties with policy oriented sectors of the
society':

> Policy makers [in Britain] for their part often think of the social
> sciences as a rationale required for any projected change estimated to be
> in the social interests. Before a major piece of legislation is introduced
> into the English Parliament the likelihood is that a survey has already
> been conducted, providing a form of social science legitimation. Thus
> in England, while investment in social science is relatively smaller
> than in the United States, there is a high payoff for social science
> information. . . . England no longer produces the great theories about
> society; rather it paves the way for practices intended to reshape social
> policy.[29]

The argument is, therefore, that when collaboration is willing, and
expressly in the interests of the society concerned, and there are
institutional safeguards against exploitation, there is every reason for
collaboration between agencies of the government and social scientists,
either by way of taking them into employment, or by establishing a
close association with them.[30] Where tension has come to prevail
among social scientists or between social scientists and policy-makers,
as in America, the notion of the functions of the social scientist as a
'policy scientist' has fallen to the ground. The scientist has been
regarded by the policy scientists as a technician who helps others to
make policy; he is not regarded as responsible in any sense for policy
as a whole. Lacking an independent basis for their professional functions, it is impossible for them to evaluate freely what policies there
should be, and this, at least in America, has not been achieved to
anything like a satisfactory extent, to put things mildly.[31]

It is hard to say what a social scientist should do in circumstances
such as these, when he disagrees with his instructions, perhaps in a case
where they are given with the best of intentions, with the object of

attaining some seemingly praiseworthy goal which is nevertheless objectionable to him. It is perhaps easy enough, to decide what to do when the purpose is simply to make money, or to win general compliance with the wishes of a third party, as when one is helping to sell some useless or harmful commodity such as a cosmetic, or winning the loyalty of the workers to a manufacturing undertaking by 'scientific' persuasion and bribery, rather than by truthful explanation in the common interest. There is, however, no simple solution to many dilemmas of this kind. The best that can be done, and the method that should now be followed, is to establish a code of professional practice akin to the medical code, which should be formulated and applied by the social scientists' professional bodies. They should explain their difficulties to the public, and invite as much public discussion as possible. Issues must be faced and fought. In the 'closed' society this cannot be done, and it is perhaps no coincidence that the social sciences do not prosper in such societies. In 'open' societies it can be done, and it desirable and necessary for their wellbeing that it should be done. This is easy enough in Great Britain, where the social scientist has only been made use of as a mere technical assistant to a relatively small degree by industry, commerce and government; by and large, it is still his to reason why. But in America, this may not be the case. There, the future of the social sciences, especially in universities, is largely dependent on the securing of 'contracts' between research organisations on the one hand, and consumers of research on the other; their future is very much in doubt.

A tremendous problem has therefore arisen which has resulted from the inadequacy of the idea of a 'policy science', save as developed by Professor Merton, and it remains to be seen how far the constructive elements in it can be salvaged and put into practice either in Great Britain or in the United States. The proximate cause of this has surely been that the notion of freedom *from* values has resulted in the idea of responsibility for the shaping of policy being inadequately based on a science that has been held to be necessarily devoid of any content of value. Professor Horowitz has come to the following conclusion:

> The proud announcement in the early 'fifties of the policy sciences has given way to a profound scepticism of such a concept in the 'sixties. Perhaps the notion of a policy science is a contradiction in terms. . . . From the point of view of the social scientist the concept of policy

science must be challenged because in the final analysis the scientific community can never accept an exclusively therapeutic definition of social life. Social science can never take for granted the things which make for political sovereignty.[32]

The only way out of the dilemma is to mount a direct attack on the logical status of values, as establishing the problems which the 'policy sciences' seek to solve, and as accepting or rejecting one kind of social expedient or another to solve them. A value is logically prior to the policy which carries it into effect; this is also true of situations which call for the exercise of political power.

It must be made plain, then, that values are deeply influential in the lives and work of sociologists, who are, in fact, far from being the 'objective' scientists the positivists would suppose. A recent account of a survey of the opinions of the members of the American Sociological Association has shown rather surprising results. As the authors say, 'sociology as a science is often said to be value-free', but most sociologists do not believe this to be true; 73% of the 3,440 sociologists who completed the questionnaire agreed with the statement that most of their colleagues merely paid lip-service to the 'ideal of being value-free': 66.9% also agreed that 'as teachers, sociologists can express their personal values to students'. So far as the depth and breadth of sociology are concerned, 84.8% agreed that 'in designing research, it is at least as important to be inventive as it is to be rigorous', and 91% voted in favour of the statement that 'the sociologist, like any other intellectual, has the right and duty to criticise contemporary society', whilst 85% favoured the statement that the sociologist should not only think about communicating to his professional colleagues, but he should also attempt to speak to a wider public.[33]

The general impression that the results of the survey make on one's mind is that the vast majority of American sociologists believe that sociology should have something important to say about the life and times of their fellow-citizens, and that they should convey their ideas to the general public in a way that can readily be understood. More than three-quarters hold that 'the most basic sources of stability in any group are the beliefs and values which its members share', whilst more than 60% agree that 'the problems of modern society are so complex that only planned change can be expected to solve them', though they also think that 'planned change is sometimes dangerous because of possible unanticipated consequences'. The cast of mind of this group of sociologists seems to include an awareness that the ills of modern society must be made the concern of public policy, and that this will have to be directed to the strengthening of beliefs and values.

Still, the American sociologists recognised that this would have its dangers; this seems to arise from the fact that their confidence in the intelligence of their ordinary fellow-citizens is not as strong as they would, perhaps, like it to be. Only just over a third agreed that 'many sociologists underestimate the importance of rationality in human life', whilst slightly more disagreed with the statement. Although it is a hopeful sign that over three-quarters did not think that 'active involvement in efforts to remedy social problems' would 'seriously bias a sociologist', it was doubtful to many whether it is possible to accept involvement without disturbing sociology itself. 30% agreed that 'sociology will be unable to hold on to its value-free ideal in the face of increasing public demands for application of sociological findings', though it is possible that this decision may be influenced by a fundamental distrust of the idea of value-freedom in any event. A much less ambiguous statement was contained in the opinion that 'many social scientists are too prone to let foundations and government agencies determine the problems they will study', agreed to by two-thirds of those answering the questionnaire, or exactly three times as many as objected to it. In these circumstances, it is doubtful whether sociologists will be able to play a leading part in changing the American Way of Life into something more in keeping with the needs of our times, especially as over a third agree that 'much of current sociological theory is tacitly grounded in a conservative political ideology'.[34] We are finally left with the impression that whilst most sociologists would like to see more criticism of contemporary society, half object to the idea that sociology should try to help society out of its difficulties. The role of the sociologist is seen, in other words, as prophet rather than as doctor or engineer.

The question as to what the values are which influence sociologists as a matter of fact is an interesting one. It has been found that most sociologists share a value-system in a very general way, together with the specific values they adopt, though they may be rather fogged and imprecise. They tend to be humanitarians, stressing the dignity of the person and strongly asserting 'the right of each man to pursue his own way, [accepting] a reasonable, tolerant and kindly philosophy, religiously neutral, and tending to be independent of tradition'. This

F

liberalism has even been said to amount to a bias, which is carried into professional work, favouring the point of view of minority groups in relation to the majorities which encompass them. 'One might', one author concludes, 'question whether the empirical evidence justifies the one-sided picture that sociologists present.' The blame for bad intergroup relations tends to be laid at the door of majorities, though this 'may not be entirely due to the objective evidence, but may be due at least in part to a humanitarian philosophy which inclines the social pathologists both to collect and to interpret their facts in a specific way'. This also happens with the sociologists' account of crime. The sociologists' tendency is 'to shift the blame from the offender to . . . poor home environment . . . bad adjustment in school, [or] the causation may be found deep in the offender's unconscious. Seldom is it admitted that the offender decided freely and in cold blood to commit the crime.'[35] The troubles that occur as the result of the collision between what may be termed the sociologists' values and other value-systems arise from the fact that it is difficult for the sociologist to rest easily in his own beliefs, and at the same time to adopt an attitude towards others of live and let live. The problem of the sociologist's concern with values will be one of the main themes discussed in the concluding chapter of this book.

4. The Impact of Weber's Ideas on the Logic of the Social Sciences

I

The state of affairs described by Robert S. Lynd in *Knowledge for What?* was a disturbing one, describing as it did an attempt to develop the social sciences as what amounted to a technology. Many of the proposals advocated in *The Policy Sciences* were an extension of this, based as they were on the idea that there should be a complete separation between the functions of the social sciences, viewed as a collection of methodologies and techniques, and those they might be deemed to have if their main purpose were regarded as establishing the principles of social action. This latter function would deal with the betterment of man's societies, rather than the means or technique of attaining the ends of social or political action that would be determined in an entirely different way.

In order to examine the logical problems that thus arise, the continuity of the argument of the present book must be interrupted. If the treatment of its subject-matter were to continue to be primarily historical, as it has been so far, the next step should no doubt be to describe how the handling of sociological problems in Britain might be compared with the treatment they were given at the same time in America, where it was more narrowly sociological. Before this can be done, however, it must be made clear that another and most important influence greatly affected the course which events took in America; this must now be described and its significance appraised at some length.

This influence originated in Weber's assertion that, as sociology was a science, it could not take sides in matters of value, and must be developed as a theoretical rather than as a practical study. American sociology came to lean that way in the interwar period, and when Weber's works, especially his essays on 'Objectivity in the Social Sciences and Social Policy' and 'The Meaning of "Ethical Neutrality" in Sociology and Economics'[1] were published in America in 1949, the impact on American sociology was both speedy and profound.

American sociology had shown itself to be hesitant to pronounce on public policies or to venture on anything like an appraisal of American society and culture in the interwar period, and Weber's writings were a powerful stimulus to this tendency when relevant sections became known after the war.

In Germany, sociology developed in close association with philosophy, and the course it took demonstrated that problems of value and purpose had to be solved before more substantial advances could be made by the social sciences than those they had achieved by the turn of the century. Weber's work grew out of an intellectual collision between those social scientists who thought of their work in primarily 'scientific' terms, and those who wished to develop a scholarly study which might assist the solution of the social problems that had become associated with industrialisation and urbanisation. The argument, sometimes bitter, that raged amongst German academics, administrators, and intellectuals around this central collision between the two opposed schools of thought, ultimately attracted the interest of colleagues in America, and afterwards and more recently those in Britain. It has deeply affected the ways in which social scientists have conceived their study, and has strongly influenced the rapidity of its growth. It has often determined the manner and the direction in which it has developed. The next two chapters will therefore endeavour to explain the reason why this controversy took root in Germany, and the course it took in its early years. This was of the utmost importance to work in the social sciences in general. First in Germany, then in America, and more recently in Britain and elsewhere it soon became the fashion for social scientists to deny that they had any concern with the validity of values; their own preferences were, it was fashionable to suppose, merely matters of taste; though they could, of course, take a legitimate interest in people's feelings about values as social facts, which thus became part of the data of social behaviour out of which it was hoped one day to build a comprehensive social science. The immediate reason for this was, no doubt, the rapid spread of the philosophic ideas concerned with logical positivism in the period immediately before and after the second World War,[2] but for all that, Weber's teaching about 'value neutrality' was an independent and for a time dominant influence in the social sciences. Over and over again, the battle has been fought over the nature of the gap between philosophic and scientific knowledge,[3] and values and the process of evaluation have been one of the main grounds on which it has been waged. Are they matters of personal preference, or do they possess any degree of validity in their own right? Are we condemned to live a divided existence in two intellectual worlds of 'is' and 'ought' that are becoming increasingly estranged from each other? And what of man's purposes? By what standards is he to live? Is his life to have any meaning for him, or is he to devote it entirely to the service of one kind of technology or another, motivated by some sort of individual psychological drive, and spurred on by some kind of social one-upmanship?

Simple as they may seem, these issues are coming more and more to the fore in the social sciences. Social and political scientists alike are split between two camps; the one, linked with philosophy and morals, opposed to the other, to which the 'naturalists' and positivists belong. From the psychological point of view, 'behaviouralists are likely to regard political theorists as pedantic, moralistic, uninterested in and a hindrance to the development of science; political theorists are likely to regard the behaviouralists as philistine'.[4] There are many signs that the dichotomy between these opposing attitudes of mind has caused so much concern that a reappraisal of the fundamental assumptions on which they rest has been forced upon many of us. David Easton has pointed out in this connection that the extension of political science to include the problems of policy-making has compelled those concerned to admit that it is impossible to formulate policy otherwise than in terms of values, and that the political scientist is inadequately equipped, philosophically, to give a satisfying account of their logical status. The best he can do is to try to derive the 'ought' from the 'is' of personal preference or whim, and to build a model of man on this foundation. This amounts to a revival of an old form of positivism. 'In essence', he writes, 'this attempt to remarry science and philosophy through the bond of human nature is symptomatic of the pressure to which social scientists are subjected today to solve the crucial problem of the relation of values. By training, social scientists have refused to pass beyond relativism; by necessity they are seeking to do so.'[5]

This is the state of affairs which arose when the full effect of Weber's thinking became established in Anglo-American sociology in the 1940s and 1950s; it is well described in *The New Sociology*.[6] As Professor Horowitz has written, the post-war generation of American sociologists became estranged from the idea that it was any concern of theirs to assume a responsibility for the discussion of values:

> The slogan is to separate facts from values; the substance, however, is
> to suppress values at the expense of facts. . . . There came in focus a
> strong current that identified social science not only with value
> neutrality, but with scholarly aloofness from moral issues. Whereas in
> the 'thirties there was a tempered and qualified acceptance of the dis-
> junction of fact and values, we find this disjunction turned into a
> veritable law of sociology.[7]

Most appraisals of recent sociological work (and *The New Sociology*
in particular) agree in finding the origins of the problem of values in
the disputes in which Weber played a leading part before the first
World War. Alvin Gouldner, for instance, calls the precept that social
science could and should be value-free a myth – a myth created by
Weber. In recent years, he writes,

> all the powers of sociology, from Parsons to Lundberg, have entered
> into a tacit alliance to bind us to the dogma that 'Thou shalt not
> commit a value judgment', especially as sociologists. Where is the
> introductory textbook, where the lecture course on principles, that does
> not affirm or imply this rule?[8]

It is necessary, therefore, for the purposes of this book, to turn our
attention first to the theory of value that Weber ultimately developed:
this having been done, the theory can be examined in the light of the
historical circumstances of its origin, in an endeavour to discover how
far it was part and parcel of the philosophical and sociological thinking
of the times. The ultimate objective is to arrive at a conclusion
as to whether the limitations which the logical dissection of the
theory imposed on it support the objectives which Weber wished to
attain as a sociologist, and whether the interpretations placed on the
theory by contemporary sociologists have not outrun the purpose
which he had in mind in placing it before his public.

The most striking of Weber's concepts, and perhaps the one that has
had the deepest impact on the subsequent development of sociology
has been his notion of *Wertfreiheit*. This embodies the idea that 'the
social sciences, which are strictly empirical sciences, are the least fitted
to presume to save the individual the difficulty of making a choice. . . .
It can never be the task of an empirical science to provide binding
norms and ideals from which directives for immediate practical activity
can be derived.'[9] This is linked with the notion that the social sciences
must be based on foundations that are objective, certain, and enduring,

in so far as they do not depend, as such, on the choice, preference, or whim of individuals. If this is not so, they cannot exist as sciences; to do so they must deal with that which lies outside the range of the personal life; their findings can only be what they are, whether individuals like them or not, or consider them to be good or bad. Their data are empirical or experimental, the existence of which can be demonstrated. The conclusions which arise from their analysis rest on rational proof. The social sciences have, in other words, come to be regarded as truly scientific in a very special sense of the term, especially by the neo-positivists. This is intended to imply that they have no moral concern, and indeed this argument asserts that the widest of gulfs exists between social science and ethics or moral philosophy. This is almost the opposite of the way in which Hobhouse conceived of ethics and social science, for it was a fundamental tenet of his that the two could be brought together under the common head of sociology.

But Hobhouse's teaching has been forgotten, and an interest in Weber's now predominates. As a result, it has often been argued in recent years that the social sciences do not include within the data they study matters of purpose, will, responsibility, intention, and evaluation, otherwise than as kinds of behaviour which can be observed. As values are considered to exist subjectively rather than objectively, the sociologist has, it is supposed, only a very limited interest in them; Weber's argument is sometimes quoted in support of this. 'All evaluative ideas', he wrote, 'are subjective.'[10] We know that moral principles influence human behaviour, but should the sociologist allow himself to be influenced by them either as a moral being himself, or in the pursuit of an interest in the problem of how values originate, or in that of how they come to acquire their social importance? In the course of the past fifty years, it has been urged, rightly or wrongly, that the sociologist, as a sociologist, must remain outside the arena of social life; he observes, describes, analyses, and concludes, but he does not guide, assist, or befriend the ordinary man, or those responsible for his welfare. If he does so in fact, it will be because he has been specifically employed to do so, not simply and solely as a social scientist, but as an official or welfare worker, or as an advertising agent or industrial consultant. Sociology is, then, only 'useful', 'significant', or 'relevant' to the maintenance or improvement of social wellbeing if it is something else as well, and the sociologist is then, as it were, living a double life and working in a dual capacity. Value and fact can be separated clearly and completely, it is thought, and the existence of the social sciences is dependent on this being done.

Is this what Weber really advocated? Is a sociologist, for Weber and his followers, a detached observer of social life, rather than a participant who is 'involved' in it in any sense? Can a sociologist really withdraw in this way? If he attempts to do so, does he not cut himself off from part at least of the fundamental nature of social life, with the result that the world to which his studies apply is an artificial one, created for the purpose of studying it, and lacking any other kind of reality? These questions are now being asked with rapidly growing urgency, and the discovery of what Weber meant when he used the portmanteau-word *Wertfreiheit* is becoming a vitally important enterprise. In what sense, if at all, must freedom 'from' values be part of the Charter of Liberties of the social scientist?

II

The answer to these questions involves, of course, a detailed study of Weber's theory of value, which is a novel undertaking. Weber's epistemology has often been examined, so far, for instance, as his concept of Ideal Types is concerned, but *Wertfreiheit* has been silently and frequently passed over, perhaps because it is a very hard nut to crack. In general, the study of value has not attracted the attention it deserves, and this has been made more possible by the misinterpretation of Weber's work; moreover, the growth of neo-positivism has deflected attention to other problems. This is a recent development, however. It must be made plain, at the outset of this chapter, that though Weber was unwilling to accept the positivist solution of the problems he set himself, he was more troubled by the idealistic thinking which prevailed in Germany at the end of the nineteenth century. He seems to have regarded positivism as a thing of the past, and idealism as the predominant school of thought of his day. Weber was a personal friend of sociologists such as Tönnies and Dilthey, who were idealists, and was deeply impressed by their work. But the lack of objectivity and certainty in their thinking dissatisfied him; it appeared to him to be far too much a matter of opinion. He had, therefore, to engage in 'fighting at least a two-front war – on the one hand against the superficialities of positivism or "naturalism" . . . on the other hand against the conventional canons of idealist thought, and more particularly its denial of the possibilities of scientific work in the field of human culture'.[11] Although, therefore, it is plain that Weber was unwilling to accept the dichotomy between the natural and the social sciences that idealism had asserted, it has become ever more plain of recent years, particularly to those who have read Weber's writings carefully, that Weber never suggested that the study of facts, 'objectively', was in any sense more important than the study of values, subjectively, or could in any way be made a substitute for it. As Fred H. Blum has pointed out, Weber's postulate of *Wertfreiheit* is not to be identified with 'mere relativism in the realm of values': 'Weber's objectivity is still further removed from positivism. It cannot be sufficiently emphasised that Weber never believed that the social sciences could be entirely divorced from value judgments.'[12]

Weber's own thoughts were stated with some precision. 'What is really at issue', he said, 'is the intrinsically simple demand that the investigator and teacher should keep unconditionally separate the establishment of empirical facts (including the "value-oriented" conduct of the empirical individual whom he is investigating) and *his* own practical evaluations.'[13] He did not argue that the sole task of the investigator and teacher was the establishment of empirical facts, and that this was inhibited by an interest in problems of values. 'An attitude of moral indifference', he specifically stated, 'has no connection with *scientific* objectivity.'[14] Why, then, did he attach so much importance to the concept of *Wertfreiheit*, when this made it hard for him not to exclude from his system of sociological analysis what was 'most distinctive in the traditional and commonsense treatment of human problems'?[15] Several explanations have been advanced. The first of these is historical. There can be no doubt that he was alarmed by the ever-present danger of 'the obstinate and deliberate partisanship of powerful interest groups' by holders of academic chairs: he was not anything like as troubled by the mere assertion of a professor's 'personal evaluations', for even though a professor might be silent on a moral issue, his silence might amount to what has been called 'pseudo-ethical neutrality'; occasions arise when silence speaks for the interests.[16] The only thing which Weber insisted on was that if the teacher believes that he should not deny himself the right of holding value judgments, he should make this absolutely *explicit* to his students and to himself.

The longer one studies Weber's argument, the more one becomes aware that what he was fighting against was not the widening of the social scientist's interests to include the problems of evaluation, so much as the utilisation of the social sciences and individual social scientists to support the propaganda of interest-groups of one kind or another, including the government, or, in other words, to concern themselves with special pleading rather than the truth. He found himself so inhibited by the warnings and exhortations of influential people in positions of authority and power, when he endeavoured to study his society and its problems, that he was compelled to try to carve out an independent area within which he could pursue the truth in his own way for its own sake. As Fred H. Blum has put it:

> His science 'free' from value judgments has a definite function in a specific social situation. It was the Bismarckian attempt to use the social scientist for his own purposes that gave rise to Weber's fight. . . .[17]

This point of view, that freedom was *for* the pursuit of truth as well as *from* oppression, is evident in his editorial statement on 'Objectivity in Social Science and Social Policy', which has a much wider significance than that of an academic discussion of the logic of the social sciences. The statement itself made it clear that the 'express purpose' of the journal in which it appeared, the *Archiv für Sozialwissenschaft und Sozialpolitik*, had been 'the education of judgment about practical social problems and . . . the criticism of practical social policy'; it was also asserted in the same context that 'the *Archiv* had firmly adhered . . . to its intention to be an exclusively scientific journal, and to proceed with the methods of scientific social research'.[18] It is obvious, therefore, that Weber thought, on the one hand, that the scope of the *Archiv* could properly include questions of social policy, and on the other that the results of the research which it was to pursue might have important practical implications, and thus transcend the significance of the conclusions based on a strictly 'scientific' analysis of empirical data.[19] It is implied by this argument that it is possible to develop a 'scientific' interest in practical social problems and social policy.

III

There is another and a much more weighty reason, quite different from this historical explanation, which led Weber to attach such great importance to his concept of *Wertfreiheit*. Briefly, he assumed (under the influence of German idealism) that the truth of judgments of fact could be established by empirical proof, whilst judgments of value, as they were the outcome of personal contemplation and individual choice, could never be validated in this way. He considered that if the sociologist refrained from value judgments, his study could be scientific, but he found himself quickly involved in difficulties when he endeavoured to follow this line of reasoning, along the road which he hoped would lead to certainty, and away from opinion. Even if it can be asserted with justification that the social scientist should not allow his own 'practical evaluations' to influence his findings of fact, it is also true that, if sociology is to have a deeper significance than would arise from the mere collection of miscellaneous information about existent social reality, it must concern itself with ideas rather than things. Ideas, however, may relate to both the True and the Good; if, then, the shaping of ideas becomes an integral part of our work, can it attain the certainties that are derived from empirical science? Is it possible to regard events and situations, on the one hand, and the social values and policies which often bring them into being, on the other, as phenomena of the same order of truth and falsehood? It will be suggested in the argument of this book that the two cannot be kept in isolation from each other, and that some means must be sought to bring them together.

The starting point of his argument was as follows:

> The historical influence of ideas in the development of social life has been and still is so great that it cannot be ignored in any 'ordering of empirical reality . . .'. The fate of an epoch that has eaten of the tree of knowledge is that it must know that we cannot learn the *meaning* of the world from the results of its analysis, be it ever so perfect; it must rather be in a position to create the meaning itself. It must recognise that general views of life and the universe can never be the result of increasing empirical knowledge, and that the highest ideals, which move us most forcefully, are always formed only in the struggle with other ideals which are just as sacred to others as ours are to us.[20]

This passage raises a difficult problem. If the increase of 'empirical knowledge' can never of itself enable us to learn the 'meaning of the world', then why all this bother about the need to keep the investigator's values separate from his concern with 'empirical facts'. For if the analysis of the latter is to lead anywhere at all we also have to concern ourselves with 'meaning'. That is surely inseparably linked with the investigator's values; for the concept of meaning implies subsidiary concepts of intention and purpose, and these are determined by evaluation; and here we are back again in the world of values once more. We have thus contradicted ourselves, as we have asserted both that we must ignore, and concern ourselves, with values. Weber recognised that the distinction between facts and values was difficult to make, and one might have expected him to refrain from emphasising the importance of making it unless he was driven to do so. If it is argued that Weber's science, free 'from' value judgments, could not apprehend the meaning, significance, or purpose of social behaviour, that it was only capable of dealing with objective facts, and that he accepted the limitations thus set to social science, then it must be concluded that his task was self-defeating. In any event, Weber sometimes argued that facts, even social facts, possessed an existence of their own, apart from values, and could therefore be analysed in accordance with the canons of the natural sciences.

Even if a fact, to be of sociological value, had to possess or be given meaning, it was also assumed by Weber (when it suited him) that 'when we distinguished in principle between "value judgments" and "empirical knowledge" we presupposed the existence of an unconditionally valid type of knowledge in the social sciences, namely, the analytical ordering of empirical social reality'.[21] On the one hand, he wished to promote to the best of his ability the spiritual freedom that was for him the supreme value, and to attain the autonomy of the person by way of an attempt to 'preserve the dignity of individual choice in a world of conflicting values'.[22] On the other hand, Weber was equally determined to lay the foundations of an 'objective' social science. But this required him to perform a dangerous balancing feat. He had to make it plain that, somehow or other, necessity governed the world, for the notion that values were only subjective had to be supplemented by another line of argument which made it possible to distinguish between the 'objective' social processes that ultimately governed social behaviour, and 'subjective' courses of action that stemmed from individual judgment and desire. If it was nothing but subjectivity that set processes of social change going, then the social wisdom of officialdom (and Bismarck) was as good as that of anybody else, viewed as the product of social causation like everything else. How could he lay the foundations of an 'objective' social science, and yet preserve the essentials of spiritual freedom? Was the sociologist to be a man of the world, then, concerned with the formulation of a social policy designed to promote social welfare, a value-laden concept,[23] or not? Was sociology a science restricted to the discovery of man's social nature, and the ultimate fate of his societies perhaps, or was it to participate in the arena of public affairs? Or was there a *via media* between the two?[24] If the sociologist was to be deemed to possess special knowledge of the world, was he not to be expected to act on it, and if so, how was he to do so?

IV

In one sense, therefore, a sociologist was to be a man of practical affairs, but in another, Weber thought of him as a scientist whose life was shielded from the errors and the exploitation of the world by the walls of his study. This conflict was hard to resolve, because of the underlying conflict in his thinking. He could write of the 'sciences, both normative and empirical' (thus implying a wider definition of 'science' in terms of 'scholarly study'); he also accepted the idea that the sanctioning of means by ends, and arbitration between conflicting ends, are 'entirely matters of choice or compromise. There is no [rational or empirical] scientific procedure of any kind whatsoever which can provide us with a decision here.' And he speaks, furthermore, of the social sciences as seeking to 'understand' human conduct, and by means of this understanding to 'explain' it 'interpretatively'.[25] At this point, a fundamental tension becomes apparent. 'There is', it has been said, 'no doubt that anti-emotionalism, rationality, passion, and irrationality are strangely mixed in Weber's world.'[26] As a man of action, truth was for him as much a matter of personal and emotional conviction as of reasoned demonstration. But the recognition that this was so brought him no peace of mind; in fact he was disturbed and even tormented by the thought. He recognised that it was the researcher who had to decide for himself what to study and how to study it, but he allowed himself at the same time to be deluded by the belief that the research itself could be conducted as a more or less mechanical process. His mind wavered between the two extremes:

> All knowledge of cultural reality is always knowledge from particular points of view. . . . If the notion that those standpoints can be derived from 'the facts themselves' continually recurs, it is due to the naïve self-deception of the specialist. . . . Without the investigator's evaluative ideas, there would be no principle of selection and no meaningful knowledge of the complete reality.[27]

But Weber also spoke with another voice, when he denied that the social scientist was compelled to make value judgments because the selection of the subject-matter of his researches depended on his own evaluation:

> All research in the cultural sciences, once it is oriented to a given subject matter through particular settings of problems and has established its methodological principles, will consider the analysis of the data as an end in itself. It will discontinue assessing the values of the individual facts in terms of their relationships to ultimate value-ideas. Indeed, it will lose its awareness of its ultimate rootedness in the value-ideas in general.

But even this was not his final word, for he added a last qualification that

> There comes a moment when the atmosphere changes. The significance of the unreflectively utilised viewpoints becomes uncertain, and the road is lost in the twilight. The light of the great cultural problems moves on. Then science too prepares to change its standpoint and its analytical apparatus and to view the streams of events from the heights of thought.[28]

A truly Weberian conclusion!

In sum, therefore, his argument is complicated and in many respects self-contradictory. Social science can only exist as a science if its data and conclusions are kept rigorously apart from the values which guide the sociologist in his selection of problems, and influence him in his choice of categories of analysis. But social realities, especially the meaningfulness of events and phenomena, are largely created by the values which must ultimately dictate the objectives (points of view, standpoints) and methods of scientific enquiry. It is only in the short run that the social scientist can be wholly scientific, because he cannot understand (have 'meaningful knowledge of') the processes of social change without the 'evaluative ideas' which make it possible to recognise the significance of the ideas and ideologies which lie behind outward appearances, and to reflect upon them. How then can any hard and fast line be drawn, and maintained, between the facts of social behaviour and ideas about their significance and purpose? How can one analyse purposes adequately if one restricts oneself to problems of scientific truth? Sooner or later, one also finds oneself facing the problem of the good, which is an integral part of the exceedingly complex story of human motivation.

An extension of Weber's line of reasoning might run as follows: The starting point in social research implies a value judgment that the study of social behaviour is worthwhile, and that some ways of studying society are better than others; it therefore cannot be surprising that the ethical presuppositions of sociologists have been found to be similar. They are, it has been concluded, engaging in much the same tasks, for much the same reasons.[29] This, however, leads to the ultimate conclusion that 'understanding' implies evaluation,[30] rather than the analysis of values, a conclusion which directly contradicts Weber's own views.

Weber imposed on the social scientist an obligation to develop a means of understanding our social affairs which would take individual motivations, values, and purposes into account in our explanations of human conduct; he found the essential truth of sociological generalisation, as such, to lie not so much in its accordance with an existent reality as in its contribution to the understanding of the social purposes underlying social change. These purposes may be evaluated by the sociologist in terms of the valid and invalid. This implies that our knowledge of social behaviour will be of a different order from that which we have of the natural order of things. There were, he appears to have thought, two systems of learning or scholarship, and though he tried to argue that there is no logical distinction between them, the understanding of society we derive from the one (*Verstehen*) differs fundamentally from the knowledge of the external world which we get from the other (*Begreifen*).[31] In order to have any valid sociology at all, we have to start with the 'value-free' study of facts; even so, they must bear a significant relationship to an hypothesis. If this is so, they can then, but only then, be examined 'for their own sake', to use the hackneyed phrase. We only become sociologists rather than mere collectors of miscellaneous information about societies when we investigate the facts of social behaviour from the point of view of meaning and purpose. But this is to write a gloss on Weber, rather than to clarify Weber's ideas. The *Verstehen/Begreifen* dichotomy does in fact provide an escape-route for the modern Weberian to free himself from the contradictions in which Weber had involved himself. But neither Weber nor his followers have taken advantage of it to any significant degree.

V

Today, it is usually considered that Weber's system broke down at
this point. Although he has been thought to have been 'able to bridge
the chasm between positivism and idealism', this was only by paying
the price of abandoning the realm of the irrational to the unconscious, a vast field that could never be more than partially comprehensible.[32] Since he could regard the process of evaluation as an object
of scientific analysis only from the limited point of view of determining its overall results, its inner consistency, and its outward com-
patibility with other social phenomena,[33] it was relegated to the limbo
of the irrational, where it has remained, by and large, ever since.[34]
The results have been tragic, for it is this conclusion, more than anything else, which has led sociologists (with certain notable exceptions)
either to have steered clear of matters of social policy, or to have
accepted the study of it as an 'applied' social science, a precarious and
logically unsatisfactory expedient which has done much to hinder the
development of this important branch of the subject.

The general verdict on Weber has, indeed, been unfavourable. In
the opinion of Professor Talcott Parsons, for instance, he 'failed to
complete the process [of the analysis of social action], and the nature
of the half-way point at which he stopped helps to account for many
of the difficulties of his position';[35] in particular, the illogicality of his
argument made it impossible for his theories to be 'assimilated to the
pattern of science'.[36] But is this all that is to be said? It is possible to
agree with Professor Voegelin when he concludes that Weber 'knew
what he wanted, but somehow could not break through to it. He saw
the promised land, but was not permitted to enter it'; he saw not only
all the defects of German idealism, but also many of the shortcomings
of positivism. It is also true to say, with him, that 'in the work of
Max Weber positivism has come to an end', but only in the sense that
it was Weber who gave it the *coup de grâce*. Weber's achievement was,
however, by no means merely negative. Though he did not solve any
of the fundamental problems of the logic of the social sciences, he was
able to prepare the way for renewed attempts to do so by getting rid
of much of the lumber (especially the apparatus of thinking of the
idealists) which cumbered the ground at the turn of the century, and
inhibited the development of new lines of argument. He asked the right
questions, and his discussion of them was relevant and highly penetrating.

The whole novelty of Weber's sociology lay in his determination to construct a system of thought that sought to deal with situations and problems that lay outside the scope of the natural sciences. It was truly scientific in the sense that desire, prejudice, whim, and special pleading were rigorously excluded from it. But it was based on the tacit assumption that human conduct, and in particular his social behaviour, was influenced by man's reason and his values as well as by social influences and physical environment. Social behaviour, he recognised, only occurs when, 'by virtue of the subjective meaning attached to it' by the person concerned, 'it takes account of the behaviour of others'.[37] It is this which provides the subject-matter of sociology, the 'science which attempts the interpretive understanding of social action in order to arrive at a causal explanation of its course and effects'. Although there is a certain flavour of positivism in this ('causal'), there is nevertheless also a recognition of the fact that the whole truth cannot be embodied in cause-and-effect formulations ('interpretive understanding'). In other words, Weber was asking himself here what really does make human beings behave as they do, and his answer was in terms of their intelligence, and their motivations; they were by no means overshadowed in his account by social influence.[38] In the last analysis he was not a 'natural' scientist, or, for that matter, any kind of empirical scientist at all, in the strict sense of the term.

Weber, therefore, was attempting to establish a *via media* between, on the one hand, realism (in its positivistic form), and, on the other, philosophical idealism. He accepted both alternatives, in the sense that he sought to establish a synthesis between them. Empiricism was inadequate, because of its inability to deal with the specifically human phenomena of intention and evaluation. Idealism was also inadequate because of its neglect of existent reality. But the synthesis in fact eluded him. As a German critic has put it:

> The ultimate problem which Marx set out to solve: how can the dignity and freedom of man be made compatible with the inescapable 'fate' of capitalism was also the ultimate problem of Max Weber's political sociology.[39]

This quotation may be generalised so as to apply to *verstehende* sociology as a whole. What this lacked, first and foremost, was force and solidity in its conclusions concerning evaluation. Judgments of right and wrong cannot be regarded only as part of the data of sociological analysis; the problem of their 'meaning', which Weber set himself, must be answered in terms of their justification as well as in those of their interconnection with other social phenomena. For instance, Weber's analysis of the significance of the rise of bureaucracy in the modern urban and industrial community was well documented and most compelling, and his vehement denunciation of it carried conviction. But this was insufficient. He never went at any length into the question of why it was that bureaucracy was to be opposed. If Weber had been able to show what exactly it was that made bureaucracy so dangerous an element in modern society, otherwise than by way of saying that it led to the 'depersonalisation' of the individual, and leaving it at that, practical recommendations might have come out of his argument. (In any event, he only assumes that depersonalisation is bad; he does not explain why. The weakness of the logical framework of his argument does not allow him to do so.) So, too, we find that his whole political sociology was deprived of any underlying moral philosophy which might have given it (in his own terms) an ultimate meaning and purpose. His political objectives were rigidly linked with his notion of the moral autonomy of the nation-state, whose destiny and justification was its own preservation and aggrandisement, and nothing more. Political generalisations were, he thought, always about the use of force,[40] and that was all there was to say about it. Germany's political objectives were thus to protect herself against Russia, and to this end to secure her frontiers against Russia's allies in the West as well as against Russia herself in the East, and so much the worse for them if that collided with their autonomy.[41]

In general, his political creed was determined by 'reasons of state' rather than by any kind of humanitarian or liberal, still less international, ideal.[42] This left him with political ideas that were both highly confused, and exceedingly pessimistic. If the onset of bureaucracy was inevitable, and utterly destructive in the long run of man's liberty, there was nothing that could be done about it. If the ever-increasing elaboration of modern industrialism, and in particular the growth of an industrial bureaucracy, was equally pernicious, no hope lay in the state ownership of industry. This would only mean that

> the management of the industry would also become bureaucratic. . . .
> A power struggle against a state bureaucracy is hopeless . . . no
> appeal is possible to any organised group interested in curtailing the
> power of the bureaucracy. . . . If private capitalism were to be eliminated, the sovereign state bureaucracy would rule supreme.[43]

VI

As Weber left things, there was little room for hope in the future, and he gave sociology an impulse towards pessimism of which it has not been able to rid itself even up to the present day. In consequence, so far as industrial and political affairs are concerned, modern sociology is apt to carry with it a somewhat distressing reminder of George Orwell's *1984*. But Weber did leave behind him at least one indication that, if he had taken the problem of the future really seriously, he could have shown that there was some hope for humanity, after all. His general theory laid it down that even if a situation was firmly established by reason of the existence of a set social structure, a process of change might eventuate if new social values were brought to bear on it. The concluding paragraphs of *The Protestant Ethic and the Spirit of Capitalism* are exceedingly illuminating in this regard.[44] The pursuit of wealth in the United States, he argues, may strip social life of 'religious and ethical meaning'; this may lead to 'mechanised petrification, embellished with a sort of convulsive self-importance'. But this is not the last word that can be said about the situation which may thus arise, because this line of analysis

> brings us to the world of judgments of value and of faith. . . . No one knows who will live in this cage of the future, or whether at the end of this tremendous development entirely new prophets will arise, or there will be a great rebirth of old ideas and ideals.

The materialistic and the spiritual interpretation of history (and of forecasts for the future) were, for Weber, equally possible, even though it seemed to him that 'modern man is in general . . . unable to give religious ideas a significance for culture and national character which they deserve'. This is more hopeful, in so far as the prognosis was at least in doubt. But why, one may ask, has modern man been unable to give religious ideas this 'significance', especially as they 'deserve' it? If we understood, could not existing tendencies be reversed, and a means perhaps be established for arresting man's head-long descent to servitude? The continuation of Weber's enquiries into the sociology of religion, therefore, seems on his showing to be highly relevant to the outcome of the crisis of the future.

Weber's ideas on the impact of judgments of value and of faith on a future society cannot be finally assessed until these somewhat random thoughts have been clarified. We find Mayer speaking of the 'tragic character of his moral stature', and of his conviction that 'the believer in an absolute ethic' cannot 'stand up to the ethical irrationality of the world'.[45] His dilemma is even more difficult to unravel because it was not his own; it was even more that of his nation, and to a large extent that of Western civilisation as a whole. As Weber's friend and colleague, Ernst Troeltsch, put it:

> The political thought of Germany is marked by a curious dilemma . . . look at one of its sides, and you will see an abundance of remnants of Romanticism and lofty idealism; look at the other, and you will see a realism which goes to the verge of cynicism and of utter indifference to all ideals and all morality. But what you will see above all is an inclination to make an astonishing combination of the two elements— in a word, to brutalise romance, and to romanticise cynicism.[46]

Weber might have been pessimistic to the point of despair, and his thinking may be so confused as to deny him any vision of the way ahead to a more effective comprehension of the epistemological crisis of our age.[47] But we now know that he was right in attaching such great importance to the acute problem involved in the dichotomy between 'objective' fact and 'subjective' value. As things have turned out, our apparatus of sociological investigation has become increasingly lop-sided as it has developed since his day, in so far as it has been ever more heavily tilted towards fact rather than value; the study of the interaction between them has been so far neglected that it is Weber's own work on religion and capitalism that provides what is perhaps one of the few important exceptions to a general rule.

Furthermore, Weber has left behind him an important legacy of sociological theory which is now part of the heritage of sociological scholarship, providing the base from which advances into the future will be made. It was a study of Weber's work which led Dr Runciman to make the remark that 'we must try to behave as though we could be positivists, but . . . this on condition that we realise that positivistic procedures must be supplemented (or preceded) by a further which is different in kind'.[48] A valid sociological generalisation can, it is now plain, only be made if there is some kind of proof that its subject-matter does in fact exist; even more imporant than this, it must also be shown that it makes sense in terms of its intrinsic meaning. It must embody a statement which is not only true in terms of fact, but it must also afford an explanation of a state of affairs or course of events which makes it comprehensible as a matter of human concern. It is not what exists that is important in this regard, so much as how it has come to be, and what its human significance is, both for today and the tomorrow whose reality will be so largely shaped by social policy.

The springboard into the future is surely Weber's tacit realisation that the study of values is essential to the study of society, but that neither raw empiricism nor ethics can reach the heart of the matter alone and unaided.[49] Each needs the assistance of the other. Far from being a mere matter of emotion or the irrational preference or prejudices of individuals, experienced or expressed under social influence, there is also a strong component of intelligent choice which has to be taken into account in the investigation of the problem of how values are created, and how they exert their influence on social conduct. In so far as he was able to transmit a vision of the importance of this kind of sociological understanding of the ultimate truths of men's social being, even though his thinking was confused and confusing, Weber may be said to have written the Charter of Liberties for the sociologist who wishes to live to some real purpose in the world of today. His closest followers and disciples are those who accept a responsibility for the identification of the true nature of the problems which endanger our civilisation, and for the discovery of the methods that are best suited for understanding, if not solving, them. We remember today the slogan which gave the *Archiv* its objective and its purpose: the 'education of judgment about practical affairs'. Weber's triumph was to show how this could be done in accordance with the requirements of sound scholarship, and thus to establish the sociologist's role in his own society.

The sociologist of our own times is thus fortunate in so far as he can, if he will, consolidate a position that has already been won for him in this way, and use it as a foundation on which he can build anew.

5. Value Freedom: The Historical Origins and Significance of the Idea

I

From the logical analysis of Weber's theory of value, and its bearing on sociological work, we turn to the examination of the origins of the theory itself, in the hope that this will explain some of the obscurities, and the confusions, latent in it. In particular, the explanation of the manner in which the bitter conflict it provoked amongst social scientists changed its nature from a mere account of the formulation of social policy to a critical contribution to the logic of scientific discovery, cannot but be expected to be most significant for our present purposes.

The whole complex of the argument has itself aroused intense disquiet amongst sociologists throughout the past half-century, but there is no really up-to-date account of what its significance was at the time when it burnt most fiercely so many years ago. Mostly conducted today in the lofty jargon appropriate for philosophical discussion, rather than in the very practical or mundane language of its administrative origins at the turn of the century in the affairs of administrative organisations, the problem is now generally regarded as rather esoteric. In Weber's day, however, this was not so. The idea generally accepted then was that social scientists, particularly economists, had to undertake the responsible task of producing a rational and ordered view of society and its problems, on the assumption that this would contribute to the betterment of the general state of society, and social welfare especially. The notion that social scientists should keep aloof from the daily concerns of politicians and administrators, and refuse to entangle themselves in the discharge of their practical responsibilities, was therefore a revolutionary one at the time. Yet that was what his contemporaries thought he was advocating, and he appeared to do so with passion. The dispute he provoked was correspondingly explosive; the issues involved were both basic and timeless.

There is, therefore, considerable practical importance today, as well as much theoretical interest, in the study of the way in which Weber immersed himself in the debate about values before the first World War, and in trying to understand some of the complexities of his position and the contradictions in his argument. There can be little prospect that progress will be made with the solution of the problems of value at the present time until it is clear to us how it arose sixty years ago, and how it influenced the discussion of practical social and political problems at that time. It will be seen that though Weber is often spoken of as the champion of the freedom of science *from* values, the discussion arose in the meetings of an association devoted to the appraisal of social legislation from the standpoint of its impact on social welfare. If Weber is to be regarded as the protagonist of science *against* values, what was he doing, it must be asked, at these meetings anyhow, and why was it that the line he took there was not so much to protest against a scientific body giving attention to so value-centred a theme as social welfare, but to launch a passionate attack on the idea that social welfare was to be achieved by supporting employers against workers, and the absolutist state against the masses of its citizens? In this, Weber appears as the champion of the idea that the academic and the intellectual have much to contribute to the formulation of social policy, by way of the testing of the viability and intrinsic rationality of social values. But that is the exact opposite of what he is so often deemed to have advocated. This has become an exceedingly important issue at the present time when so much depends on building a solid academic or intellectual foundation to underline the formulation of social policy, and the processes of social administration, if not national policy at large.

II

For many years, academic social scientists, especially in Germany, were suffered to play with the idea that men of scholarship and learning could possess themselves of special knowledge concerning the objectives of social policy and participate in its rational and beneficial formulation.

In 1864, when Weber was born, the German middle-class liberals had been decisively defeated by Bismarck in their fight for a share of political power; from the 1860s, German government represented a compromise between the strength of landowning Junkers and the capitalist bourgeoisie, with the imperial government very much in the saddle. The middle classes were given protection against growing proletarian unrest and the opportunity to exploit expanding internal and colonial markets, though they failed to gain any really effective political control over internal affairs, which remained in the hands of the old conservative ruling classes. The outlooks of Max Weber and his younger brother, Alfred, were shaped by this collision between the middle classes to which they belonged, and the policy of Bismarck, and ultimately the imperial government.[1]

The second half of the nineteenth century, from its midpoint onwards, was a time when German imperialism was being steadily fostered, and Bismarck's internal policy was to develop a nationalist programme of legislation and administration, the most striking features of which were to build a tariff barrier to make the quick expansion of industry and agriculture possible, and to pay careful attention to the social needs of the masses of the working classes brought together in the industrial centres. From the practical point of view this meant the inauguration of health and other insurance schemes, attention to housing and other aspects of urban development, trade union legislation, and the like. From the philosophical point of view, it was the era of idealist theorising, ushered in by Kant and Hegel, leading to the glorification of the state by such writers as Gumplowicz and Ratzenhofer, and the period when philosophers and political theorists justified the absolutist state, and gave academic cover to the autocracy of Bismarck and ultimately that of Kaiser Wilhelm II.

One of the results in Germany was that a school of nationalistic social policy and social history developed, led by academic intellectuals in sympathy with Bismarck's views, in particular the great social economists, Gustav Schmoller and Adolf Wagner. These men had at their disposal forces which they led into battle against the internationalists and free traders, lumped together under the opprobious title of the 'Manchester School', which was then paramount. The battleground between these two sides was provided by the Association for Social Policy that Schmoller took a leading part in founding in 1872, and it was not long before the social policies of Bismarck were welcomed by the social reformers incorporated in it. By the time Max Weber and his brother Alfred came on the scene, those who dissented from the imperialist programme of state and bureaucratic rule found themselves in a minority. As Weber came to be so outstanding an opponent of bureaucracy, we face the conundrum why Weber joined the Association at all. He did so, it has been said, because of its 'objective' interests. Social questions stood at the time in the foreground of politics, not only because of the speed of German industrialisation, but also because the law against the social democrats, introduced by Bismarck in 1878, had just been revoked (1890), and the German bourgeoisie was alarmed by the quick rise of socialism. This gave Weber his primary motive, for he was closely identified with the outlook of the middle classes; we find him telling the Association:

> The time is still far off when we shall be able to join hands with the urban proletariat for a solution of social problems. I hope that this will come, but for the time being there can be no question of it.[2]

Secondly, as will be explained, Weber was also, deeper down in his mind, identified with his working-class fellow-citizens, and the story of his life is largely that of how the latter concern came to dominate the former, though the conflict between them was never resolved. This is the ultimate explanation of the dispute about values, and it seems to have had its origin here.

The object of this chapter is to recount how the influential middle-class body of opinion which followed Bismarck was, in its turn, subjected to challenge by the Weber brothers, who came to speak for the masses, and the consequences of this for the development of sociology. But, before any attempt to do so is made, a fuller account must be given of Weber's attitude to Bismarck's policies. His early manhood was lived under the shadow of Bismarck; his father was a member of the National Liberal party which supported Bismarck against the socialists; Weber was, in fact, 'a politician's son in the age of Bismarck'.[3] He assimilated Bismarck's nationalist policies 'and made them his own in his twenties', his inaugural lecture in 1895 being a confession of belief in *Realpolitik* and imperialism generally. But, though nationalism remained with him for life, it was tempered to a steadily increasing extent in the course of his later years by a sense of identification with the interests of the common people. Very early, we find him regretting the 'horrible destruction of independent convictions which Bismarck has caused amongst us'.[4] His final appraisal of Bismarckian rule in 1917 was to recognise his greatness, and to bewail the supine behaviour of the politicians of his day. Yet though he did so, he regretted that this obscured the fact that the nation had been alienated after 1875 from its political representatives by his autocratic rule, and this prevented the exercise of the political responsibility that would have given them relevant experience and a greater sense of responsibility. Moreover, Bismarck's specific social policies carried with them a fundamental underlying weakness. If the nation depended for its strength on a mass army, based (as it was believed) on honour and comradeship between those who served in it, so too the same principles needed to be carried into effect in the nation at large. Insurance payments for the sick and the weak and the injured were good things to have, but Bismarck had given no representation to the interests of the healthy and the strong. This was disastrous. It was no mere chance, therefore, that the nation came to regard his dismissal from office with indifference.[5]

Whether it was the comradeship which he had enjoyed with private soldiers during his period of military service, or whether it was due to the influence of his mother, who left him with a keen sense of social responsibility,[6] Weber fought throughout his life for individual liberty, and his wife wrote that 'his sympathy with the struggles of the proletariat for a human and a dignified existence [was] for decades so great that he often pondered whether or not he should join their ranks'.[7] He therefore had to attempt to reconcile this with support for industrial capitalism, which he considered to be a necessary foundation for national power.[8] There were, in consequence, two separate trends in his thinking. One, towards supporting national ideals, was in accordance with the idealistic political thought of his nation and his times; the other, towards protecting the weak and the oppressed from regimentation and exploitation, appears to have had its origins in religious teaching, though they have never been clearly identified. It is obvious, however, that it was the second that proved the more powerful when he took an active part in politics at the end of his life. It is also obvious that the reason why Weber became so bitterly opposed to the *Katedersozialisten* (or academic socialists as distinct from the Social Democrats) in the Association, from Schmoller downwards, was that their teaching and their lives, as men of affairs, coincided too closely with that element in Bismarck's rule, and in that of his successors, which alienated him from the imperial Establishment. He approved of a social policy that met the requirements of the modern industrial state, but he was disgusted and incensed by the treatment of his fellows as mere cannon fodder, politically. It aroused the most fundamental beliefs and engaged the most powerful emotional forces in one of the most sensitive minds of his age.

Weber therefore joined the Association with divided loyalties. He was convinced of the necessity of Bismarck's nationalist policies, and he respected his unswerving determination to bring them into accordance with realities, but he disagreed violently with his refusal to take the nation at large into his confidence, or to trust the common people with executive responsibilities. Bismarck's foreign policy was irreplaceable, but his treatment of his fellow-citizens was, Weber thought, disastrous.

III

The idea on which the Association for Social Policy was based was to give men of scholarship and learning a chance to discuss the problems that arose from the formulation of social policy in an industrial age, and to contribute to their solution; in other words, it was intended to be a forum for the expression of opinions concerning the possibility of manipulating the existing state of affairs so as to improve the lot of mankind in the circumstances then obtaining under industrialism and urbanism. The Association was given the task of convening annual conferences at which matters of contemporary moment were discussed, on the basis of carefully prepared papers submitted by university teachers, public officials and businessmen, and others. The general trend of the Association's work during the first thirty years of its existence was to present a businesslike and unemotional treatment of troublesome problems, and to investigate them on the assumption, so common in the Victorian age, that the progressive spirit of the times could solve them in a commonsense way if enough care and trouble were taken to do so. The Association thus established by the 'academic socialists' was inclined towards the introduction of ethical ideals into economic policies, and accepting, in particular, the idea that the state should regulate contracts of employment.[9] The result was to bring an organisation into existence that was on the side of 'progress', and was itself a means of encouraging it. To this end, doctrinaire beliefs and actions were carefully prevented from influencing its work, and harmonious and well-informed discussion, and the bringing to bear of 'know-how' in an unspectacular but creative way were valued much more highly than knowledge of and wrangling over abstract truths unpalatable or otherwise. The various conflicting interests and classes would, it was hoped, be enabled to arrive at compromises which would reconcile them to each other, rather than provide opportunities for them to express irreconcilable opinions, or for the various interest groups to explain how sharply and why they were in conflict.

Academic teachers such as Gustav Schmoller and Adolf Wagner, Brentano and Knapp, played a leading part in the movement, and representatives of newspapers were also active in it; it is of much interest that industrialists and civil servants were present at the opening meeting[10] and participated in the Association's affairs. Schmoller gave the opening address, and he quickly became the most prominent figure in the movement. Max Weber joined the Association as a young man in his late twenties, and made his maiden speech when he was 29 at the Berlin meeting of 1893, when the socialists were present for the first time. The proceedings quickly became controversial, and we find Weber at loggerheads with the socialists over the causes of agricultural unrest in East Prussia.[11] All the same, he and his brother Alfred established themselves as leaders of the radical left wing, developing their own analysis and interpretation of phenomena such as the Prussian *Junkertum*, and their own explanation of the preference of their workers for the insecurity of seasonal employment in the west, to the security of collective living in the east, due to their dislike of patronage and oppression. The tension between the two opposed schools of thought gradually grew, as it became evident that the issue was one of fundamental principle, and of social and political policy, until at the Mannheim conference in 1905 the right and left wings fell apart, and the right began to feel that they were oppressed by the left. Schmoller, as President, went so far as to write to his colleague, Brentano, thanking him for preventing Weber from giving publicity to the dispute in the newspapers; the only thing that actually appeared in them being a general report of the Weber brothers' attack on bureaucracy, which provoked a certain sensational interest in the world at large.[12]

The dispute finally came to a head at the second Vienna meeting in 1909. This centred on the mundane business of municipal trading, with special reference, of all harmless things, to tramways. Some optimistic members had compared the pay of municipal workers favourably with that given by private industry; this seemed to the Webers to be mere sentiment, Alfred Weber opposing the whole idea that municipalisation was a vehicle of social progress. Max supported him energetically, arguing that the increase of bureaucratic controls would, if pursued too far, lead to man's enslavement rather than his liberation. A whole day was devoted to the argument, and there was much talk about the damage people had suffered from the 'bureaucratising' (*Verbeamtung*) of administrative services. Something of a scandal arose out of this, and we find another member of the Association (Knapp) writing to Schmoller that:

> Our Association has become a comic opera. I can hardly find words to describe the uproarious nonsense in which the shrill quarrelling of impromptu speakers has landed us. My solution for these difficulties is that the Association should concentrate on practical issues. Well prepared papers may embody theory without the latter becoming the object of discussion by the Association; this should arise incidentally. Warm discussion should only be allowed to take place where it is unavoidable, namely when political matters arise.

Schmoller answered:

> I was astounded by the Webers' attitude to my contribution, and by the tone with which they launched themselves against me.
> If they restrict political economy within the bounds of an exact science, as Schumpeter and now Alfred Weber do, they cease to say anything about the part economic affairs play in the life of men. I don't see anything difficult in emphasising the necessity for purely objective observations. I only see at the ultimate end of the kind of understanding which we arrive at through the social sciences, the appraisal of what is known from the point of view of the whole, of which it is a part.

Yet another colleague (Carl Joh. Fuchs) recorded his impressions of the Vienna debate as follows:

> In my opinion the search for a way to deal with theoretical problems in the General Assembly of the Association has not been successful. It would on that account be better for our Association, and also for theory, if this were entrusted to a special society which might meet without the press and without calling on anybody to contribute papers. The declarations of the bankruptcy of our science we have just had made to us must do infinite harm not only to our study, but also to the social and political effectiveness of the Association. Disputes about membership are to be kept for the professional literature, and are the affair of professional colleagues; they are not for the press or the public.[13]

At this point there began what has been called (as a term of art) the *Werturteilsdiscussion* – the 'evaluation discussion'; literally, the 'judgment of value discussion', that has been wrangled over ever since, in one way or another, dying down and burning up again from time to time, always a chronic cause of muddle and obscurity of thought in the social sciences. The examination of the handling of theoretical problems led on, in fact, to the wider question of the status of values; and the Webers' attack on the complacency of their contemporaries produced in the end the specific demand, in a letter from Knapp to Schmoller, that the main consideration in the choice of theoretical subjects for examination should be the avoidance of emotional and personal difficulties such as these.

The dispute then began to get out of hand. A letter from the chairman of the Association was sent to all the members saying that the problem of values would be discussed at an enlarged executive committee meeting. In order to prepare more adequately for this meeting, the following points would be given special preliminary attention, namely:

1. The status of moral judgments of value in scientific economics;
2. The relationship between development and practical values; and
3. The relationship between general principles of evaluation and special problems of academic teaching.

The members of the committee were asked to put their views on these problems succinctly, and the response appears to have been good; a small book of 134 printed pages was produced by assembling together the statements that were received as a result, which included contributions from Eulenburg, Hartmann, Oldenburg, Oncken, Schumpeter, Spann, Max Weber, von Wiese and Wilbrant. A limited edition was produced 'as a manuscript' in 1913, but only distributed amongst the members of the committee, and those members of the Association who asked for copies, as it was only intended to serve as a basis for discussion. The text was neither included in the Proceedings of the Association, nor was it published commercially, then or later.[14]

The controversy was therefore burning brightly immediately before the first World War, and it was given special attention at one of the sessions of the Düsseldorf meeting, held in January 1914. It was agreed on Schmoller's suggestion that no shorthand notes should be taken of the proceedings, in pursuance of his wish to 'preserve their intimate character, and prevent, above all, the strong differences of opinion that were expected to arise from being held against the Association, or indeed against science itself, by outsiders'.[15] There was no general agreement on this, but even Max Weber assented to it, and he had a friendly word for Schmoller; this is important, as it demonstrates a weakening in his hitherto somewhat contemptuous attitude.

Despite these precautions, it was inevitable that opinions should clash sharply. The available notes of the proceedings do not suffice to give a complete account of how they went, but it is understandable that there should have been some uproar, and that Max Weber was the ringleader, finding his most bitter opponent in Grünberg, who intervened in the debate repeatedly. Contradictions or partial contra-dictions multiplied, only Sombart expressing real agreement; Max Weber rose once more to present a weighty exposition of the issue which gave those who had opposed him so sharply, an understanding and insight into the origins of his beliefs, and he left the sitting reluct-antly. The older generation played only a small part in the discussion, and associated themselves only to a small extent with Max Weber's standpoint. The middle-aged and younger generation gave it little support, or even disapproved of it, so that one concludes that the discussion must have failed to please its sponsors.[16] The outcome was therefore most unsatisfactory, and sharp differences of opinion still existed when the first World War broke out, and the discussion was suspended for the time being.

IV

So much for the history of the strife that the dispute about the status of values in the social sciences provoked amongst academics and their colleagues, just before the first World War. The version given by Dr Franz Boese in his *History of the Social Policy Association 1872–1932* tells us a great deal about its origins, but it does not really explain very clearly why it occurred at all. Some may have considered that it was merely troublesomeness on the part of the Weber brothers that provoked it, but with hindsight at our disposal today, we know that that was an absurd belief. If we go to the originals of the speeches Max Weber made to the Association in this context, however, we can understand much more clearly how the events arose.

In 1905 we find him speaking at a meeting of the Association on the seemingly harmless subject of industrial relations in large-scale undertakings, but in such a way as to foreshadow the troubles that lay ahead.[17] His aim in this speech was to identify himself with the workers' cause against their employers and the state, defending them against charges of irresponsible breaches of contract, made because they had gone on strike without having given the notice required by law; a certain insincere astonishment had been expressed at the meeting at the low moral standards this was assumed to imply. But, Weber said, a contract which amounts to a subordination of one party to the interests of the other must, lawyers would hold, be set aside. The situation was deplorable, because Prussian rule deprived working men of their liberty, and weakened their characters. The phraseology of the German labour law was, he said, policemen's jargon: whoever does this or that will be punished, or given a reprimand. If a man on strike says to a blackleg, if you don't join me you shan't dance with my daughter, he renders himself liable to punishment. That was no joke, but valid law, and the existence of such a law in Germany was, in Weber's opinion, disgraceful. 'I am', he told the meeting, 'personally of the opinion that, no matter whether trade unions are factions in open war, they are valuable in themselves. They are the only means we have of mass education. I oppose every proposal which threatens their being, no less strongly if to do so would be to serve the national interests.'

At the same meeting of the Association, he spoke with similar effect on a subject that appeared to be equally harmless: 'The Relationship between Cartels and the State'.[18] This gave him a chance to express liberal-minded (but, it must be admitted, somewhat irrelevant) views concerning the shortsightedness of oppressing the social democrats, and the stupidities of governments generally. Prussian ministers, he said, might be matter-of-fact men of business, but none of them would claim to be statesmen. There was assumed to be a community of interest between the state and heavy industry, which was regarded as a businesslike affair, but was this really so?

> There will not be forgotten in German social history the scene in the Saar court when a miner, called as a witness, said 'Shall I lose my job if I tell the truth?' That shows once more how strangely the state appears to the workers in its mines. . . . Have the representatives of heavy industry (and the agrarian parties united with them socially and politically) really any interest or concern that social democracy should be kept down? Everyone who thinks politically must say no, just the opposite; every socialist who enters the Reichstag at the expense of the

parties supporting social reform is pure gain for their opponents. Every increase of radicalism in social democracy, every increase of social democracy at the expense of liberalism, especially social liberalism, represents pure gold for them. On the other hand, it is pure gold for the social democrats if we accept reactionary policies.

Then again, taking part in the discussion on the 'Constitution and Administrative Organisation of Cities',[19] he spoke as a sociologist who tried to base his political ideas on realities.

We can and we should now trust the social democrat party, which is in control of so many large local authorities. . . . When the contradictions between the material concerns of career politicians, on the one hand, and revolutionary politicians on the other, are allowed to develop freely, then for the first time internal problems will begin to arise for the party, in earnest; this will also happen if, further, one no longer throws democrats out of the army's old comrades association, and if they are allowed into Church committees, instead of being thrown out as they now are. For then the real danger of revolutionary virulence will flourish, and it will become apparent for the first time that in the long run it is not social democracy that will conquer the state, but on the contrary that it is the state that will conquer the party. And I do not expect that middle-class society will see the former as much of a danger.

This shows Weber to have been a man who had a novel under-standing of the main trends of development of the industrial society of his day, and a determination to influence the formulation of social policies according to his ideas. This was all very well of itself, but the pace of progress seems to have been too slow for him, and the opposi-tion of the conservatives amongst his academic colleagues and the bureaucracy to have been too strong. Be that as it may, he was led in 1909 to abandon any endeavour at temperate explanation and per-suasion; he came into the open and spoke his mind in the course of his notorious speech on Municipal Trading, which he delivered at the Vienna meeting.[20]

His opening was deliberately controversial, for he flatly contra-dicted the opinion expressed by one of the elder statesmen of the Association that Prussian railway profits benefited the poorer classes, by saying that it was mainly from their pockets that they were drawn. He continued by asserting that this was likely to proceed unchecked, as the technical superiority of the bureaucratic mechanism stood un-shaken, in the same way that machine production surpassed handwork; the forward progress of bureaucracy was therefore irresistible.

H

We willingly admit there are honourable and talented men at the top of our administration . . . [but it is] horrible to think that the world could one day be filled with nothing but little cogs, little men clinging to little jobs and striving towards bigger ones – a state of affairs which is to be seen . . . playing an ever increasing part in the spirit of our present administrative system, and specially of its offspring, the students. This passion for bureaucracy, as we have heard it expressed here, is enough to drive one to despair. It is as if in politics the spectre of timidity – which has in any case always been rather a good standby for the German – were to stand alone at the helm; as if we were deliberately to become men who need 'order' and nothing but order, who become nervous and cowardly if for one moment this order wavers, and they are torn away from total incorporation in it. . . . The great question is therefore not how we can promote or hasten it, but what we can oppose to it in order to keep a portion of mankind free from this parcelling-out of the soul, from the supreme mastery of the bureaucratic way of life. . . .

We should rather ask ourselves, what are the social or political prospects under this advancing bureaucracy which you so passionately applaud. Gentlemen, I could not but shake my head at the illusion which seems to have possessed all of you here that, when the private employer has been replaced to the fullest possible extent by the state or municipal official, the result will be anything other than the administration of state authority from the employer's point of view. . . .

What will then happen if state and municipal officials gain authority over ever-widening classes of workers? Will they acquire a greater sense of the importance of social policy from the friction with the workers' organisations that will inevitably continue? It has even been thought that if the state were to take a share in the coalmining syndicate, this cartel would be run on social lines; what, then, is the fate which will await the state if this wholesale surrender takes place? . . .

It is common knowledge that the conditions in state-owned mines are the worst that exist in terms of social politics. . . . Only a community which is independent of the employer's outlook can, in the long run, cultivate 'social politics'. . . .

The principle of ever-widening nationalisation and commercialisation has found varying degrees of expression in the Association for Social Policy since the beginning of its history. . . . An essential factor in the predilection for bureaucracy which exists among us in varying degrees, is a purely moral sentiment: namely, the belief in the unshakeability of the undoubtedly high moral standard of German officialdom. Here, however, the 'ethical' aspect of the machine today plays a decidedly minor part.[21]

It was these rather tactless observations that started off the debate on the status of values in the social sciences. But it must be borne in mind that Weber's was the attacking position as against that of his more conservative colleagues in the Association; his was the moral standpoint of the person who asserts the importance of values against that of his opponents who base their arguments on the 'objectivity' of hard facts. His primary intention was to castigate them for conniving at the oppression of the working classes, and for failing to resist the advancing power of the bureaucrat, not for confusing facts and values. For oppression and bureaucracy were essentially evil things, and would never prevail against essentially democratic values; that was his passionate assertion at this point. It was only when he had to face the uproar that the virulence of his attack aroused that he changed the direction of argument; it was only then that he complained that scientific appraisals of fact were being confused with value judgments, because the majority of the members of the Association had seen fit to take the other side against him in a political dispute, on grounds that were, as a matter of fact, much less moral than his own.

This was highly illogical, and Weber was in a weak position; it is not surprising that, in his later contribution to the discussion (on 'The Productivity of a National Economy',[22] at the same conference), he seems to have recognised that he had gone too far in his earlier speech, and to have attempted to make amends to the other side. For he admitted that, if one studied the history of the Association, it became understandable why value judgments should be introduced into the debates. But the damage had been done, and the consequences followed that have already been described. His endeavour appears to have been to switch the discussion over from a dispute about the realities of political affiliations and policies to the academic subject of the relations between science and values, emphasising that to bring what should be questions of value into scientific questions was 'an affair of the devil', which the Association had allowed to happen with a splendid lack of concern. As it was Weber, rather than his opponents, who had done this, the latter may be excused from expressing a certain degree of exasperation, and feeling a measure of irritation. Hence the explosiveness of the discussion; the fact that he felt he was fundamentally in the right made matters worse, especially when he saw fit to change the direction of his argument in mid-stream, and to defend himself in a way that was fundamentally illogical.

At the outset of his remarks, Weber asserted that social welfare was, of course, an idea which had plainly involved in it all the ethics in the world that there were. To free the debate from these entanglements, it was now being argued that 'social welfare' was identical with maximising the wealth of all the members of the economic group concerned; this brought up the question of productivity, which was assumed on these grounds to be a 'good thing'. Ethical assumptions thus became involved. But the problem, he continued, was that an empirical science has nothing to contribute to learning otherwise than on the basis of what actually exists; it says nothing about what should be. To say that there was no common agreement about value judgments did not dispose of the matter, because scarcely had that been said than the argument about the desirability of 'productivity' had to be resumed again. 'Average judgments' might be relied on to determine what it was popularly thought should happen, but it was the concern of science to criticise beliefs of this order, and to clarify the problems that were implied in them. It might be true that, from the historical point of view, the Association had come to life as a practical and not as a scientific body. All the same, the notion that the struggle for economic advantage was the *causa movans* of social life was inadequate; they had to get this generally understood. They had become concerned with values (regarded as motives) in this way. But the point had been reached where it had become plain that it would do a service both to science, and to practical affairs, if a line were drawn between the facts of behaviour and the notions underlying it. We had to admit, with a certain regret, that mutual differences in value judgments were sharper than they used to be. This was a cause of social insecurity, but we could not preserve our dignity as men if we were to allow ourselves to dream life away in a fool's paradise.

This was, however, imprecise, and the argument really led nowhere. Weber would have done far better to have stood his original ground, and to have developed the arts of tact and persuasion rather than to have attempted to further his purpose by confusing the issue. In sum, Weber presented the discussion of values as a red herring, to deflect attention away from the discussion of politics by refocusing it on the examination of philosophical rather than practical issues. Whether the result was not to do a disservice to the social sciences can only be a matter of opinion, for it must be doubted, to say the least of it, whether philosophical discussion is capable of dealing effectively and decisively with the kinds of problems that had been raised in this way. The ultimate result has been to provoke a sterile dispute, in which energies have been wasted that were much needed elsewhere.

The controversy about value judgments seems, therefore, to have been occasioned by an unfortunate lack of understanding, on Weber's part, as to how he might play a constructive role in the affairs of the Association, and counterbalance the influence of the bureaucracy in it. It is plain that he had no desire to cling to the psychological safety of a life in an ivory tower, but the arguments he ultimately presented to his colleagues were such that he was assumed to be striving to obtain the unattainable: philosophic certainty concerning matters of human motivation and evaluation, rather than the straightforward but uncertain objectives of political and social organisation he set out to attain. He relinquished these at least temporarily at the outbreak of the first World War, perhaps because they seemed to challenge too directly the values and beliefs of his contemporaries, and though he made strenuous efforts to resume the analysis of political objectives during the period of postwar reconstruction, his mind was too divided and his outlook too uncertain to allow him to propound any simple and straightforward solutions to the problems with which he had faced himself.

The nearest we can get to the reality of his reasoning today is to say that certain moral beliefs were implied in German social life (such as the idea of comradeship on which the armed forces were dependent), that this was incompatible with the oppression of the working classes by industrialist and bureaucrat alike in the interests of productivity and nationality, and that the highest good, utterly unattainable in the Prussian state as long as it remained strictly Prussian, was self-determination. To make this viable required agreement about the possibility of establishing a hierarchy of values, and constructing a form of social analysis in which it might be applied. But Weber himself was neither intellectually courageous enough to admit the need for it even to himself, nor was he willing to face the consequences of applying anything like it to his own society. The *Werturteilsdiscussion* was, in fact, a gigantic rationalisation of his own inhibitions.

v

It will thus be concluded that the part which Max Weber played with his brother in the affairs of the Association was revolutionary, but that the revolution they started was very incomplete. He introduced overtly party-political issues into an organisation whose members liked to think of themselves as an eminently 'objective', non-political, and impartial body. It must have been singularly hard for them to restrain their impatience when Weber preached at them about 'objectivity' and 'freedom from values'. They were undoubtedly an especially influential part of what we would now call 'the Establishment' because the Association was dealing with governmental problems (such as the organisation of trade unions, taxation, and municipal government and administration), by finding methods of dealing with them that were administratively viable, which meant making itself useful to Bismarck, the Kaiser, and the German bureaucracy. The shock to the self-esteem of those responsible for its affairs when they began to encounter the social problems of the 1900s was all the greater when they were subjected to a frontal assault from Weber, in the course of which he pointed out ruthlessly how spineless their attitude was, making it mercilessly plain that to act in this way was to betray their original aims, and to identify with the oppressors against the oppressed, and with the exploiters against the exploited.

It was not the main run of Weber's sociological thinking that troubled the minds of his contemporaries so deeply, stung them so painfully, and led to such passionate outbursts at the Association's conferences, but his declarations that what it was trying to do amounted to an intellectually dishonest attempt to deal with political issues non-politically, a theme which has cropped up over and over again in the business of government and administration ever since then. It was not Weber's work as a sociologist *qua* sociologist that created the uproar, nor his assumption (which had so profound an influence on the development of sociology) that the foundations of an 'understanding' sociology are general concepts or analytical ideas (or 'ideal types').[23] The general intellectual current in his times was idealistic, and this sort of speculation was easily assimilable into the thinking of his age. What was the cause of the trouble was his burning conviction that the bureaucrats whose work he deemed to be so dangerous should be recognised for what they were – threats to the liberties of mankind, and a disruptive element in society which would, sooner or later, destroy the liberties of the people by acting as the agents if not the authors of their enslavement. What lay behind the bitter dispute within the ranks of the Association was his keen concern for social questions, and the warmth of his support for the idea of self-determination as a goal of social policy.[24] His breakdown can be understood in terms of the conflict within his mind between his belief in social justice, on the one hand, and his loyalty to his class, on the other. From this stemmed the inhibitions, and the frustrations, that have been so profound a cause of trouble to sociologists ever since.

For Weber, the rationalising intellectual and the nationalist army-officer, 'policy-making is not a moral trade, nor can it ever be'. However much one might deem pacifists to be, ethically, 'our betters',[25] national policies had to be agreed to, and the corollary followed easily enough that the tough-minded amongst politicians and bureaucrats must see to it that the national advantage would overcome merely humane social policies and good intentions. In fact, 'the manifold tasks of the so-called policy of "social welfare" operate in the direction of bureaucratisation', because these are 'saddled upon the state by interest groups', or 'the state usurps them either by reasons of power policy or for ideological motives'.[26] Weber tried early in his academic life (in 1887) to find an answer to this contradiction:

> We reach a totally new world [with regard to the moral conscience] where a quite different part of our mind pronounces judgment about things, and everyone knows that its judgments, though not based on reason, are as certain and clear as any logical conclusion at which reason may arrive.[27]

But this argument is not good enough; he left a disastrous gap in his sociology by saying this, and no more, in his endeavour to heal the breach he had created between reason and values. Though the need to go on with the intellectual fight became plainer to him in his later years, he never made any substantial endeavour to resume it, in terms of sociological theory at any rate.[28] It must now be asked whether his final conclusions were due to his failures in this regard. Given the strength of the idealist component in his sociology, he could have developed an idealist's solution to the problem of values, and it remains to be seen whether the inhibitions which prevented this also prevented him from tackling the closely allied problem of incorporating into his system of thought a more sophisticated attitude to values and social welfare.

We start with the *Werturteilsdiscussion*. The substance of Weber's complaint against the Association, when examined with due care, amounted to a charge that the values of its leading members such as Schmoller were untenable, not that they had stepped out of the bounds of science by concerning themselves in any way with values as such.

Nor, in the last analysis, that its members erred in taking up an attitude to social welfare, but that their attitude in this regard had been wrongly decided. The oppression of the social democrats, and the destruction of political liberty were what Weber objected to, rather than these involved values which were 'the affair of the devil', by which scholars and scientists should not allow themselves to be contaminated. His own values were, in fact, as plain as they were controversial. His opinions lay very much in the direction contrary to those who thought that the academic should mind his own business, and leave political problems to the government. But he did not hold to this line without flinching; his opinions were often contradictory. When he deflected the discussion away from broad political issues, and towards the technical or logical question of the status of value judgments in scientific affairs, the social democracy in which he believed then became a secondary issue, and he started a discussion that ultimately proved to be most embarrassing for social scientists. Weber became a kind of Sorcerer's Apprentice, and we today, rather than he in his generation, have come to pay the penalty.

The discussion of values for which he was primarily responsible was, unfortunately, widened in its scope by enlargements in the form he gave to his theoretical views after it began. The original version of the memorandum he wrote for the Association's special committee, on 'Contributions to the Discussion of Value Judgments',[29] started with a statement that the observations made in it were expressly limited to *empirical* disciplines like the kind of sociology that is of interest because it is factually[30] based (including politics), and similar social sciences such as political economy (including economic organisation), and history (of all kinds, including legal, and cultural history, and the history of religion). Weber added that he would not personally like to argue in the committee, if it were allowed to cross the boundaries of empirical science, whether questions of points of view, or more precisely practical or political evaluations, had their place in the work of the Association. Neither did he wish to discuss any further (at the stage the argument had reached) whether account should be taken in academic teaching of aesthetic points of view, or of practical evaluations. These limitations, though fairly precise, were wide enough for the discussion itself, but Weber soon widened them still further, until they lost most of their meaning. In the revised version of his original memorandum[31] he entered into those questions he had said so explicitly in the earlier draft he did not want to discuss, with a good deal of relish. The result was that he became closely identified with the discussion of the problem he had raised (namely, values), in the widest terms, and he left the impression with contemporaries that he was too much of a 'scientist' to participate in the muddle, for instance, of an ethically-determined economics. The view is over-simplified, but it is nevertheless true that he came in the end to demand the strictest separation of purely empirical or causal sciences dealing with existing facts, from the politics of what ought to be.[32]

The ultimate and complex climax of the argument must also be remembered. As time went on, Germany's political fate under the Kaiser, and the bureaucracy which was obedient to him, became worse and worse, and Weber took an increasing interest in practical politics. He became concerned not only with the negotiations which led to the Versailles Treaty but, much more important than this, he took an active part in the drafting of the Weimar constitution itself, and in assisting with the political education of the German people, by newspaper articles and in speeches.[33] This, it might have been thought, would have given him a better appreciation of the moral realities of political power, and the significance of values in the social sciences. But no. In the middle of this final phase of his life, in an article published in the *Archiv für Sozialwissenschaft und Sozialpolitik* in 1915, he repeated his notion that the bureaucratic state had to be regarded as less influenced by moral considerations than were the patriarchal societies of past ages, as the state's systems of justice and social administration were conditioned 'by the objective empiricism of "reasons of state" in spite of all social welfare policies'.[34] The result was that no amount of endeavour on Weber's part to bring bureaucratic officials under the control of responsible ministers by following the English precedents, with which he was familiar,[35] lessened his reputation as a 'realpolitiker' to any perceptible extent, and he was commonly deemed to be both a reactionary nationalist, and one who wished to keep sociology out of politics and free from value judgments, to maintain its academic respectability and 'scientific' integrity.[36] Which was, of course, if not the opposite of the truth at least very far from it. He was, it must be confessed, in two minds even at the end of his life.

Still, it is plain that it was the side of his mind which defended the interests of the common people so unreservedly and gave rise to the beginning of the dispute about values just before the first World War, that proved to be much the more powerful influence over his behaviour at the time of his death. It was the theoretical sociologist in Weber, rather than the man of practical affairs, which injected so much gloom into his life, causing him to agree with Nietzsche's devastating critique of those 'ultimate men' who had invented happiness. For, in the endless struggle between creative charisma and rationalising bureaucracy, it was the latter, in Weber's opinion, that was bound to win, if only because it had every material condition on its side. He thought he had already discerned a foretaste of the coming age of un-freedom in the social realities even of his early days: 'in the "benevolent feudalism" of the Americans, in Germany's so-called "welfare institutions", in the Russian factory-made constitution – the new House of Enslavement stands ready everywhere for occupation'.[37]

The acceptance of pessimism and hopelessness for the future is, perhaps, the impression of Weber's outlook that prevails today. But it is vitally important to note that he subjected these conclusions to very real and almost successful criticism; his views on 'the primacy of national interest [for instance] . . . stood in stark contrast to [his] democratic and individualistic assumptions'.[38] Although it may be true to say that his attitude was one of 'heroic pessimism',[39] the force of his ideas and his faith in the future have been gravely underrated, to the lasting detriment of his reputation. He left behind him views attuned to genuine political realities as well as theoretical explanations, and it may even be that the political sociology of today may follow the interests of the man of affairs rather than those of the theoretical sociologist, in the years that lie immediately ahead of us.

6. An Alternative Analysis: Mannheim and Myrdal

The preceding three chapters have given an historical examination of the intellectual struggle that took place in the U.S.A. and in Germany during the past half-century, concerning the extent to which the social sciences could be said to embody social purposes in them, and whether this was integral to their nature. This account was interrupted by a lengthy discussion of the way in which the struggle could be said to have arisen out of the idea, for which Weber was responsible, that a complete separation has to be made between scientific methods, when these are embodied in the social sciences, and other or more subjective ways of looking at a social situation or problem. On the one hand we have the proponents of 'social science' as a quasi-natural science, with the accent on the need for objectivity and freedom from personal ties; on the other there is the comprehending of the subject as a means of studying the more intimate realities of social life, in the sense of a concern with the aspirations of man, his ideals and motivating ideas, his achievements, satisfactions, frustations and denials. These latter it is held by the second school of thought, are of paramount importance to social scientists, and it is in more intangible ideas rather than 'objective' facts that they find qualities of compelling reality.

Developments in the U.S.A. have brought the argument back to Weber, but they could also have easily been linked, logically if not historically, with the work of the Webbs and Hobhouse in England. The story would have been interesting, but not very profitable, as the personal connection across the Atlantic was too remote. Instead of this, it is much more rewarding to continue with the main thread of the argument, which leads forward to and onwards from the work of Mannheim and Myrdal. But it is only too easy to conclude, before this is done, that the main controversy, especially in its early stages, is not one which readily repays the labour of following it in all its details. An examination of its beginnings may appear, indeed, to

describe a deadlock or stalemate, since it continued for so long: and
its subject-matter has been gone over so often without bringing to
light much new material, or any new method of solving human
problems, new ways of looking at human societies, or acquiring new
knowledge about human institutions. Nevertheless, the dispute has
recently become much more topical; it has shown few signs of dying
down, to put things mildly. It must now be asked, therefore, whether
this is all that can be said. The deadlock, in so far as it still exists, is
frustrating, and must be resolved; re-examination may show that it can
be approached from a new direction, perhaps more profitably.

II

The position has changed somewhat in recent years, in so far as it
concerns the work of two social scientists that is essentially 'practical';
Karl Mannheim's criticism of the logic of social enquiry relates,
broadly, to the validity of the policies of the totalitarian state in
Central Europe in the 1930s, whilst Gunnar Myrdal attempted to solve
the problem whether or not the social movement in favour of the
emancipation of the Negro in America in the same period could be
said to originate in movements of public opinion, or had a more
objective foundation. Both these lines of thought, then, were thus
fundamentally 'practical', but it has always been plainly evident that
they ultimately concerned the nature of social truth, particularly in
regard to their ultimate objectives and the values which defined them.
And the longer time has elapsed, the more it has become evident that
they involve us in issues that are truly logical, philosophical, and
moral, rather than matters of 'hard fact'. National politics or economic
or social organisation.

The starting-point may be found in Louis Wirth's discussion of
the relevant logical problems in his Preface to Karl Mannheim's
Ideology and Utopia.[1] This leads on to Mannheim's own work and continues with a discussion of the work of Gunnar Myrdal, a Swedish
economist, employed during the 1940s in an investigation into race
relations in America.[2] Neither set of conclusions, however, has had
anything like the influence it should have had on the development of
the social sciences, and this requires a great deal of explanation. When
Mannheim's work appeared, it had come to be admitted that values
were in fact highly important influences in determining the actual

course of the development and the content of the social sciences, and it was necessary, therefore, to examine the precise relationship between fact and value, as it was expressed in current research and teaching. His preliminary study, *Man and Society in an Age of Reconstruction*,[3] was strictly logical in form; as such, it was much more conservative in argument than his later works since it emphasised the importance and the possibility of dealing with the social problems which threatened the welfare of men, by rational and commonsense methods. 'Planning', he wrote,

> means a conscious attack on the sources of maladjustment in the socialist order on the basis of a thorough knowledge of the whole mechanism of society and the way it works. . . . Planning is foresight deliberately applied to human affairs, so that the social process is no longer merely the product of conflict and competition.[4]

Even so, he saw no problem in relating fact and value. He went so far as to believe that 'we have now reached the stage where we can imagine how to plan the best possible human types by deliberately organising the various groups of social factors'; the way ahead, he thought, led towards 'the planned guidance of people's lives on a sociological basis. . . . The apparent limits of the transformability of man are not themes for abstract philosophical discussions but for realistic approach, education, and social research.' At the same time, he found it necessary, at least in the English edition of the book, to emphasise in a footnote that 'all thinking is determined, both by the actual situation' and 'the will'. The over-emphasis on power for which the Fascists were responsible, however, might have led one to think that power and violence were the really decisive phases of planning, and the 'situation' had thus come to overshadow the 'will'. But this, he concluded, could only produce violent crises, rather than 'the best chances of discovering new adaptations'.[5] Philosophic doubts began to creep in.

These doubts were reinforced by the actual experience of the Hitlerite dictatorship in Germany. The steadfast determination many opponents of Fascism maintained against the Nazis showed clearly and positively that attitudes could be firmly based on values that originated from sources quite other than specific relationships and structures. Values required explanation; they had obviously come into existence otherwise than as the mere outcome of social influence. First, the fact of Fascist government had to be explained, irrational as it was. Secondly, the facts of the opposition to it also had to be dealt with, more significant and more compelling than Fascism itself as they were to men of reason and religion, to the scholar as well as to the saint.

Two things had become clear by the time *Man and Society* was finished. It was necessary to understand not only how the day to day social life of the ordinary man was shaped, including his everyday thinking. It also had to be understood how the social values that motivated the routine of his social behaviour could be examined critically, so that higher standards could be achieved, and social habits and institutions improved, in the interests of establishing a cumulative improvement in patterns of culture. Was this possible, Mannheim asked, or was man condemned by his nature to a perpetual and permanent intellectual slavery in a dark age? *Man and Society* was for the most part an optimistic book, in so far as it was devoted to illustrating ways in which this could be done that were fundamentally reasonable; but the work that followed it, *Ideology and Utopia*, explained with some force the reasons why man's thinking had become dominated by his times. This was predominantly pessimistic, though it was qualified by flashes of optimism. Louis Wirth's well-known Preface, which he wrote in 1936, was also pessimistic, in so far as he sought to show how it was that the thought of his own generation had become dominated by the disturbed conditions of the historical epoch through which they were passing, and why it was that his contemporaries had come to question the essential basis of social existence, the validity of the truths they had inherited, and the tenability of the norms associated with them. 'It should become clear', he wrote, 'that there is no value apart from interest, and no objectivity apart from agreement.' But, he added, and this is where a more optimistic theme was introduced,

> the classification of the sources of [disagreement] would seem to be a precondition of any sort of awareness on the part of each observer of the limitations of his own view. . . . It is in some such tentative fashion as this that social scientists, even though they are in disagreement on ultimate values even today, erect a universe of discourse within which they can view objects from similar perspectives and can communicate their results to one another with a minimum of ambiguity.[6]

This, then, was the starting-point of a discussion that has become familiar to all social scientists in the mid-twentieth century. The dilemma in which they have found themselves is that whilst it is necessary and possible on the one hand to be 'objective' and 'impartial', to rid oneself of prejudice and bias, and to steer clear of the influence of the tides of emotion that sweep across any society from time to time, on the other hand, it has to be accepted that to obtain knowledge of a society one must keep in touch with affairs, sharing the feelings and sympathies of one's fellows. Any work undertaken must be approached with an organised mind, which implies an outlook and interests that give a sense of direction and a method of approach that make it possible to gather relevant data and provide at least the beginnings of a means of analysing and criticising it. The social scientist must be a member of his society, but by no means entirely a creature of it. His thoughts must be part of its 'universe of discourse', but they must also be communicable to others within the same society. But the essential thing to note is the conclusion that, if the preconditions are satisfied, results can be obtained from the individual's work, and they can be communicated to others.

There is another but equally important consideration of the same, dual, kind. Whilst, as Louis Wirth said, one should have no pre-conceived values or judgments in the presence of the facts, it must not be overlooked that this passage carried a footnote to the effect that this implied that 'political-ethical norms not only cannot be derived from the direct contemplation of the facts, but that they them-selves exert a direct moulding influence upon the very modes of perceiving the facts'.[7] And this, again, left undetermined the source from which these 'political-ethical norms' might be deemed to be obtained. Two streams of thought, therefore, stemmed from this. The one led to the idea that the facts themselves, and the social situation of which they were a part, determined the manner of their own interpretation; the other supposed that the intellect responsible for their interpretation could, as it were, remain outside the situation which contained them, and, by some sort of social analysis, free itself from social influence and establish its own categories of interpretation.

At this point we must leave Louis Wirth's analysis and concentrate on what Mannheim had to say, without further interpretation. It became clear that the processes of social influence might be embodied in what he called an 'ideology', which amounted to a function of the position in the social milieu occupied by the person concerned. This was what he termed 'situational determinism'. But the individual was also capable of exerting his own influence on his society, as well as being influenced by it. The process was therefore a dual one. It became clear that when this happened, a state of mind might be described as 'utopian' rather than as 'ideological'; it is then 'incongruous with the state of reality within which it occurs'.[8] That is to say, an individual not only bears the imprint of his times in his thinking, but he is also able, in some measure and in some circumstances, to insulate himself from influence, and form his own opinions, and arrive at his own recommendations as to how his environment may be manipulated and perhaps improved. It is this that gave Mannheim the opportunity to escape from the conclusion that 'all thought is ideological'; this was obviously undesirable, as it implies that no remark can be objective in the non-Marxist sense, or even be known to be objective. Mannheim, therefore, suggested that independent intellectuals, such as himself, were unmoved by social factors that forced lesser men into ideological errors;[9] this has enabled them to produce the literature of social science which 'has significant bearings on social policy and action', and for Mannheim 'to point out the lines along which a new basis for objective investigation of the controversial issues in social life can be constructed'. It is this that 'makes it possible for social scientists, even though they are in disagreement on ultimate values, [to] erect a universe of discourse within which they can view objects from similar perspectives, and [to] communicate their results to one another with a minimum of ambiguity'.[10] This was obviously of enormous importance in judging the significance of evaluation, which is obviously incompatible with 'situational determinism'.

Mannheim's work established a new interconnection between being and knowing which involved an analysis of the extent to which thought processes are influenced, on the one hand, 'by the participation of the thinker in the life of society'. In other words, the prospect is offered of demonstrating the extent to which involvement in a given social situation influences patterns of thought, and the conclusions that are arrived at; this might be called the concept of 'situational determination'. More important than this, however, it is also concluded (on the other hand) that it is possible to take a first step towards 'the solution of the problem of situational determination itself'. This arises from the sociological observation that the organisation of the groups which constitute the situations within which thought takes place, may make possible a kind of social life which has few parochial or local ties, and may be more given to abstract and constructive thinking. This, it is said, is clearly observable in the emergence of the academic or social life, and in the sociological point of view itself.[11]

The last word was said by Mannheim in his brief study, 'The Crisis in Valuation', published in 1943 in his collection of essays entitled *Diagnosis of our Time.*[12] This incorporated the idea that whilst 'valuations are partly the expression of subjective strivings, [they are] partly the fulfilment of objective social functions' ('objective', that is, in the Marxist sense). 'There is', he wrote,

> a continuous adjustment at work between what individuals would like to do if their choices were directed by their personal wishes only, and what society wants them to do. . . . The valuation process is not simply an epiphenomenon structure, an addition to the economic order, but an aspect of social change in all its provinces where changed behaviour is wanted. . . . Whereas the most important values governing a society, based upon the rule of custom were blindly accepted, the creation of the specifically new values and their acceptance is to a large extent based on conscious and rational value appreciation.[13]

That is to say, evaluation comes within the domain of both ideology and utopia. There is something more in valuation than mere preference; there is an element of objectivity in it, far removed from individual speculation, personal taste, or physical or even social influence. There is an element of desire which is involved where 'changed behaviour is wanted', but the creation of 'new values' may also be based on consciously held and rational principles. If so, we cross the boundaries between ideology and utopia, and to do so marks the inauguration of a new stage in civilisation. Values, to be valid and to win the approval of society, must appeal to reason; they must be part of the rational 'universe of discourse' which is at the disposal of social scientists. Their importance is therefore ultimate.

This marks a very definite advance in the development of the logic of evaluation. But Mannheim was undecided in his final conclusion. How could the element of objectivity in evaluation be discovered? What, as he said,

> is the use of developing exceedingly skilful methods of propaganda and suggestion, new techniques of learning and habit-making . . . if we do not know what they are for? What is the good of developing child-guidance, psychiatric social work and psycho-therapy if the one who is to guide is left without standards?[14]

What is wanted, of course, is some method of attaining a synthesis of values whereby a sufficient degree of social harmony can be established,

I

ensuring both the active functioning of the social system and the realisation of new purposes and the maintenance of the new relationships. One of the principal negative tasks of the sociologist will be to 'study the conditions under which disagreement arises, and where the process of group adjustment and value reconciliation fails to function in the context of everyday life'. Sociology, in fact, will have to assist people in their daily adjustments and mediate in their disagreements on valuations; its function is to 'discover empirically remedies for social ills, which were formerly looked upon as the result of ill-will and sin'. It will also have to 'promote a democratic value-policy' which will be directed more to caring for the growth of basic agreement than the mitigation of conflicts and maladjustments. What is needed is a more conscious knowledge and philosophy of the meaning of value dissemination, value adjustment, and value assimilation',

> a more deliberate co-ordination of their policy and a focussing of their efforts on the strategically important points. . . . It is essential to supplement the divergence [between groups] by a machinery of co-ordination and value mediation in a collectively agreed value policy, without which no society can survive.[15]

This, from the point of view of the logic embodied in it, is the ultimate end-point of Mannheim's argument. It amounts to an assertion of the over-riding importance of values, and a compelling account of the way values function in the modern and more dynamic society of our times. But it is also supplemented by a plea that some sort of machinery should be set up, with two tasks. Its first would be to encourage the emergence within society of new values which may promote in turn new patterns of behaviour, styles of life, and systems of relationships (on which Mannheim was on very safe ground); its second and more important task would be to identify the measure of agreement which is the social source which confers authority on one value or another. Far from establishing the criteria for the acceptability of values, however, or their intrinsic rightness, Mannheim found himself compelled to rest content with demanding that values should be preserved, developed, and replaced in accordance with the desires of the majority; in other words, what was thought to be good sociologically or theoretically was what was felt to be good by the masses of the people. This doctrine was plainly dangerous, especially to those seeking to find an answer to the measures taken by a dictatorship to acquire power, and perpetuate its hold on power. The reasoning employed, especially in so far as it related to the exercise of power by democracies rather than by totalitarian governments, came near at times to solving the ultimate problems, and it certainly made substantial contributions to the task of doing so. But the overall appraisal of Mannheim's work must be that the really important question was begged, namely the terms on which a value, or an institution or culture carrying a value, was to be judged. His attempt to produce a sociology of change associated with a linked sociology of value was thus a failure, but a very gallant one.

III

The future seemed at the time, nevertheless, to hold in store the same promise for both practical and theoretical achievement as it had when Booth had finished the last edition of his Survey forty years before. The initiative passed at this moment from Mannheim to a man closely associated with him, Gunnar Myrdal, whose reputation had not been primarily as a philosopher, like Hobhouse, or a social theorist like Mannheim, nor even as any kind of sociologist, but as an economist who had become deeply involved in the business life of Sweden. It was, in fact, because he sought to make theory and practice run closely together that he had become engaged in finding a solution for the problems of the theoretical economist entangled in the business world; he found he could not even discuss these facts, without becoming involved in the problem of value. The step from this to the acceptance of an offer to investigate the social tensions that were connected with the Negro problem in America was not difficult to take, and was in fact easier than it might appear to be for the race relations problem had a highly developed and extremely important economic angle to it, both in regard to the obvious question of wealth and poverty, and in regard to morals. Thus arose his concern with the 'American Dilemma' in the 1940s, and his special regard for the way in which it had come to manifest itself not only as a fundamentally moral problem, and thus as one of value in general, but also as one which was equally important as a special and exceedingly intractable form of social disorganisation, at one and the same time an acute form of poverty, a distortion of the labour market, and an unstable type of family structure; and so forth and so on.

From the strictly scientific point of view, of course, it was not one of 'race' properly so-called at all; in reality, it was purely social. And it must not be forgotten that the mere existence of the problem of the Negro in America involved a dramatic clash of values that, as it amounted to a direct assault on the American Way of Life, could not be compromised or be given a meanwhile solution. The American Dream will end if the American Negro, a citizen of the United States, continues to be denied, throughout the twentieth century, reasonably complete equality of civil rights as such. The consequence can only be, in the long run, that the fundamental rights of citizenship itself will be disastrously undermined, and the poor, the aged, and the sick, any or all of them, and many other and as widely spread classes of citizens too, will be compelled to live at similarly low levels held to be appropriate to them. Which would be a thinly disguised form of discrimination which might amount to slavery and, to an American, that cannot but be unthinkable.[16] The end of the American polity would then be at hand, or the Civil War would have to be fought again.

As an economist, Myrdal had developed a keen interest in the problems of evaluation early in his career. He had started with the conception that economics should deal with realities, with things as they were, not as one philosopher or reformer or another would like them to be.

> It should be one of the main tasks of applied economics to examine and unravel the complex interplay of interests. . . . This ought to be done by economists. . . . It would be of the greatest practical importance to reconstruct precisely the social field of interests. . . . We should want to know where interests converge, for in these cases we could make at once generally valid recommendations. . . . The solutions are of practical interest to the extent to which their value premises are relevant to political controversies, i.e. in so far as they represent the interests of sufficiently powerful social groups.[17]

This line of approach gave Myrdal a leaning towards a relativistic rather than an objectivist theory of economic values; values only became significant for him when they actually motivated the behaviour of given groups of individuals to act individually, and they therefore assumed importance, not because they were right and could be defended on rational grounds, but because they were given effect by the people who thought them to be right, or behaved as if they did. Myrdal explained this at length in *The Political Element*, and he also set his views out at length in a paper he published in Germany in 1933.[18] In the latter, whilst he made it plain that he considered objectivism to be impossible, and he took strong exception to the idea that anything like a catalogue of objective values could be compiled, he nevertheless thought that, if the facts about how individuals and groups actually behaved were analysed, the results would 'consist of norms that are objective. . . . We ought to direct ourselves towards such a relativistic, practical economic science, founded on social psychology.' His conclusion was that 'value premises must be clearly exposed, but must be related to the actual attitudes of the different social groups'.

So far as any kind of intrinsic objectivity was concerned, other than that which arose from the crude fact that a value was manifest in the behaviour of given individuals, the 'true form' of the social reality which was created in this way was, he thought, psychological rather than rational, even though it might assume a rationalised form. One's understanding of it had to be synthetic. Understanding ultimately had to be a matter of empathy, perhaps 'not science in the strict sense'; it would be mainly a matter of intuition.

> Our objective is . . . after careful psychological studies of as many groups as possible . . . to use them intuitively to set the sights of scientific analysis. . . . The process resembles the empathy of the poet and his identification with a group. . . . Practical discussions in economics must, as far as possible, be based upon modern sociological and psychological studies of attitudes, behaviour, opinions, and ideologies. . . . Practical political economy can become objective only through ascertaining the political will without disguise, in all its important manifestations, and through fitting these directly into scientific analysis as its alternative, simultaneously present, value premises.[19]

In sum, Myrdal recognised that, 'to postulate ends for social activity is a moral choice for the individual'. But, so far as a social science like economics is concerned it is best to eliminate normative concepts from it, 'for it is hardly possible to make them useful for economic analysis, no matter how we modify our definitions'. We thus get a clear division between scientific operations, value-free as Weber would have had them, and the moral interpretations that might be placed on them afterwards. The preliminary argument is simple, but things as we know them to be are much more complex. However hard we try to be scientific, and keep clear of values, we can never get away from the *a priori*, and that entangles us, firstly in the complications of logic and secondly in the adjustment of theory to fit the needs of an ongoing science, which ultimately leads to the construction of a framework of value within which theory can be contained. The large, unordered, mass of crude facts does not fall into order by itself. Without a principle of organisation, scientific observation is impossible. Naïve empiricists, particularly common amongst American institutionalists, attempt the impossible: their posture is to gaze at reality without preconceptions, and to hope that things will fall into place, and thus give rise to scientific laws. But they are, of course, the victims of an illusion. They only give the semblance of objectivity to their ideas, by carefully concealing from themselves the fact that they are entirely *a priori*. Without such ideas they could not have reached any conclusions. The ideas are themselves ultimately an expression of a valuation, which lends 'interest' to certain hypotheses and gives importance to certain relations between facts.[20]

To say this was to echo what Mannheim had already said. But Myrdal went further in the end, for he recognised that not only did a scientific generalisation imply preliminary steps in logic, and particularly in matters of judgment in general, but it also implied specific value judgments. In the preface he wrote in 1953 to the English edition of *The Political Element*, he said that the book originally contained the notion that

> after all metaphysical elements are radically cut away, a healthy body of positive economic theory will remain, which is altogether independent of valuations. Political conclusions can then be inferred simply by adding to the objective scientific knowledge a chosen set of value premises. This implicit belief in the existence of a body of scientific knowledge acquired independently of all valuations is, as I now see it, naïve empiricism. Facts do not organise themselves into concepts and theories just by being looked at; indeed, except within the framework of concepts and theories, there are no scientific facts but only chaos. There is no inescapable *a priori* element in all scientific work. Questions must be asked before answers can be given. The questions are an expression of our interest in the world, they are at bottom valuations. Valuations are thus necessarily involved at the stage when we observe facts and carry on theoretical analysis, and not just at the stage when we draw inferences from facts and valuations.[21]

It is no wonder, therefore, that however strenuous the effort may be to keep values out of scientific work, they have a way of creeping in despite everything.[22] This left Myrdal in a quandary, when he encountered the sharp realities of Negro-white relationships in America. If there was nothing more to the situation than the fact that some people's thoughts and moral ideas went one way, and some another, then all that could or need be done would be to find (by sociological analysis perhaps) some means of bringing the conflicting ideas about how social life should be lived into a harmonious and co-operative relationship; whether or not that left Negroes in a position of subordination was of no significance provided that they accepted it with docility, or at least with resignation. This was the kind of social gospel that Booker Washington had preached, but it had led to the development of signs of conflict and the beginnings of militant resistance by the time Myrdal arrived on the scene, and this has developed to a very marked degree in the subsequent twenty years. The facts of social organisation in America, therefore, did not permit the optimistic interpretation that theory seemed to make possible, and they showed no signs of being about to do so.

IV

All the same, Myrdal made the conclusions derived from his early thinking the basis on which his great report on 'The Negro Problem and Modern Democracy' rested.[23] This was, of course, inevitable; but the point to remember is that the work itself was more a matter of utilising the fundamental conclusions of *Ends and Means in Political Economy* and *The Political Element in the Development of Economic Theory* rather than the development of new thought, or the solving of old problems. In fact, only a small amount of fresh light was thrown on these in the course of the preparatory studies for, and the writing of, *An American Dilemma,* though it was succeeded by a very important phase of reconsideration that came afterwards, and has extended until the present day.

The most important of the conclusions that Myrdal had arrived at before he began his researches in America were as follows. First and foremost, as has already been made plain, he was firmly of the opinion that valuations were an essential part of the actual process of scientific work.

> Scientific terms become value-loaded because society is made up of human beings following purposes. A 'disinterested' social science is, from this viewpoint, pure nonsense. It never existed and never will exist. We can make our thinking strictly rational in spite of this, but only by facing the valuations, not by evading them.

Next, the logical operations that are an integral part of research precede as well as follow it.

Scientific facts do not exist *per se*, waiting to be discovered by scientists. A scientific fact is a construction abstracted from a complex and interwoven reality by means of arbitrary definitions and classifications. . . . Prior to research, therefore, are complicated theories. . . . The very attempt, so prevalent in recent years, to avoid valuations by doing research that is simply factual and without use for practical or political efforts, involves in itself a valuation.

Then there is a group of propositions that relate the Negro problem to moral considerations generally. This is approached as 'primarily a moral issue of conflicting valuations', but Myrdal refrained from deciding on *a priori* grounds which values are 'right' and which are 'wrong'. 'In fact', he said, 'such judgments are outside the realm of social science, and will not be attempted in this enquiry.' Value premises would, however, be relied on in it, but they would be made explicit; this would be done to serve three main purposes:

(1) to purge as far as possible the scientific investigation of distorting biases; (2) to determine in a rational way the statement of problems and the definition of terms for the theoretical analysis; (3) to lay a logical basis for practical and political conclusions.

But this had the immense disadvantage that it established the friendly attitude towards the Negro, the desire to help him, and the actual endeavour to do so, as a 'bias'. This, it was implied, was 'unscientific', and therefore to be distrusted and, if not avoided, to be dealt with as a matter of emotion, and to be supplemented and checked by other more reliable methods based more directly on 'the facts'. This left social science with an enormously important problem on its hands, which still requires final solution today. The final conclusion was, indeed, somewhat weak: namely, that the values embodied in the enquiry would be those present in the minds of American citizens, and not those of the researchers. Accordingly, no attempt would be made to explain or defend them.

In so far as we make our own judgments of value, they will be based on explicitly stated value premises selected from among those valuations actually observed in the minds of the White and Negro Americans and tested as to their social and political relevance and significance. Our value judgments are thus derived and have no greater validity than the value premises postulated.

This might seem to excuse researchers if they avoided involving themselves personally in the most bitter of the disputes with which they were concerned. Whether or not it was wise for them in the long run to do so was a matter of opinion at the time, though the hindsight available to us today has made more evident the impossibility of making a really significant contribution to the overall solution of the problem itself unless involvement is accepted.[24] Myrdal made certain tentative suggestions in *An American Dilemma* that were based on the supposition that this was possible, but he could not visualise how he could reach the way ahead, and he therefore found himself denied the fruits of his discoveries. He concluded that he had to formulate 'a scheme of principles for selecting value principles and introducing them into scientific research' which might 'present an ideal for social science'. His criteria which value premises had to satisfy for this purpose were entirely general, rather than specifically related to the validity of any given value. These criteria dealt with relevance, significance, feasibility and consistency; they were valid in themselves, yet they had, if they were to be of practical utility, to be extended to the support of an argument which established the truth or falsehood of each value, rather than used as an explanation why any given value had secured social currency. As he said himself,

> The analysis in practical terms would be elevated to the rational plane and made specific and realistic. The aim of practical research . . . is, in general terms, to show precisely what should be the practical and political opinions and plans for action from the point of view of the various valuations, if their holders also had the more correct and comprehensive factual knowledge which science provides.

This led nowhere as long as it was so definitely assumed that science could not lead towards the identification of the truth or falsehood of any value, as such, or to what indeed should be 'the practical or political opinions and plans for action from the point of view of the various valuations'. Myrdal was, of course, entirely justified in concluding that 'the scientific basis for constructing our "field of valuations" is poor'. What he wholly failed to grasp was that it would always remain poor if so far as the Negro problem was concerned, all that could be done was to strengthen the factual or 'scientific' basis by way of making our 'knowledge of the values held by different groups and individuals' comprehensive and exact, rather than allowing it to rest on 'impressionistic observation'. What was surely needed was knowledge of the underlying truth, rather than still more information about what people said and did; the invalidity of behaviour that was oppressive to Negroes, as were its consequences for the lives of both oppressor and oppressed, was more important than the fact that some people thought it was justified, whilst others considered it to be unjustified.[25]

It is Myrdal's predisposition towards the kind of truth that is embodied in 'hard facts' that led him astray. Yet, whilst he was fully justified in saying that 'by subjecting popular beliefs and scientific assumptions to the test of facts, specific biases in the research on the Negro have time and again been unmasked', this is much less than half the truth, as he himself commented time and again. He went on, in fact, to point out immediately in the same passages that 'it must be maintained, however, that biases in social science cannot be erased simply by "keeping to the facts", and by refined methods of statistical treatment of the data'. The quest for scientific objectivity in America had been a cause of regret as well as congratulation. A majority of the foremost social scientists 'have an ambition toward, and take pride in, keeping entirely free from attempting to reach practical and political conclusions from their research'. This was partly due to the possession of high professional standards, and partly to 'a conscious reaction to an earlier highly normative and teleological doctrine'.

> The reaction against reformism and philosophical system-building has been particularly violent in American sociology where a concerted drive to build a social science on the model of the natural sciences is clearly apparent.

The reasons for this are understandable, but this 'does not weaken the present author's conviction that the principle is arbitrary as a methodological rule and is detrimental to true scientific objectivity in its application'. Social scientists were often so extreme in their denunciations of those who draw practical conclusions from their work that the strong anti-practical reaction itself becomes moralistic. In sum, 'the attempt to eradicate biases by trying to keep out the valuations themselves is a hopeless and misdirected venture'. Whether this is so or not, however, Myrdal did not conclude positively what could be done to bring them in as an integral part of social research, rather than as a way to make its relevance and significance plain, or to demonstrate that 'facts' could not be regarded as scientific facts at all, unless the process of evaluation had played its part in showing how this could be done.[26] This is a grave weakness in his theories.

It is one thing to say that 'to the knowledge of the present writer, there is no piece of research on the Negro problem which does not contain valuations, explicit or implicit'; it is quite another to produce a theoretical sociology which has an essential and positive place in it for evaluations. This discrepancy seems to be due to an essential defect in Myrdal's argument; his 'primary task' was to 'ascertain relevant facts and to establish the causal relations between facts'. But how can relevant facts be established without values? His own argument proves up to the hilt that this cannot be done, and he has therefore no means of distinguishing a relevant from an irrelevant fact, unless he takes his argument on values further. It must, indeed, be extended further. It is necessary to get away from Myrdal's idea that fact is somehow prior to value, and that value is somehow dependent on fact.[27] His final conclusions are based on the assumption that 'true values' could be arrived at, and would be acceptable, if the 'correct facts' were known.

But the 'true values' must be known before the 'correct facts' can be established. A double approach is necessary; we start with imperfect knowledge of both fact and value, and we lack hypotheses and theories in the light of which our research and speculation can lead us nearer the truth. Our preliminary task is to formulate them. It is the problem of the hen-and-the-egg again; in this case the relationship is between true facts on the one hand and true theories and values on the other. this requires both the philosophical approach to values and the scientific approach to facts as Hobhouse would have had it. Even this is an oversimplification, as the two processes are simultaneous, interconnected, and interacting; they reinforce and extend each other.

v

When Myrdal wrote the Preface to the English edition of *The Political Element* in 1953, he expressed himself very modestly indeed. He admitted that his conclusions were 'very sketchy', although he added that he thought they 'point in the right direction'. His 'implicit belief in the existence of a body of scientific knowledge acquired independently of all valuations' is, as he had come to see it, 'naïve empiricism'; the argument he presented there can, therefore, only be regarded as an essentially preliminary one, and as being, at best, very partial. The point he left off at dealt with the studies of values; these, he thought, should be made 'concrete in terms of economic interests actually pursued by groups of people dealing with real human attitudes to social processes'. This idea proved to be an enduring theme in his thinking; it was pursued still further in *An American Dilemma*, but even so he

obtained no greater or more lasting satisfaction from the final conclusions embodied in it. 'I must,' he told the Annual Conference of
the British Sociological Association in 1953, 'now confess that I have
not read any major work, or written any myself, which fully satisfies
me as really meeting the demands of how properly to deal with facts
and valuations in social science.'[28]

Myrdal's long-drawn-out thoughts on this problem were as systematic as they were responsible, but they were inconclusive and indecisive.
Whilst it appeared to be true that:

> both the choice of the set of value premises, which is given the advant-
> age of being used as the 'instrumental norm', and their more specific
> definition ideally, can and should be made on the basis of a realistic
> study of peoples' actual valuations,

it was also true that we can never attain anything more than a make-
shift:

> Indeed, clarity about the perfection of all our scientific endeavours
> in the social field, and about its deeper reason is, in itself, an important
> and healthy result of methodological study. It gives a broader per-
> spective to the fact of which every writer – who is not a fool – is well
> aware, viz., that no scientific work can be anything other than a contri-
> bution to an ever-continuing process of growing knowledge through
> discussion and controversy. . . . But it will never be anything other
> than, at best, a step forward in a development. No book is definitive;
> nobody ever says the last word on anything that really matters.[29]

It was on this outspokenly modest but highly unsatisfactory note
that *Value in Social Theory* ended. An alternative conclusion is also,
of course, possible; Myrdal had really achieved far more than he allowed
himself to claim. As has been made clear, he undertook a lifetime of
work as an economist, and the specific study of the Negro problem in
America, with the belief in mind that to be 'objective' was the first
concern of the social scientist, and that if one was to be objective one
had to give the most careful attention to hard facts, which had to be
made the foundation of every research project, and underpin the
analysis built on it. Nevertheless, he came to see even more clearly
that any such idea amounted only to 'naïve empiricism' if it was
allowed to become an end in itself; in this, his work was closely
related to Mannheim's findings. But it was his special achievement to
point out that, whilst the study of the Negro problem had benefited
immensely from the fact-finding of social scientists,[30] valid research

work must perforce be based on hypotheses and *a priori* assumptions of which value judgments are an important part, and evidence incorporated which was relevant to them.

It is the fact that Myrdal understood how vital the moral issues were in regard to Negro-white relationships, and how necessary general sociological theory was in explaining the ways in which they had developed, that makes his work of such immense importance; a watershed, in fact, in the general development of the social sciences. It was in his understanding of the significance of the interplay between hypothesis and evidence, and fact and value, that Myrdal's work reaches the summit of its achievement. *An American Dilemma*, indeed, provides a multitude of examples of how this can be done. Myrdal's creative abilities have, therefore, been much more impressive in themselves, and of much more value to the methodology of the social sciences than he has realised. So far as the Negro problem in America was concerned in itself, the social facts were peculiarly difficult to disentangle from a moral conflict that was of the greatest importance in its own right. Indeed, the problem, as Myrdal pointed out,

> would be simpler to handle scientifically if the moral conflict raged only between valuations held by different persons and groups of persons. The moral struggle goes on within people and not only between them. As people's attitudes are conflicting, behaviour normally becomes a moral compromise. There are no homogeneous 'attitudes' behind human behaviour but a mesh of struggling inclinations, interests, and ideals, some held consciously and some suppressed for long intervals, but all active in bending behaviour in their direction.

This demonstrates that Myrdal was only too well aware of the complexities and the explosiveness of the situation with which he was dealing; he ultimately came to realise that it was 'as complicated as life itself', and that it was 'permeated by the most intense valuations', which 'clash violently'. It was expected of him, nevertheless, that the study he was commissioned to carry out would 'be undertaken in a wholly objective and dispassionate way'.[31] His greatest achievement lies in the fact that he triumphed over the limitations of his instructions. The foregoing account of his methodological difficulties, especially in regard to fact and value, will have shown how far from being 'wholly objective' his study was or could be made, and how regrettable it would have been had it been developed in this way, if 'the facts alone' had been relied on to 'speak for themselves'.

Myrdal was fully conscious of this fact. The truth ultimately became apparent that the value is as much a part of social reality as forms of institutional life, such as those of the Negro church, the matriarchal family, systems of government in the South, or something even more specifically 'objective' than this, such as the conditions of the share-cropper in Louisiana, slum conditions in Harlem or any other Negro section of a large town, or the plantation system of tropic agriculture.

If it is the values motivating behaviour which are a main distinguishing factor between the way of life of industrialised populations, for instance, in Britain and India, Russia and China (not to speak of Negro and white), values have to be regarded as something which can, on occasion, create a whole style of life, and ride supreme over physical or technical factors, climatic or traditional. Values may change, and often do, and with them the culture of societies, cities, and families may change correspondingly. What we need to enable us to understand how this may come about is a new concept of a constructive or dynamic element in social science, which operates through the discovery of a new conception of the interaction between fact and value. Such understanding of the purposive nature of values and of the manner of their functioning within the cultures that are so largely dependent on them, and their influence on the social life contained within social structures, is essential to the creation of a fully developed social science. This must be able to explain why change occurs in the manner it does, and how a change in values may come to have so profound an influence on the course of social history. In the long run, *a priori* ideas about the significance of facts, which are so essential to the construction of theories about their nature, run parallel with *a priori* ideas about significance itself. The one is as important to the construction of a sociology as the other, and this must always be borne in mind.

The final and ultimate point is, therefore, not that the study of values is dependent on the study of those individuals who hold them, and how they have come to be held as in fact they are; it must be devoted to the examination of their essential characteristics. Despite Myrdal's distrust of paying too much attention to the metaphysical aspects of values, we need to know how the influence of a value within a society can be justified, having regard to the circumstances which obtained whilst it acquired its influence and became accepted. There is, as Myrdal pointed out in his early paper, *Ends and Means*[32], an element of empathy in arriving at a complete understanding in depth of the full meaning of a value, and of the influence it has on given individuals. It is only through this kind of sensitive appreciation, likened by Myrdal to the intuitive imagination of the artist, and the identification of the poet with the experiences of the group, that the full truth will begin to become apparent. For the most part, the kind of 'objective' and 'dispassionate' understanding which Myrdal was asked to apply to the Negro problem cannot come alive and be given full general assent unless it is supplemented by the equally important subjective and emotional understanding, of the importance of which he was equally well aware. This might mean a sacrifice of certainty in one's results in order to increase the depth of their applicability, and this may, at times, be a price that it is well worth while to pay; at others, that may not be so. It all depends. But it is plain that the choices that have to be made between the linked pairs, subjectivity/objectivity, and reason/emotion, are never easy to make; it is more profitable to associate them together in research, and the future development of the social sciences largely depends on how this can be done, and the skill and insight employed in doing it.

Finally, we must be conscious of the debt we owe to Gunnar Myrdal for the tentative way in which his conclusions were formulated, the wide understanding with which he has presented the results of a lifetime of research and endeavour, and the courage with which he has insisted that his work is necessarily incomplete and his achievement only provisional and open to improvement by those who follow after him. Myrdal's work is a challenge to all scholars, not so much to go over his material again, and check his analysis, but to discover how this analysis can be made to correspond more closely with reality and be brought nearer to the human problems with which we are confronted.

7. The Difficulties of 'Pure Science': Problems of Ideology

I

The outcome of the previous chapters has been the conclusion that the segregation of fact from value gives the social scientist a distorted idea of reality. A necessary *a priori* operation is to determine the significance and meaning of any investigation in the social sciences, expressly or by implication, before any scheme of research can be designed, or any social analysis of a situation carried out, which contributes to the social sciences; in a word, before the result can be scientific in any true sense. It now remains to examine the converse of this proposition, and to discover what can be achieved when an argument assumes that the 'facts of the case alone' are sufficient for scientific purposes, or that a research scheme can deal with the 'objective' evidence alone, to any satisfactory degree.

This will lead to the conclusion that the failure to make values an integral part of sociological explanations of the course of events, and social research schemes, is, in fact, disastrous. The failure to do this has resulted in the fact that many social scientists behave far too often as if the subject has acquired a vested interest in the *status quo;* if a generalisation has been accepted as valid, then the intellectually idle and the morally timorous will try to preserve the values and beliefs which were current at the time it was established. This self-interest will lead them to keep things as they were, lest what may have been shown to be true in the past will become untrue in the future; which, for many, would be most undesirable. There are those who have the effrontery to admit this openly by making the assumption, sometimes explicit, that all problems that might arise out of the discussion of ends have been solved, for instance, by the success with which the democracies have mastered their own social and political difficulties.[1] Which is, of course, rarely anything like the everyday truth as we know it.

This may be given pointed emphasis by an example. It is strikingly evidenced by the way in which the study of positive or materialistic values has overshadowed the more realistic and rewarding examination of the nascent ideas and ideals that showed signs of developing in Africa: the encouragement of these would have made possible the growth of new societies in which new cultures might flourish, and the local peoples might develop a confident and carefree but responsible attitude to the problems of political and social life. The tragedy of Africa has been that with some prominent exceptions, those who have come from overseas to live in African countries have rarely made their homes there.[2] They have never assumed the responsibilities of full membership of the societies, or made their contributions to the cultures as such. In consequence, when the ways in which these countries have developed have been studied, and their problems examined, it has been assumed more often than not that the person undertaking the task will share the outlook of an 'expatriate'; he has been called upon to be 'objective' in the sense that his own hopes and fears, beliefs and aspirations, have not been involved in his work. He has written about the lives of the people concerned, as it were, at arm's length emotionally.

It will be suggested that the very objectivity on which the sociologist has often prided himself has caused the full reality of the situation on which he has reported to escape him. The consequences have often been deplorable; they are still with us. But this is quite unnecessary and, indeed, positively harmful. There is no reason in the nature of things why the social and political attitudes of the expatriate upper classes to societies under colonial rule, and those newly enjoying independence, should be as unforthcoming as they have been during the present century.[3] Lack of imagination has inhibited the development of new values which might have facilitated the exploitation of the many opportunities for development and betterment inherent in the changes in their way of communal living. The main trouble that has arisen in coping with the problems of such new societies has come from the extent to which material values have been allowed to preponderate over cultural and spiritual in controlling and planning their growth and regulating their daily lives in recent years. The same confusion has been allowed to arise in regard to the values governing the objectives that administrators and political and social leaders have set before them-

K

selves; this has made chaos out of many systems of colonial rule. The very notion that white is better than black, and that so-called 'half-castes' are of less worth than anybody else, white or black, has been so destructive as to render impossible, on occasion, almost any sound policy-making at all.

This has been written at a time when the affairs of the so-called races have been so tense in several parts of the world and the outcome has been so fraught with such horrible consequences that it would be no exaggeration to speak of an explosion in race relations.[4] In the Congo, events have been so dramatic and so terrible as to amount to a disaster of worldwide importance, which exists as an historical fact that must be faced. Acute tension is only too obvious in the United States, whilst, though the same state of affairs may be hidden from view in South Africa and the Portuguese colonies, the situation in those areas is more grave, and may well be all the more dangerous for the future because the discontents of coloured people living in them have been so ruthlessly suppressed. And although appearances may lead one to believe that there is little to worry about in Western Europe, that is because the proportion of coloured people living amongst us is small, as yet. In Great Britain, for instance, where it has increased substantially, so has tension. The growth of sub-cultures is one of the more striking features of our urban scene, and it is only too easy for segregation of this kind to become associated with colour. We appear, indeed, to be on the verge of producing our own Harlems in several cities. And the current situation in the United States needs no emphasis.

Bearing this in mind, it is by no means a pleasant experience for a sociologist to look back on the results of the work accomplished in this field by social scientists in the period that has elapsed since the last World War. Large amounts of resources have been devoted to researches in race relations, but, it appears, to only small purpose. Few warnings have been given by social scientists to their fellow-citizens of the seriousness of the situation that has arisen. So far as the United States is concerned, Professor Everett C. Hughes asked in his Presidential Address to the American Sociological Association: 'Why did not social scientists – and sociologists in particular – foresee the explosion of collective action of Negro Americans towards immediate full integration into American society?' This is, he added, 'but a special instance of the more general question concerning sociological foresight of and involvement in drastic and massive social changes and extreme forms of social action'.[5] There seems to be, as Professor Hughes suggested, something which inhibits the social scientist from entering into and recognising some of the most acute problems and dilemmas with which mankind is faced, let alone discussing and participating in the solution of them.

The same state of affairs has confronted us in Africa, particularly in the Congo. A number of surveys and enquiries into social and political conditions have been carried out under the direction of Unesco that more or less cover the central parts of the Continent. The research groups employed on them have included sociologists and anthropologists of international reputation. Yet the reports, when read by those who look for the living reality, make disappointing reading.[6] The point of view of the authors is narrowly restricted to certain aspects of the situations they endeavour to describe, and, for the most part, the results of the researches are more determined by the methods that have been developed during the present century by social scientists, and are available for use, than by the events and situations to which they are supposed to relate. Much attention is given to somatic types, social structure, population, housing, poverty, health, employment and education, but the lives of the people themselves, their hopes and their sufferings, seem to elude the social scientist. The difficulties that arise from intellectual confinement within bounds set by the random sample and the interviewing schedule are sometimes recognised, as well as the need to adopt at times freer methods of 'intensive enquiry',[7] but this has not made it possible to give more than the most cursory attention to the values and the motives of the inhabitants. The need for work along these lines has, indeed, been emphasised, but it has been seemingly impossible to produce anything of this nature on the basis of the surveys reported, for instance, in the 743 pages of the Unesco volume dealing with African studies.[8]

The existence of a 'malaise' has, it is true, been recognised: this has seemed to arise from the apathy or despair connected with the social insecurity and frustration of Africans living under 'westernised conditions'.[9] Yet the general picture presented of the now superseded colonial rule is of a reasonably satisfactory, if not a blissful, accommodation of Africans to the way of life established by the colonial powers. Groups of artisans in the Congo, for instance, 'appear to be animated more by the desire to fit into the foreign world with which they come into daily contact than by any wish to dominate'.[10] Sociometric testing in the Congo led to the conclusion that 'good behaviour' is regarded by the Africans as evidence of 'civilisation'; the whites are supposed always to 'behave' well. This stereotype is proof against direct experiences, which occasionally brings the Africans into contact with whites whose conduct is held to be 'not always exemplary'.[11] And so on.

It is recognised in the *Report on the World Social Situation*, published by United Nations in 1957,[12] that the development of a new African culture 'is without question one of the most challenging and complex problems of the contemporary world', but the Report also contains the comforting tautology that 'as African society becomes more settled and stable . . . it will doubtless also acquire greater social stability'.[13] The same complacent mood dominates the Unesco publication on *African Elites*; it is stated, for instance, with special reference to the Congo, that 'an African society has been brought into being which . . . succeeds in maintaining a harmonious balance between the various élites and social classes'.[14] Of the Portuguese African colonies, where tension is hardly less great than it has been and now is in the Congo, it is said that 'The native may have, and on occasion proffers, complaints, but they are always against a particular person and not against the white community or the Portuguese administration as such. There never has been an instance here of hatred of the [white] race or culture due to the errors or excesses of individuals.'[15] These are all classic examples of the misunderstanding of social relationships and degrees of tension by social scientists, as the hindsight now available to us has proved beyond any possibility of mistake.

Moreover, when an international conference, preponderantly of social scientists, was convened in Honolulu in 1954 to study race relations, it proved to be very difficult to determine the angle from which the subject should be approached. The idea that the conference should determine whether 'race' and 'culture' and levels of achievement had any necessary connection, was rejected by an overwhelming majority of participants, as was the notion that the conference might result in the establishment of an 'action' organisation responsible for the examination of everyday social problems associated with the idea of 'race'. In other words, all proposals to examine the nature and the outcome of social ideas about race, and determine what could be done about them, were rejected. Instead of this, an endeavour was made to set up an International Society for the Scientific Study of Race

Relations, whose main function would be the encouragement of research, in the belief that if the studies contemplated were carried out with precision and objectivity 'they would be of important aid to other scholars, administrators, observers and politicians'.[16] This Society was stillborn, however: it is interesting to speculate how far this was because of the emphasis placed on the need for 'objectivity' in its work, or because the conference attempted to shelter from the perils of social responsibility under the mantle of 'science'. The conference worked under severe tension, provoked in greatest measure by conflict between the coloured and white participants from South Africa. The issue soon arose whether race relations in general could be made a matter of 'scientific' analysis rather than social evaluation, and it was the failure of the conference's attempts in this regard that led to ultimate break-down.[17] Experimental science, it became evident, is an insufficient means of analysing and resolving conflicts that arise from fundamental and tenaciously held differences in matters of social policy, especially where they are expressed in irrational and emotional terms; though, of course, this might be done if the term 'science' were expanded and reinterpreted.

In sum, it is the basic collision of values which has created the problem of race. As Godfrey and Monica Wilson put it of Central and South Africa, 'the conflict of values in the Union has resulted in the defeat of the policy of "equal rights" for all civilised men', and the triumph of the policy of racial discrimination.[18] It is the attitude of superiority on the part of white people that has led to so much resentment and frustration for 'coloured' people, and the building up in their minds of an intense desire for political automony and self rule. As it is also said in the same work, 'to slight Africans is, in the European group, itself a convention, whose breach leads to embarrassment'.[19] References to demands for 'freedom from contempt',[20] and as far as South Africa is concerned, similar references to 'deepening, irresolvable, unbalanced conflict',[21] are scattered throughout anthropological literature. But though this literature carries with it overtones of doom, they are only overtones. Race and conflict are regarded as side issues, briefly alluded to when mentioned at all, and only rarely dealt with by a frontal attack on them.

There are, of course, exceptions. In *The Uniform of Colour*, published by Dr Hilda Kuper in 1947,[22] the social and psychological attitudes of coloured and white people are analysed in some detail, particularly in sections devoted to 'The White Man's Myth of the Black Man' and 'The Black Man's Myth of the White Man'. In general, the book provides an analysis of the impact of 'white' culture on the life of the Swazi people, and concludes that 'the present criterion of social inequality is not a rational criterion, but a blend of sanctioned prejudices'.[23] It is a great pity that it has not been followed up by similar work, perhaps conducted in other parts of the world; but it is nevertheless true that the *Race Relations Handbook*, published for the South African Institute of Race Relations in 1949, contains a somewhat guarded account of 'Inter-Racial Co-operation' and a very indecisive study of 'Race Attitudes'. The conclusions reached are summed up in the sentence 'In a multi-racial society as we know it [in South Africa], the social system is in a state of extreme disaccommodation or disequilibrium, since the dominating-dominated pattern of relations between white and black is not accepted by the dominated group, and can only be maintained, in the last resort, by force'.[24] This is far-reaching, even if imprecise.

Otherwise, little work has been done along those lines. In South Africa the reasons are only too obvious, but it is strange that it could not have been carried out elsewhere. The Report of the East Africa Royal Commission, 1953–5,[25] for instance, contained a short chapter on Race Relations, but when it is read with what is known of the Mau Mau explosion in mind, it can only be regarded as superficial to the point of complacency.[26]

Professor Anthony Richmond can take the credit for pointing out in 1955 what the essentials were of the situation between the races in Africa.[27] In the second edition of his book, published in 1961, he followed Professor Myrdal by declaring that 'the colour problem is ultimately a moral problem'. This is more generally recognised today, and its implications have been discussed at some length by Miss Margery Perham in the broadcast talks on 'Thinking Aloud About Africa' which she delivered in 1965. In her view, it is the crisis which now confronts us about 'race' which has given the power to African leaders to win approval and support from the masses to demands for self-government. It is what it 'can still mean to be a Negro' that has given some Negro leaders the opportunity and ability to prevent their fellows from suffering 'from the offence of being black' and to 'fasten on all white men . . . a common guilt'.[28] It is this state of affairs that social scientists have failed to observe in the past, and it is this failure that has blinded their eyes to perhaps the most important of the social realities of our times.

The reason for this inability to face the brute facts of race relations seems to be that anthropologists, and to a large extent sociologists as well, suffer from a compulsive desire to develop their study as a 'science' directed to the discovery of 'invariable relations' between events; perhaps it is hoped that to do this will be to relieve the individuals concerned of responsibility for action. Objectivity is a word that seems to denote an unwillingness, paradoxically enough, to endure the pain of accepting the reality of social conditions. These conditions are frequently the outcome of the will and intentions of man, and as such, cannot be understood otherwise than as the product of his disposition to produce a world in accordance with his notions of what ought to be. The results may be both good and bad; they are to be condemned when the latter predominates over the former. The sympathies and deeper understandings of social scientists may be kept on so tight a rein in an endeavour to steer clear of responsibility, that they are sometimes not suffered to show themselves at all.

The argument is really a very simple one. Professor Radcliffe Brown believed that the advance of the 'pure science' of anthropology made it possible to develop colonial administration as 'an art based on the application of discovered laws of anthropological science', especially if, as Durkheim and his intellectual descendants sought to show, 'the moral is what is normal to a given social type at a given phase of development'.[29] But what if the moral ideas of the anthropologist, however arrived at, differ from those of the government in office, perhaps tied to the interests of a determined minority? What is then to be the justification of his work? An anthropologist of the seventeenth century has said that 'the perfection of man does not consist in seeing much, nor in knowing much, but in carrying out the will and good pleasure of God',[30] a formulation which the social scientist of today would probably be unwilling to accept. Only one thing is certain, the inadequacy of 'pure science' to serve as his justification or to provide meaning and purpose for the study of the sociology of 'race'.

III

These and other researches provided social scientists with experiences which, it might only too easily be concluded, showed how difficult it was for them to remain detached from the policies, objectives or purposes that were embodied in the situations they were called on to examine professionally. Despite this, the argument on which the Policy Sciences movement was based assumed that this could be done. This line of argument was continued and developed, however, in a general way, though the movement itself made little headway in the United States, the country in which it originated, or elsewhere. A somewhat complex and indeed paradoxical notion came to be advocated as a result, which led to a rather surprising conclusion. This was, indeed, evidenced by the mounting of an attack on the conventional social and political principles of the Western world by a group of Western intellectuals. A conference called at Milan in 1955 was asked to consider their ideas. The American-financed Congress for Cultural Freedom was responsible for it; but it had no overt connection with the activities which had led to the publication of *The Policy Sciences* four years before in America. The social and political theories promoted at it could only be regarded, nevertheless, as an extension of the same basic ideas.[31]

The general idea discussed at this Conference was that science had superseded moral or ideological speculation. The application of this, it was suggested, would establish much more valuable methods of enquiry, and more reliable ways of dealing with political and social problems or issues. The argument was summarised in 1960 in *The End of Ideology: On the Exhaustion of Political Ideas*.[32] As the title of this suggests, its author offered a somewhat tendentious explanation of current politics, and suggested that the West would have to accustom itself to doing without the driving force of ideologies, which had been so prominent a feature of public life in the past century and beyond. In contemporary political life, however, it is argued in the book that:

> In mass society, the old primary group ties of family and local community have been shattered; ancient parochial faiths are questioned; few unifying values have taken their place. . . . Mores or morals are in a constant state of flux, relations between individuals are tangential or compartmentalised, rather than organic. What [now] gives ideology its force is its passion. . . . One might say that the most important, latent, function of ideology is to tap emotion.[33]

In other words, the strength of ideologies was to be found in a basic consensus of morals and faith, and a translation of this faith into reasonable programmes, intelligently formulated. But this is now over:

The ideologies which emerged from the nineteenth century had the force of intellectuals behind them. . . . Today these ideologies are exhausted. The events behind this important sociological change are complex and varied. Such calamities as the Moscow Trials, the Nazi-Soviet pact, the concentration camps, the suppression of the Hungarian workers, form one chain; such social changes as the modification of capitalism, the rise of the Welfare State another. . . . One simple fact emerges [from recent history]; for the radical intelligences, the old ideologies have lost their 'truth' and their power to persuade.[34]

The consequence is that if the clash between ideologies has lost its bitterness, it has also lost its purpose; liberals and conservatives are no longer prone to argue that the State should stand apart from the operation of the economy, or that the Welfare State is the road to serfdom. There is a rough consensus in the western world on these questions, and in that sense 'the ideological age has ended'. But there was an important reservation to this:

And yet the extraordinary thing is that while the old nineteenth-century ideologies and intellectual debates have become exhausted, the rising status of Asia and Africa are fashioning new ideologies with a different appeal for their own people. These are the ideologies of industrialisation, modernisation, Pan-Arabism, colour, and nationalism. In the distinctive differences between the two kinds of ideologies lies the great political and social problem of the second half of the twentieth century. The ideologies of the nineteenth century were universalistic, humanistic, and fashioned by intellectuals. The mass ideologies of Asia and Africa are parochial, instrumental, and created by political leaders. The driving forces of the old ideologies were social equality and, in the largest sense, freedom. The impulses of the new ideologies are economic development and national power.[35]

A large part of the argument stemmed, of course, from the United States, and was specific to that country,[36] where there has been a long-standing tendency to deal with ideologies in a pejorative way. Something of the kind has also been bound to arise in the minds of intellectuals who have read Mannheim's *Ideology and Utopia*, due to its one-sidedness, and perhaps even more so to Louis Wirth's introduction. If the matter is looked at dispassionately, however, there is little reason to be made upset – still less indignant or downright angry – by the idea that a man is influenced intellectually by the nature of the times in which he lives, if this is supplemented by the idea that the process is two-way, for a man may influence his society and his times, as well as be influenced by them. But this is often forgotten, and ideology is used as an explanation of everything unfortunate that happens. No wonder that the notion that ideologies have come to be invalid in the modern world received such ready approval.

IV

The planners of the Milan Conference had all this in mind, and a great deal more of the same kind. Its purpose, as Professor Shils (who participated in it) has explained, was

> To forward the process of breaking the encrustations of liberal and social thought, to discover their common ground, and to push forward with the task of formulating more realistic and more inclusive ideas on the conditions of the free society.[37]

One of the subsidiary intentions of those who planned it was

> the persuasion of the intellectual leaders of the free societies with underdeveloped economies that they should not think that by renouncing the ample political liberties which they now enjoy, they will be able to make more rapid and better economic progress.

The simple fact had to be faced that these societies

> would have to go through an industrial revolution which, for the severity of the life it inflicted on the people as consumers, would not be less painful than the industrial revolution in the West or the development of Soviet industry.[38]

Whilst on the one hand, therefore, the intention was to pour cold water on the enthusiasms of ideologists and doctrinaire politicians in the Western world, on the other it was not intended to persuade those who came from 'underdeveloped' societies that the mere abandonment of ideologies (including political liberty) would solve all their economic problems. All the same, it is hard to avoid the conclusion that the objective of the Conference was to get the political leaders of the world, particularly those in countries behind the Iron Curtain, to abandon their 'old-fashioned' political and social ideas and ideals, which had compromised them so seriously in the minds of Western thinkers, particularly in Western Europe. If this were achieved, the bringing into existence of One World could be achieved sooner than was generally realised. It was argued that, so far as the world as a whole was concerned, the recent past had shown that men in positions of intellectual leadership had become accustomed to subordinating everything else to the one over-riding value of winning the war. They had discovered for themselves what a pleasant experience it was to collaborate together, and to achieve common agreement; this enormously added to the effectiveness of their endeavours, and acted as a means of adding to the strength of the social bond that united them. Could not this kind of collaboration, and the sharing of common tasks that had resulted from the necessity to fight the war in harmony together, be carried over into peacetime conditions, if ideologies could be forgotten?

The intellectual climate in which the Conference met was therefore the belief shared between many of the participants, that the political ideologies that had divided the nations of the world in the past had succumbed to the harsh realities of the necessities wartime needs had imposed on the Western allies, and had left the United Nations in a mood of practical co-operation rather than of theoretical disagreement. This had, it was thought, continued in peacetime:

> The first sessions dealt with the growing hollowness of the conventional distinction between socialism and capitalism. . . . The programme went forward to . . . examine the extent to which the Soviet economic system, simply by virtue of being a large-scale industrial system, was forced to meet the same conditions and to face the same problems as the capitalist countries of the West.[39]

The world, it was claimed, had 'been freed from the harassment of ideologists and zealots'; there had been a turning point in the thinking of the last few years, which had been 'the end of ideological enthusiasm'. It was pointed out that 'the underpinning of the great ideological conflicts of the first part of this century had largely been pulled out'. The full awareness that British socialism 'has not resulted in tyranny' had 'materially weakened the ideologies of thorough-going socialism and thorough-going neo-liberalism'. The once clear distinction between 'left' and 'right' had become obscured; the identity between them was now more impressive than the differences. The ultimate conclusion was that the age had been freed from intellectual tyranny, and the scientific millennium might begin at once.

Small wonder, then, that we find Professor Shils writing that it seemed to him 'that the conference had in part the atmosphere of a post-war victory ball', and that 'there was in a variety of ways, a sometimes rampant, sometimes quiet conviction that Communism had lost the battle of ideas with the West';[40] there was a widespread feeling that there was no longer any need to justify the West *vis-à-vis* the Communist critique of capitalist-run industry. Small wonder, also, that this optimistic and somewhat complacent[41] point of view could not be shared by the representatives of the under-developed countries, in particular the Africans, Asians, and Middle Easterners, or that a storm burst in the middle of the Conference. There was, in fact, a totally unexpected reaction to the attempts of the organisers to influence them, in so far as what was intended to be a 'subsidiary intention' (namely to bring the policies of the underdeveloped countries into line with those of the democracies), in fact, became a major issue. It was, indeed, these countries that caused the trouble. Their reply to such argument was to ask for aid

> from the more advanced countries, [stressing] how precarious was the situation of liberty amongst them, and [expressing] their belief that without an impressive rate of economic progress, liberty might collapse.

The rejoinder to this was not to submit these conclusions, and any value judgments that might be embodied in them, to rational analysis, or to point out the ways in which they might be defective. On the contrary they were confronted with a hostile and emotional contradiction. A delegate from a western country

> with angry eloquence denied the obligation of the richer countries to provide economic aid to the poorer countries, in a voice which expressed resentment against the resentful overtones which were noticeable in remarks of some of the Asians. ... [Another] vigorous criticism [was] of the intellectuals of underdeveloped countries for their excessive demands, which generated hopes which could not be realised.[42]

V

At this point, the Conference broke asunder. On the one hand, the Western delegates sought to demonstrate to their colleagues 'the baselessness of ideological pretensions'; on the other, the representatives of the emergent nations showed that they possessed 'nationalist sentiments as a part of the love of liberty', despite the fact that, for the Westerners, this was merely 'an unfortunate distraction, at the worst a source of great troubles springing from the passions'.[43] But no serious attempt seems to have been made, then or afterwards, to bring the two sides together, and the consequences have been unfortunate. Professor Shils was content to admit, even after the onset of the storm, that advances

could only have been made, 'amidst the ruins of the ideologies'. He
was unwilling to draw any really precise or important conclusions
from the Conference, and the fact that he was unable to do so was
evidence of its failure, and, indeed, of the lack of practicality of the
ideas of the modern social scientist. He went on to underline the
necessity to 'reconstruct our beliefs', though that should only be done,
he thought, without 'yielding to the temptation' to reconstruct rigid
ideologies. In general, his view was that:

> We must rediscover the permanently valid elements in our historical
> ideals. . . . In our rejection of ideologies we must study what can be
> salvaged from them, and just what in them should be kept alive, how
> and in what measure grandiose visions and austere standards have their
> place. Every society needs a certain amount of these ideals just as it
> would be ruined by too much of them.[44]

This is, in effect, a somewhat cautious and qualified plea for the
reconstruction of ideologies, rather than for their abandonment, and
in that sense the Conference marked a return to old ideas, rather than
the acceptance of new ones. The direction in which the line of argument might have proceeded is evident, instead, in a long quotation
from a speech of an Indian colleague, wise, well informed, pointing
out the contradictions inherent in the Western point of view, and
presenting a *via media* between the strong and the weak nations, the
old and the new.[45] And the report of the Conference ends with an
abstract of Professor Michael Polanyi's closing speech, in which he
admitted that the interventions made by Asiatic, African and South
American delegates had given him, as a Westerner, a 'new sense of
perspective', and that this had revealed

> the power of their political thought, which on a number of occasions
> [had] commanded not merely intellectual appreciation, but the respect
> due to greatness of mind.

While, then, the Conference revealed an obvious need for the
reconstruction of ideologies, values, and policies that might provide
the basis of a working partnership between the nations of the world,
and lead to the re-creation of an international polity,[46] it could only
make plain the need for doing so, rather than take even preliminary
steps towards achieving this end. And, most unfortunately, it was the
supposed fact that the influence of ideologies had no longer to be
reckoned with, rather than the need to reconstruct them, that was left
much more clearly in the minds of the intellectuals of the West as the

aftermath of the Conference. The means of providing a framework within which this task could be attempted was completely ignored.

When, four years later, Professor Lipset published his book on *Political Man*,[47] he recorded his opinion that the Milan Conference had shown that there was

> general agreement among the delegates, regardless of political belief, that the traditional issues separating the left and right had declined to comparative insignificance. In effect all agreed that the increase in state control which had taken place in various countries would not result in a decline in democratic freedom. The socialists no longer advocated socialism, they were as concerned as the conservatives with the danger of an all-powerful state. The ideological issues dividing left and right had been reduced to a little more or a little less government ownership and economic planning. No one seemed to believe that it really made much difference which political party controlled the domestic policies of individual nations.[48]

He also made his view plain that

> The only occasions in which debate grew warm were when someone served as a 'surrogate Communist' by saying something which could be defined as being too favourable to Russia.

From this, it might be deduced that nothing was said about the bitter dispute between rich and poor nations, and that this could be ignored, whatever Professor Shils' views might have been. Professor Lipset admitted at the end of his book that in the underdeveloped countries

> the problems of industrialisation, of the place of religion, of the character of political institutions, are still unsettled, and the arguments about them have become intertwined with the international struggle. . . . The socialist in power in an underdeveloped country must continue . . . to lead a revolutionary struggle against capitalism, the western imperialists, and, increasingly, against Christianity as the dominant remaining foreign institution. If he accepts the arguments of Western socialists that the West has changed, that complete socialism is dangerous, that Marxism is an outmoded doctrine, he becomes a conservative within his own society, a role he cannot play and still retain a popular following.[49]

With these qualifications, Professor Lipset endeavours to bring the events of the Milan Conference within his general argument. His thesis was that politics is now a somewhat trivial and boring activity, concerned with a little less or more on the price of milk, or the level of wages, and is therefore hardly a matter which is likely to excite 'intellectuals'. Controversies about cultural creativity and conformity reflect the general trend away from ideology towards sociology. But the growth of sociology as an intellectual force does not necessarily demonstrate the loss of interest in political enquiry. Professor Lipset therefore ends his book on a note of concern about this trend; there is, he thinks, still a real need for political analysis, ideology, and controversy within the world community, if not within the Western democracies. Democracy

> cannot be achieved by acts of will alone, of course, but men's wills expressed in action can shape institutions and events in directions that reduce and increase the chances for democracy's development and survival. Ideology and passion may no longer be necessary to sustain the class struggle within stable and affluent democracies, but they are clearly needed in the international effort to develop free political and economic institutions in the rest of the world. It is only the ideological class struggle within the West which is ending.[50]

The view, then, is optimistic. Some might say that it bears only remote reference to reality; if the need to study the gap between the rich and poor nations is admitted, the same might be said of that between rich and poor people, even in so-called affluent societies. For poverty is, after all, a relative term, and in any event poverty amongst the sick in body and mind, the disabled, the aged, and in families in which the chief wage-earner is incapacitated for some reason may be severe, and this applies to large numbers of people. And in any event there are the enormous issues waiting to be faced which arise out of the problem of 'race', especially in the United States, where the nation has a most dangerous situation on its hands, calling for urgent attention. This has grown increasingly critical since the publication of *Political Man*. Indeed, the measures called for to relieve the poverty and inequality of coloured people sum up the dilemmas of modern man, which range from the substandard living of the inhabitants of the decayed districts of large urban areas (and the social dislocations that are chronic, for that matter, in all cities) to the miseries and oppressions suffered by 'coloured' peoples everywhere. These problems call not merely for minor readjustments in the mechanism of modern living; they concern the objectives of social life itself, and the conditions under which it is lived which arise out of these objectives. They relate to social policies and therefore to social values, and ultimately to ideology itself.

VI

The debate on the 'end of ideology', such as it has been, has left us much in the same position as the preceding discussion about the 'policy sciences'. Indeed, the whole concept of 'the end of ideology' was attacked in a paper for which two American scholars were responsible. This was published in the *British Journal of Sociology* in 1963;[51] just as Robert K. Merton had pointed out the weaknesses of the policy sciences notion, they punctured the idea that ideologies had ended, and needed no replacement. They were prepared to agree that there was much truth in what had been said about the poverty of ideologies in the modern world,[52] but looking at the problem from the point of view of fundamentals, they argued with much force that no kind of political or social criticism, development or policy (one that embodies the idea of growth and change, that is) is possible unless it is constructed on the basis of some sort of idea or value. Their point of view was that:

> 'Liberals such as Lipset are proud of the progress which has been made in the Western world, but it is curious they never acknowledge the fact that we have gotten as far as we have, precisely because of the ideologies which have stirred men to action.' If ideology had, in fact, ended, 'then we have the best explanation of why we in the West are standing still'.[53]

In other words, the situation may in some ways be worrying, in so far as modern social and political life displays so much apathy. But if this is so, the remedy surely lies, not in allowing or encouraging disbelief in so-called ideologies to go still further, and in destroying the influences they have on men's minds, but in setting in motion the deliberate reconstruction of ideology (in the basic sense of values) in such a way that men will achieve a new sense of purpose. This will motivate their lives, and give them the determination and the encouragement to be up and doing, and to display in a very real way the awareness that it is 'not in their stars, but in themselves that they are underlings'.

Wright Mills defined the end of ideology as 'an intellectual celebration of apathy' which had 'collapsed reasoning into reasonableness'. In attacking the idea that programmes and policies might be expected to emerge with the help of skill and perhaps effort (rather than any stirring of the soul) from 'the facts themselves', and that normal social processes might be entrusted (when aided, perhaps, by social science) to make them evident whenever they might be required, Wright Mills retorted that this might be true; yet it was still possible that the baby might be emptied out with the bath water:

> The disclosure of fact . . . is the rule. The facts are duly weighed, carefully balanced, always hedged. Their power to outrage, their power truly to enlighten in a political way, their power to aid decision, even their power to clarify some situation – all that is blunted and destroyed.[54]

This kind of theorising, therefore, seems much more suited to a member of a fatalistic Hindu sect, contemplating the infinite whilst standing up to his navel in the Ganges, than to a responsibly-minded citizen of the Western world. Least of all should this come naturally to the citizens of modern industrial towns, who are not prone to the philosophy which invites them to put up with things, and suffer their evils in silence; on the contrary, such people are accustomed to translate their notions about responsibilities into action. 'Along these lines', Rousseas and Farganis say, 'Wright Mills would agree that the end of ideology makes a fetish of empiricism and entails an ideology of its own – an ideology of political complacency for the justification of things as they are.' On the other hand, 'progress, as distinct from mere change, can be defined meaningfully only in terms of some "vision". For progress is relative to an ideal which reflection creates. And it is here that, perhaps, the most serious criticism of the end of ideology can be made.'[55]

Writing on the subject of 'Humanising the Future', Dr Visser 'T Hooft has made the point very clearly indeed that, though in the second half of the twentieth century the most far-reaching opportunities are opened up for mankind, 'We are in the greatest uncertainty about the desirable objectives and about the choices we should make'. The problem that confronts us is not merely the technical one of programming computers, so as to secure the right answers. The future is not simply the sum total of technical development, because what we have to contend with is the choice men must make between values:

> At this point we see again the fundamental difference between the exact sciences and the sciences having to do with man, and his individual or collective behaviour. . . . These sciences must operate with some criteria about what is important and what is not, with some sort of presuppositions about what kind of a being man really is. Whether

L

they like it or not, they must make value judgments; and it is precisely at the point of the ultimate values that there is no real consensus amongst us.[56]

These are moral and philosophical issues, which go to the root of social and political theory. It is this which compels us to recognise the very high importance that must be attached to philosophy in our own age, and the impossibility of the expectation that a purely technical approach to social and political problems is likely to make a significant contribution to their solution.

8. Science, Natural and Social, and Value Judgments

Earlier chapters have shown that the foundations laid by English Empiricism up to the first World War were strong enough to provide the basis for a social science that was able to meet the needs of our society as it then was, with a fair degree of adequacy. It now remains to be seen whether these foundations can be extended still further, so as to meet even more urgent and fundamental needs. Before this question can be answered, it is necessary to discuss some of the problems which arise when an attempt is made to bring values even more closely into consideration. More difficult theoretical problems become relevant when the social sciences are asked to undertake the examination of elusive problems of motivation, belief, and value, such as the problems of religious organisation, the treatment of the offender, industrial productivity, and community life. The present chapter attempts the more detailed examination, therefore, of the dilemmas of fact and value, belief and action, which now arise.

The status of values in the social sciences becomes much clearer after consideration of the issues discussed in the preceding chapters. There is no short cut to finality on any of the problems contained in them; in fact the more evident it becomes that the human characteristics of a social situation determine its nature, the more one is called on to show oneself willing and able to live with uncertainty. This conclusion is by no means retrograde, from the scientific point of view. Even in the natural sciences, certainty becomes more and more provisional; that is the main reason why the sciences have been able to assimilate the radical changes of the present century so successfully. A scientific generalisation, if it is to be truly scientific, is one which invites disproof, and is stated in such terms that it can be disproved, and replaced by something better. Although there may be a type of science composed of classificatory statements, such as the determination of the genus and species of animals and plants, this is now regarded as being comparatively old-fashioned. The developing end of science, where the interesting work is done and the reputations are made, is to be found in the amplification and consolidation of evolutionary theory, rather than in the collection of what may be regarded by some as 'incontrovertible facts' or 'raw data'. However positive the data may be, the scientist is not content unless he is able to show how their significance can be established theoretically. The result may sometimes be speculative, but this does not dismay him: modern developments are towards the propounding of possibilities and probabilities that can be argued, as well as conclusions that can be proved. Though it is nice to know that the earth really does go round the sun, that has ceased to be a matter of much scientific interest or importance except to a few cranks such as 'flat earthers', and to those emotionally crippled people who seek to establish a few certainties in their lives to give them a measure of security and safety. In the meantime, and for most of us, natural science has become increasingly a venture into the unknown, and a matter of intellectually dangerous exploration.

The operations of the social sciences result, in fact, even more strikingly in varying degrees of certainty, in the measure that they are directed to the examination of characteristically human phenomena, or situations charged with values and intentions. A high degree of certainty can result from the analysis of demographic data, or statistics of road or rail traffic. Information derived from the census can be subjected to quite elaborate methods of statistical analysis with a high degree of precision, as in the case of reproduction rates. There is an area such as this in which the techniques of the social and the natural or biological sciences approximate. To this extent we can agree without qualification with the statement that social behaviour 'is just as amenable to scientific investigation as any other natural phenomenon'. However it cannot be conceded that such obstacles as are encountered if this claim is generally applied come 'not from the subject-matter itself, but from the limitations placed on the investigator by his own society'. It is true that the investigation may be scientific in the sense that 'the emotions of the investigator do not influence the observation and explanation of the facts'.[1] But where the more complex forms of social behaviour are investigated, profound modifications in scientific techniques have to be adopted to deal with the data, and it may be argued (perhaps mistakenly) that the methods of the social sciences become so individual that they are not sciences at all, but 'studies'. This is not because social scientists may take sides in moral, political, or social issues, but because their conclusions may be based on opinion rather than evidence. It is hoped to demonstrate that this need not be the case.

Complex situations have sometimes to be investigated, as with the feminist movement, which cannot be undertaken without a prior understanding both of the facts of economic change during the previous two hundred years, and the values that were attached to the individual personality by judaeo-christianity. These preliminary assumptions and the relevant knowledge that goes with them make judgments possible of the ways in which phenomena are related to each other, together with a sympathetic awareness of how the individuals involved might have reacted to social stimuli. This may lead directly to significant conclusions, which are not based on critical experiments, or demonstrations. As such, they are not part of the conclusions of an experimental science, but prolegomena to them. It is the construction of an imaginative hypothesis that is so important in such instances; it is this that is so typical of the social sciences, rather than painstaking empirical proof, particularly proof that is watertight and incontrovertible. Proof of an argument of this latter kind is of an entirely different order. Because the natural sciences, particularly the physical sciences, have undergone revolutionary changes in this regard in the present century, the contrast between the certainty of the physical sciences and the degrees of freedom with which the social siences have to contend is rather out of date.

Science, as such, has now developed new approaches to knowledge, and new methods of understanding, that could profitably be studied by those who tackle the highly elusive problems of human societies. If the statistical certainties of population trends tell us so little about the fluctuations of intensity of feeling, as in the case of Negro élites, we must search for less familiar, if more relevant, kinds of knowledge. If the needs and desires of humanity in general, or of the masses employed in industry in particular, are often inexplicable, irrational, and deplorable, as Weber found them to be to upper-class officials in Germany, we must allow realities to impose themselves on us, and reject the certain and the safe as categories of social explanation. This is what Weber told his colleagues to do. The pursuit of knowledge requires us to fashion new tools of social investigation and new theoretical concepts on which to base hypotheses, which will lay bare the truth, irrespective of the class, 'race', or sex of those involved, or the opinions they have inherited from their own societies. Something approaching universal assent as to the why and wherefore of what happens in the social world must be sought. We have to face the difficulties of doing so, intimidating as these may be, and try to forge ahead. Each science must fashion its own methods, and those of the social sciences cannot but be expected to differ widely from the physical or biological. The social sciences, the life and the physical sciences, have so little in common that the value of 'general science' may be small. That can be no cause for surprise, since the social behaviour of human beings, is fundamentally different from the properties of inanimate matter or the characteristics of plants or animals. Although the methods of the several sciences may be many and diverse, their existence as sciences must be undoubted, however widely they come to differ. It is the universal search for objective truth that binds them together, rather than a common methodology.

The social sciences, therefore, will have to develop a means of dealing with a subject-matter which is their own speciality. They must perforce examine, describe, and assess the truth and importance of the values which play so characteristic a part in the make-up of the daily life of man's societies. Values will have to be understood and explained as a dynamic factor influencing events which, if they are treated as things-in-themselves, cannot be regarded as anything more than the outcome of chance and circumstance, to the exclusion of any reference to the ideas by which men are, in fact, swayed. The course which human history takes must otherwise remain much of a mystery. Knowledge about it cannot extend to the reasons for the rapidity or slowness of social change, or the course it takes. The receptiveness of societies to new ideas, or the degree of rigidity with which any given society faces innovation, cannot be other than an unknown quantity. This problem is the central and essential one in the situation now confronting the sociologist. It is the hardest of all those with which sociologists have to deal and this is especially true if they attempt to do so plausibly and to some purpose.

Social science, like any science, comprises an endeavour, amongst other things, to reduce relevant data to order for the purpose of understanding them; it is different from other sciences by reason of the relatively low degree of certainty or proof that it is able to command. Its main distinction as a science is in working from theories, particularly social theories, to hypotheses, and from then on to the relevant data, rather than the converse. It also differs from other sciences in so far as its hypotheses are often much more remote than theirs from the data. It must take the broad general sweep of theory into account in formulating them. Value in the form of social theory plays an important part in the determination of what data must be examined, both to establish a sociological generalisation, and to enable the social sciences to develop: value and fact have to be taken into consideration simultaneously in social research, to a much larger degree than in science generally. It is obvious, says one student of the logic of the social sciences, that 'human beings are end-pursuing creatures. The ends pursued are evaluated, individually and socially, and these evaluations are part and parcel of the facts of social living – the very subject-matter which the social scientist studies and interprets.' This does not concern values merely as factual matter for analysis, which is a different thing altogether, so much as values as explanations of human behaviour. Human beings consciously and deliberately pursue ends which they value – and what they actually do comes to pass because this is so.

> If this fact is not taken into account, human behaviour, in so far as it is purposive, remains inexplicable, and social science cannot advance beyond the stage of mere description. . . . Explanation and prediction are impossible without reference to the basic value commitments of the agents involved. A change in those commitments may alter the whole series of events with which the social scientist is concerned. But once basic value commitments are understood, many otherwise inexplicable phenomena fall into a coherent pattern in their relation to these commitments.[2]

What we are talking about, therefore, is value as an explanatory category; it is this characteristic which is of really crucial significance for the social sciences. Values may stimulate and influence conduct, and promote change and the activities that go with it. An outstanding example is to be seen in the reactions of the leaders of coloured people to oppression (or supposed oppression) the world over. Nothing short of an understanding of why it is important to the individual that his intrinsic worth as such should be recognised by his fellow-citizens, can explain the conduct which his membership of a 'race' can evoke. Without comprehension of this bind, there can be no explanation of the way in which peoples' minds can be set ablaze with fury by a sense of injustice, or made malleable and submissive to it by the consciousness that the following of another's leadership is the best way to attain common goals. Such an understanding may lead to a grasp of the course of events, public and private, and enable one to forecast the trends of current history with some accuracy: this implies an awareness of the significance of both fact and value, and their complex inter-relationships.

Much more controversial is the supposition that it is the sole function of social science to undertake the direct and commonplace application of reason to the understanding of societies or social processes. Here it will be suggested that the reason satisfies a much wider and deeper purpose in judging the validity of values. Values are, of course, inextricably linked with facts, and it is both hard and rare to discover examples where values or facts can be dealt with separately or autonomously. There is a tendency for those who wish to examine societies and social behaviour according to what they may conceive to be the canons of science, to deal with facts almost exclusively, and then only as existing in their own right, 'objectively' or materially. Their assumptions are that values are nothing more than another order of social facts, and that the dimension of value therefore need not be examined as a way of looking at things or as a mode of thinking. From this point of view values are not, as has been suggested above, a way of establishing or changing the meaning of events for individuals. This may be disastrous for the social scientist, because it seems undeniable that values are forces which lie behind the creation of events; they must not be mistaken for the events themselves.

It has been widely recognised that a misconception of this kind arises from positivism; which is correspondingly inadequate to meet the complex demands of a real situation. To approach reality, the process of enquiry, if positivist, must be either preceded or supplemented by a method or methods that are essentially of a different order.[3] The trouble arises from the nature of the 'facts', and the manner of the attempt to deal with them 'scientifically', as the positivist would wish. Few can be profitably examined in virtue of their own independent existence, rather than in the dynamic context of human endeavour and intention. Facts are much more elusive than they are commonly thought to be. It is true that a class of facts may exist, as it were, in virtue of their own self-sufficiency, uninfluenced by desire, will, or obligation. The facts that result from the operations of the census organisation may appear at first sight to be of this order, but it must be remembered that it is only true of some facts such as those relating to birth and death. These questions form part of the census solely because somebody considered them to be of significance for some purpose. The Registrar General does not have questions asked merely to satisfy an idle curiosity, and waste time and money in doing so.[4] All the same, facts may be 'hard' or 'brutal' to the point that they may be deemed to have an autonomous existence of their own, as they have for the losers of a battle, a man suffering from a mortal disease, and a person or nation facing bankruptcy.

This must not be forgotten, and it involves an admission that there is a degree of truth in the positivist system of thought. Far more important than 'hard' facts of this kind, however, so far as the general run of social life goes, are those facts that are of interest to us because they accord with our ideas, or because we believe we can make something out of them, or (if they are contrary to our aspirations and beliefs) because we think we can overcome them, and carry into effect the way we think things ought to be, despite them. Attitudes between the sexes or races are not made up out of a simple awareness that one is a woman or a Negro, and that one must acquiesce in the inevitable, and accept one's lot in life. They may provoke us to believe its contrary, that the socially unequal position of women is an injustice, or the oppression of Negroes is a crying shame. The harder the facts, the stronger our determination may be to overcome them. One may fight against fate, as well as accommodate to it hopelessly and with resignation. An anxious search for more knowledge 'for its own sake' of the class, employment, and the group membership of women and Negroes, may be merely escapist. Facts may be a stimulus to action, and action may change facts; values as applied to fact may demand that one does what one can about them. The action that arises in this way may be much more than a simple fact, or mere raw material for sociological analysis. It may amount in itself to a dynamic factor in growth and change.

Facts, therefore, may have a very complex existence. They may, of course, be of significance to the proving or disproving of specific theories, of an impersonal order. But they may also be of the greatest importance to the sociologist because they occasion the development or abandonment of values, which may, in turn, emphasise their existence or require their abolition or transformation, as has been argued. It is for this reason, and in so far as the social world owes its origin and its future to this manifestation of the human mind, that values must be given a prominent part in the sociological explanation of the way in which societies function. The complexity of fact becomes only too obvious when the methods are examined whereby an understanding is arrived at of their significance. Theoretical significance is attributed to a given theory by a process of induction; there is very little to be said about the way this is done over any part of the range of the sciences, natural as well as social, and there are no rules or expedients that can be adopted for improving inductive processes. But there is a great deal more to be said about significance from the point of view of understanding what it is that given individuals consider to be significant to them. What part do values play in terms of the satisfaction or the reverse which people get from the experiences of life, what joys and sorrows have come to them as a result of their pursuit of values and what stimuli and motives are associated with the values they adopt? These are very sensitive phenomena, and are not to be discovered, still less to be understood, by the rather superficial methods often used today, such as the questionnaire and institutional analysis.

It is, in other words, involvement in the lives of others that sensitises the mind about their feelings and about their conduct, and gives one the impulse to understand that urges one on to the creation of hypotheses, and thus to the starting-point of science. An intimate interest in another person, especially when it is associated with a genuine concern for his well-being, may be so deep that it involves components of understanding, as well as feeling, and moral obligation;[5] 'empathy' is a more technical name for this very human relationship; it is, the *Shorter Oxford English Dictionary* has it, 'the power of projecting one's personality into, and so fully understanding, the object of contemplation', and something of the kind has been found by many writers to be essential to the development of a social science that is able to deal with realities of life, rather than with the superficialities and the spinning of somewhat dubious concepts and theories about social phenomena. Social scientists have already written authoritatively about the problems involved, and there is a considerable measure of agreement with the view that an understanding of social change, especially the rise and fall of minority movements, or the troubled life that is lived in the borderland between deep emotion, convinced belief, and cold reason is dependent on the use of methods of observation and a conceptual system that is peculiar to the social as distinct from the other sciences. It involves an ability to share other men's experiences with them, and to project one's thoughts from the fact that one has done so. To some extent this is a *sine qua non* of all social research, because without it we can no more understand or assess run-of-the-mill social behaviour than we can considered action or calculated policy. Sorokin has expressed himself on this uncompromisingly:

> A scientist observer who has never experienced joy and sorrow, love or hatred, religious or aesthetic bliss, justice or injustice, creative or dull moments, certitude or doubt, can never obtain even the remotest knowledge of these living, feeling, wishing, emotional and thoughtful states. With all his statistical, logical, observational techniques, he can get only shadows of the dead shells of these meaningful, living miracles. . . .
>
> The same is true of social systems. Only through direct empathy, coliving and intuition of the psychological state, can one grasp the essential nature and difference between a criminal gang and a fighting battalion; between a harmonious and a broken family. . . .[6]

Put more succinctly, the argument leads us to conclude that, in matters of social concern, a man can only understand; what he has previously experienced.[7] It is indeed true a man can understand more clearly if his knowledge of life is correspondingly wide and deep, but it is at least doubtful, however, whether we have to go the whole way that this argument implies; some people have, as it were, a gift for synthetic understanding by learning from others, and an ability to explain and describe that enables others to learn from us. But although the assertion that there can be no social learning without empathy goes too far, the main point is true, that it is the ability to share experiences that lies at the bottom of understanding, particularly the kind of understanding that leads to social action.[8]

German psychology and sociology has made much of this in the past, but this has proved to be a blind alley, and the idea has not been followed up with any great degree of determination at the present time. Insight and intuition were valued much more highly in Dilthey's day (in the late nineteenth century) than they are now. According to Dilthey:

> To understand is to know what someone is experiencing through a re-opening in my own consciousness of his experience, which, though in

my consciousness, is projected into him and perceived as his. To sympathise is to have in my own person experiences analogous to his and related to them. . . . It is not normally possible to understand without sympathising.[9]

Perception of this kind is aesthetic, so far as it is a matter of the direct apprehension of the quality and content of another person's life. But it is also scientific, firstly because it is directed towards a pre-determined object in a predetermined way to a much greater degree than perception usually is. It is in the second sense scientific because it is made use of as the raw material for an ordered explanation of the way of life of the subject. It can be matched with other material, and be built into an organised whole as the result of a critical examination and appraisal of its worth as evidence. Professor Redfield has distinguished the 'outside' from the 'inside' view in anthropological work, which is undertaken in this way, and what he says goes for the social sciences generally. The latter is derived from the making of intensive relation-ships such as those Dilthey was writing about. The former are the more distant observations of the social scene, involving more impersonal methods, such as the collection of documentary and perhaps historical material, and statistical analyses of behaviour, sociograms, records of meetings, and the like. He suggests that the latter is a necessary part of the study of individual lives, or of primary groups or small face-to-face societies which live an independent life of their own, detached from that of the modern world at large. He writes:

> The necessity to take the inside view on the way to systematic under-standing is the peculiarity of the study of the personal and the cul-tural. . . . The student can begin with the outside view. . . . But the sentiments, ideas, and judgments of good and bad that make up the mental states of other people are the very stuff of the personal and cultural studies. On the other hand, these mental states of other people do not become data, do not enter into abstract and general know-ledge, until they are looked at from the outside and given names that relate them now in the minds of outside students to other such data.
>
> This tension between the inside and outside view, the obligation to manage correctly the relationship between them, is the central problem in studies of culture or of personality. . . .[10]

We have been reminded by Lord Lindsay that this idea is as old as Plato's *Republic*; following Dilthey, he states that in his view 'this instrument of imaginative sympathy needs to be cultivated and educated as assiduously and carefully as the faculty of scientific observation. If we neglect the cultivation of the re-creative imagination – especially in an industrial civilisation which naturally starves it – our hopes of understanding ourselves and our civilisation are doomed from the outset. . . . For if insight into man depends upon experience, failures in our experience will affect our insight.'[11] Although there is thus a general recognition at least of the desirability of associating oneself as closely as possible with the subject of one's researches, in order to present as true an account as possible of their life or lives, it is not realised that the argument goes much further than this. Lindsay seems to regard this kind of 'imaginative sympathy' (Dilthey's idea) as something which can be compared with 'the faculty of scientific observation' rather than regarded as a special example of true scientific observation which can be used in the social rather than the natural sciences. This is disappointing, and must be regarded as something of a lost opportunity. Lindsay's argument may have to be taken further, and it is encouraging that Max Planck was prepared to do so with his immense reputation as a physicist behind him. Writing of 'those sciences which deal with human events', Planck advanced the following opinions:

> Here the method which the scientist follows can have nothing like the same exactitude as that which he follows in physics. The object of his study is the human mind and its influence on the course of events. The great difficulty here is the meagre supply of source materials. While the historian or the sociologist strives to apply purely objective methods to his lines of investigation, he finds himself confronted on all hands with the want of data whereby he might determine the causes that have led to general conditions in the world at the present moment. At the same time however he has at least one advantage which the physicist has not. The historian or the sociologist is dealing with the same kind of activities as he finds in himself. Subjective observation of his own human nature furnishes him with at least a rough means of estimation in dealing with outside personalities or groups of personalities. He can 'feel into' them, as it were, and may thus gain a certain insight into the characteristics of their motives and thoughts.[12]

The problem as stated by Max Planck, therefore, is not whether empathy of this kind can or cannot be used scientifically as a means of scientific discovery, but the degree of exactitude which can be derived from it. It is much easier to use it as a means of formulating hypotheses than of validating or disproving them, though it undoubtedly has a part to play in this task. It will readily be seen from the foregoing argument that the methods of proof adopted in the social sciences must to a large extent be *sui generis*, and that many of them could not be used in the physical or biological sciences at all. Indeed, the logic of the social sciences, as might be said by a modern philosopher, may be a universe of discourse that is autonomous and self-sufficient, but it is also one which has close links with moral philosophy. The explanation of social conduct must take into account both rational and irrational factors, both logical argument and emotional and other psychological or social influences, and it is the emotional influences that can be understood best by empathy. And the same applies to morals. In so far as the judgment is expressed that an act is right or wrong, or a given way of life good or bad, it has an influence on its social viability. In so far as individuals are influenced in their conduct by normative ideas, it is necessary for the sociologist to have an acquaintance with the notions of morality which run parallel with them.

If empathy involves the exercise of judgment of one kind, the identification and selection of moral values requires another, and it is to that that we now turn. But before doing so we should note that the argument about empathy, and in particular what Max Planck had to say about the social scientist's direct insight into his subject's motives and thoughts, must accustom us to the idea that the methods of the social scientist are very different from those of his colleagues in the other sciences.

We now know as the result of the foregoing argument that knowledge about human conduct and the inner life of individuals can be acquired in several ways. This is important for our present purposes because, as has already been emphasised, values are especially influential in determining the conduct of any individual person; in order to be able to have some idea of how a social process works, it is to peoples' values that we must look in the first instance, and knowledge of their functioning may well be acquired by sympathetic insight in addition to other more conventional methods. Next, we need to know how the values themselves are determined. The argument in this regard is usually conducted in terms of morals, which are undoubtedly a very important, if not the most important, type of values which influence the conduct of the individual. We may well expect to find that if sympathetic understanding gives us a special knowledge of the how and the what of other people's lives, our knowledge of why it is that they have come to hold the values they do and to believe what they do is deeply influenced by two factors: firstly, the intensity of social influences, and secondly, the degree of rationality or plausibility embodied in the values themselves, which plays a very important part in making them as powerful as they are socially, by predisposing the individual to embody them in his own conduct.

This is primarily the business of the moral philosopher. In our own society, and in the western world generally, philosophy has emerged only very recently from an idealist phase which lasted roughly speaking up to the first World War. In Germany this began with Kant and Hegel, but its collapse was evident in the work of Weber, who attempted to be both idealist and realist at one and the same time; though his attempt was a courageous one, it failed conspicuously, and though it opened up issues for further exploration, it did not give the sociologist the firm philosophical foundation he needed. His handling of the problem of morals was particularly unsatisfactory, and left sociology adrift in this regard. In Great Britain, idealism assumed the form given it first by T. H. Green, and finally by Bernard Bosanquet. This school of thought, although it was immensely influential in Oxford in the nineteenth century and up to the first World War, collapsed utterly under the strains imposed on it, although its inadequacies were plainly visible before the war began. Unfortunately, the extensive ethical teaching which was a prominent feature of idealist philosophy at the time collasped with it. All that filled the gap that was left behind was an attempt to deal with morals as a matter of instinct rather than reason; or as something that, because it was non-rational (if not irrational), was to be regarded as part of the subject-matter of the social sciences viewed positivistically as extensions of the natural sciences, rather than, as has been said before in regard to values in general, as part of any philosophical system of explanation of human conduct. This left the sociologist with a very shaky foundation for the analysis of social relationships, if they were regarded as being influenced by rational concepts at all; this, in turn, left the social sciences in the hands of 'pure' scientists and the positivists. Human behaviour seemed, indeed, to provide excellent material for the creation of a natural science of society, based on Weber's ideas about freedom from values.

The situation was particularly difficult because this period was one during which the philosopher was uninterested in the problems of sociology, due largely to the chaotic state into which philosophy sank during the 'twenties and the 'thirties, when the philosopher had no surplus energies left to enable him to interest himself in anything other than technical problems. When the philosophers came to adopt a more definite attitude towards public affairs and problems during the next decade, it was the negative and destructive ideas of Wittgenstein in his earlier years, and the logical positivists generally, that prevailed. Today, logical positivism has been succeeded by the school of philosophy developed by Wittgenstein in his later period, namely linguistics, which may be said to amount to a very self-conscious apotheosis of common sense. This has been much more realistic and helpful; it is still very narrow technically speaking, but the philosophy that has come to the fore during the last decade has had the great merit that it has at least cleared the ground of most of the wreckage left behind by English neo-idealism, and the subsequent philosophising that succeeded it. At long last, support has begun to manifest itself for the sociologists, whose most acute problems have now become real problems for the philosopher once more, and this has bolstered their self-confidence, particularly by making possible the new start in their thinking, for which we have been waiting for so long.

The present position is therefore that the wide-ranging and nebulous theories of Hegel and his successors, up to and including the English neo-idealists, have been completely deflated, whilst the work of the philosophers of the inter-war period, which had reduced philosophy to logic-chopping and the lengthy discussion of issues of no great intrinsic importance, has had the wind taken out of it some years ago, and has now been brought to an end. This has been followed by a period which was one of negative criticism at the outset, but has nevertheless become one in which philosophy has to an increasing extent been a helpful contributor to the solution of problems of modern social life; this is particularly so in the field of morals.

As logical positivism and linguistics left things, it was supposed that a statement which embodied a moral judgment implied merely a personal preference or inclination, and that this was a question of emotional feeling, taste, or whim, and nothing more. As Professor Emmet has put it:

> Ethical propositions, it was said, asserted nothing true or false; to say 'stealing is wrong' would simply be to express an emotional abhorrence of stealing on the part of the speaker, and also, perhaps, to try

and arouse a similar emotional abhorrence in others, but not to be saying anything which could rank as rational argument.

This has been generally thought to make only a very inadequate account of the relationships between reason and emotion possible, and to deny more than vestigial meaning to expressions such as 'reasonable', 'responsible', or 'moral' (as distinct from 'moralistic'). To quote Professor Emmet again, 'In ethics, aesthetics, religion, it is not plausible to say that whatever is said ranks equally as an expression of feeling and no more'.[13] When all is said and done, it is only in very exceptional circumstances that poetry is really as good as pushpin (as Bentham had it), and guns are to be preferred to butter (in Hitler's jargon), and we all know perfectly well that there are good reasons for saying this. Linguistic philosophers have, indeed, made it their business to discover how words can be used meaningfully, and to warn us against the other ways, which are nonsensical. If there are meaningful uses of language, then philosophy must give them due regard in any system of thought that may be constructed, and it is thus that common sense has come into its own again. If the 'plain man' has a word for it, then it exists for the linguistic philosopher, and no amount of critical analysis robs it of its real existence for him. It is then held to describe something, which requires clear understanding. This argument has been accepted, knowingly or unknowingly, by some contemporary sociologists, who are now more influenced by a somewhat sophisticated common sense than classical metaphysics. Conversely, the age-old problem of freedom versus determinism may be solved by declaring it to be a nonsense or no-problem, in the manner of recent philosophers. The fact, to repeat, that responsible people are worried by something which is seen as a problem by them, makes it a real one for philosophy. As Peter Worsley says:

> We emphasise choice instead of positivistically enunciated 'laws' and 'predictions' because social science cannot tell us what 'will happen'. It can enable us to understand what forces are at work, to assess the significance of the values according to which we act, and the likely practical implications of our choices. It enables us to choose rationally, and not blindly or dogmatically. What we lose, in dropping the spurious certainty of deterministic dogmas, we compensate for in other ways, for this width of uncertainty carries with it a corresponding share of hope and freedom, and an enhancement of human choice and human values, whatever the constraining conditions, which some men have to take account of. Social influences, evident in the form of

M

probabilities, do not re-establish deterministic forces in a new guise, 'for men have minds, and can die rather than submit'.[14]

The first approach of the modern moral philosopher to the problem of moral behaviour has, accordingly, been the negative one of denying that positivistic explanations have been adequate. Professor Stephen Toulmin starts his *Reason in Ethics* by rejecting both the 'objective approach', which explains moral behaviour by way of asserting that it is the outcome of social influence, and the 'subjective approach', which explains it in terms of emotion; these are held to be inadequate ways of dealing with the facts. It is sufficient for his purpose to argue that men exposed to similar environmental influences agree about the physical facts they perceive, but not about their value, or the morality of given actions; furthermore, he points out that the validity of an ethical judgment of an action does not depend on its acceptability, as evidenced by the frequency with which it is performed.[15] What he finds to be the necessary element in an ethical judgment, which makes it good or bad, is 'the reasoning behind [it]'.[16] The foregoing passage is directly related to a consideration of abstract moral reasoning, but in so far as this is both an individual and a social process, it is also very relevant to the ways in which societies function. The attribution of truth to a system of morals, and its acceptance as a guide to conduct, is closely associated with the recognition of the existence of a social system which contains the moral system, and the willingness of its members to identify themselves with it, and to give it viability and vitality. We decide

> which value systems shall be relevant to a certain kind of situation and which shall not. In choosing a way of life we make a given system relevant or not relevant to a given situation. . . . Such a choice is our ultimate normative commitment. The only kinds of reasons which can be given to justify the principles of a way of life are reasons which justify the way of life as a whole. . . . Such reasons consist in showing that the way of life is rationally chosen.[17]

The starting-point of the contemporary moral philosopher, there-fore, is an assumption that we are able to understand what is going on in any given society 'if we have identified and assessed the established methods of reasoning and criticism in that society', and this 'brings us into the sharpest conflict with any sociological school of thought which holds that questions of the truth or reasonableness of beliefs either ought not to be or cannot be raised by sociologists'. The whole field of judgment, and the testing of the truth or falsehood of ideas and beliefs by some standard other than the raw empiricism of the positivists, is reopened. Furthermore, it is also made clear that it is the tension between social life (and other factors such as the criticism or appraisal of social life), and 'the delineation of a society's concepts', that are necessary to 'the delineation of its life'.[18]

So far, then, as morals are concerned, the paths of the moralist and sociologist tend to converge. The task of the sociologist has been made easier, because his philosophical colleagues have shown that they are now prepared to accept a view which is more in keeping with common sense than the ideas of their predecessors were, on such matters as social causation and social determinism. It now seems to be more generally agreed amongst philosophers today (if rejected by sociologists as a whole) that the existence of a society or 'social system' also implies the logical pre-existence of an at least partially rational and consciously adopted way of life that goes with it, and that this, again, presupposes the existence of a system of ethics which provides a means of dealing with the social problems for which every society must find solutions. It is the way of life and the ideas that underlie it that really are more sociologically significant than the pattern of day-to-day social relationships which actually take place within any given normative system, because it is these ideas that give rise to such conventions or values as justice, truth and well-being; and it is these which give a society its stability and generate an ongoing process of development. The life of a society is created by its values, in the long run, and is more determined by them, than the reverse. But it is perhaps more of a mistake to take a society for granted, and to deduce the system of morals current in it from its organisation, than the converse, though both ideas are unreal. The truth is complex, which is that societies and systems of morals are simultaneously existent, and the one cannot be separated from the other; their inter-dependence cannot be broken. A society should be regarded as being both based on and giving rise to a way of life, which is composed of moral ideas and other values, as well as of structures, institutions, roles, and relationships. The process is essentially ongoing and dynamic. But which are the more basic from the point of view of its overall constitution, and more important from that of its continuity, stability, and prosperity, and the experiences, including the welfare, of its individual members, is arguable, to say the least of it.

We can now advance one stage further towards explaining everyday realities, from the very abstract and unreal position adopted by the logical positivists in matters of morals, and the neo-positivists in matters of social behaviour. The contemporary philosopher has, in fact, taken up a position that enables him to collaborate with the sociologist in providing practical explanations for choice, evaluation, and change, permitting the two to conduct an amicable conversation with each other rather than continue the sterile argument or maintain the sullen silence of mutual incomprehension, which has been only too much their common habit until recent years. The next problem we can deal with, therefore, if we start from a base such as this, and take the existence of a moral philosophy for granted, is to ask what assumptions we must make if a social science is to exist, and how philosophy and social science can be brought into relation with each other in their daily tasks. If we agree that choices must be allowed for in our everyday experience, as a function of the free-ranging intelligence in the fulfilment of its opportunities, responsibilities and obligations, the simple but troublesome question must be answered: how it is that this freedom of the will can be combined with any degree of scientific determinism, and any social science at all be possible? For that matter, the position is no clearer if we take Professor Winch's submissions into account, when he argues in *The Idea of a Social Science*[19] that the mind can exercise creativity and inventiveness in constructing concepts about society, and that is how social science comes into existence.

We must accept, it seems, that the causal category must not, and for that matter cannot, be applied inflexibly to the universe of social events, and that these events cannot be understood only in terms of those that have preceded them; for if we tried to do so, we would assume that it would not be possible to make valid choices, and for man to live as a moral being. But, again, if we allowed the converse, or positivist, argument, to prevail, and supposed choice to be an appearance rather than a reality, it would not be possible to understand how any fundamental social changes could take place; which is perhaps why the positivists seem only to talk about trivialities. So, it must now be asked, have we really got to go to one extreme or the other, and say either that no scientific explanations at all are possible of social phenomena, or that morality is a mere sham? Some people find themselves compelled to say that this is so in one way or another, as the positivists' argument is a forceful one, especially in the present technological age; but the philosophers are beginning to develop a coherent and a telling position of their own in reply, which is the more or less exact contrary. (One cannot help remarking in passing how welcome it is to a sociologist to have their help available to him in this field of study again, after being virtually absent from it altogether for so many years.) Louch credits Winch with saying that sociology is a matter of conceptual analysis 'akin to philosophy instead of to empirical science'.[20] That reduces (or extends) sociology to philosophy, and gives the sociologist a *locus standi* in a real sense. But Louch is much more precise in his own writings. He holds that this is so, but that sociology, because it is a philosophical study, can only be a moral science. In his view sociology focuses attention

> on prevailing or important ingredients in a way of life, and [shows] how these relate to and follow from other presuppositions, attitudes and practices, whether they are religious, moral, scientific, political, or economic.
> In morally explaining human practices, the sociologist is not merely cloaking actions in the respectability of one's own moral convictions, but enriching the factual detail so as to see what it is in the situation that could possibly provide the agent with grounds for acting.[21]

So from this angle the sociologist is seen as a moralist with an extensive view of social fact, and there is undeniably a large measure of truth in that idea. But trouble seems to arise from our doubt about what social facts really are, for in saying this we are trying to cope with the substantial traces left behind by the age-old Cartesian division of experience between body and soul, and the existence of social facts on the fringes of the two worlds simultaneously. It seems often to be thought that there is some sort of material or matter which constitutes a society or a personality, which can be experimented with scientifically, or (conversely) some kind of influence, force or field which is set up by the mind, which permeates the universe to which, in the last analysis, it owes its being, and controls the precise manifestations which matter assumes from time to time. These are all primitive ideas like the Victorian's phlogiston, however; they are most unhelpful, and should be scrapped once and for all. Neither modern science nor modern philosophy can tolerate a complete separation between body and soul, matter and mind. It is now generally recognised that it is unreal to do anything like this, and it is also a gross over-simplification of the facts.

Man's mind is the originator of science and all its triumphs, whilst man's physical equipment undoubtedly conditions his mind. From one point of view it rises above and beyond physical or bodily facts; from another it is part of them. It all depends on one's point of view at the moment.

Man, as the possessor of an animal nature, is the subject of scientific exploration; the brute facts of life and death and of his physical needs are the subject of generalisations which can be wholly scientific. In so far as the basic needs of food, clothing and shelter (and innumerable other facts too) are part of the data of sociology, therefore, sociology can be truly scientific. But in so far as man is the possessor of a moral, aesthetic, and spiritual nature, he also creates an elaborate code of evaluation which he follows in his daily life, and in so far as he does so his animal and his moral natures may interact. The fact that a man may be gluttonous is no more 'real' than that a woman may deprive herself of material comforts in the religious life.

The crux of the matter is thus that the same facts can be much more than the raw material for any one interpretation. But the science of which man is the originator, and social science itself, is a tool in man's hand which can be used for creative purposes; when we deny positivism, or assert that there is more to science and to knowledge than is in general to be distilled out of 'the facts themselves', and when we agree that in many senses body and soul, or matter and intellect, are one, we do not admit that for that reason mind is, any more in reality, conditioned by matter than the converse. It is illogical to suppose that the statement was any more true one way round than the other; the argument is circular, and leads nowhere. The neo-positivist's belief that social action arises out of specific and concrete (and measurable) social influences, irrespective of the life of the intellect and any ideas or beliefs it may contain, is therefore a meaningless assertion which cannot be proved, and is not worth arguing about. The social reality of an orchestra, which is composed of its physical equipment of one kind or another, and the dispositions of its members and their relationships with each other, is no more a 'reality' than the music it finds itself able to play under a given conductor. The supreme reality to a given audience may, in fact, be its re-creation of a Beethoven symphony, and all the values and the meanings that it may have for the players and the people who listen to them.

Furthermore, when the argument is developed along the converse line, and it is attempted to show that social practices have their basis in nothing more substantial than concepts which are developed so as to fit in with the way of life of any given society, we are asserting that our notions of reality are completely independent of the material. In his paper, 'Understanding a Primitive Society',[22] Peter Winch argues that any kind of notion about magic, rain-making or medicine is true or false according to whether or not it 'fits in' with other practices or beliefs. He criticises Professor Evans-Pritchard for saying that a distinction can be made between 'logical' and 'scientific' explanations, and objects to his conclusion that:

> A pot has been broken during firing. This is probably due to grit. Let us examine the pot and see if this is the cause. That is logical and scientific thought. Sickness is due to witchcraft. A man is sick. Let us consult the oracles to discover who is the witch responsible. That is logical and unscientific thought.

Professor Winch thinks that a great deal of this is right, in so far as both magical and scientific processes can be held to be logical in appropriate societies, but that Professor Evans-Pritchard is wrong 'in his attempt to characterise the scientific as opposed to the magical in terms of what is "in accord with objective reality" ', because 'the scientific conception agrees with what reality actually is like, whereas the magical conception does not'. This is not so; 'the concepts used by primitive peoples can only be interpreted in the context of the way of life of those peoples'. It is illogical, he suggests, to judge Azande practices by standards that are 'part of the way of life of Western peoples'.[23] But surely that cannot be prevented from happening, and the practice of doing so may often be logical in itself. It all depends on how it is done. If an explanation is put forward which is logical and magical, when another is available in the present state of the culture that is logical and scientific, this is an error. Some explanations are applicable to material phenomena, others to the facts of conduct. Some are scientific, others moral; explanations have to be chosen which relate to the nature of the facts, as they can be seen and recognised to be at the moment. And we may be wrong in seeing them as explained by magic; or we might get at the truth more adequately if we were to rely on a scientific explanation. Professor Winch says:

> A Zande would be utterly lost and bewildered without his oracle. The mainstay of his life would be lacking. It is rather as if an engineer in

our society were to be asked to build a bridge without mathematical calculation.

It is intelligible, of course, if a Zande does actually go to a magician to explain sickness. We know he does, and that is a simple statement of fact or definition (that is to say, if we define him as a Zande) rather than a total explanation. But it will also be probable that, over the years when Westerners arrive in his country, he will go to the surgeon to cure appendicitis rather than to a magician, and that will not be because he has become a Westerner through and through, but because he has learnt something about Western medical science, and enough of the West's culture to incorporate it in his own,[24] without becoming a Westerner, perhaps. That makes medicine 'superior'. It is not the culture as a whole and acculturation in general, which is responsible for happenings of this kind, but the effectiveness of the rational learning process within it. Western medicine must in fact be superior to Zande magic where either medicine or magic can be preferred, and there is not a free choice between them in an entirely Zande society.

Western medicine is so dramatically superior where anything like a comparison and a free choice is possible that it does not need a total superiority of Western culture to popularise it. It is a preference for Western medicine that is apt to carry a preference for Western culture with it, rather than the reverse. This is another reason why Dr Louch's admonition is apposite that social scientists need to keep minds clear as to what they are talking about, and should not, in pursuing research, perpetrate logical howlers, such as to try to discover whether two and two make four by counting apples.[25] Logical processes, as well as research techniques, need to be used only when they are suitable for the purposes for which they are intended to be used. Cultural relativism can easily go too far, and can result in a stultifying excess of caution if care is not taken. In one society two and two do not make four, because there is no word for 'four'; but when counting is an unlimited process in another society, two and two do make four. It is absurd to suggest that a single process is 'just as good' for either society. Where there are no limitations, apple counting is better done by the decimal system, and that is how science has got ahead.

This argument therefore leads one to the conclusion that though there are two universes of discourse, the scientific for the material or objective world, and the philosophical and moral for the subjective or personal world, there is a social aspect of reality that is common to the two, and can serve as a link between them. Hitherto, there has been no inkling of how they interact; no explanation of how, though a scientific or objective fact can quite easily be seen to have a subjective quality, a subjective fact cannot be given an objective quality without losing its essential nature. One can have an artist's impression of an operation or discovery of the natural sciences, like a chemical reaction, or a fermentation, or the atom, or the solar system, but the converse is not true.

Natural science takes a more restricted view of the world than philosophy, and the two simply cannot contradict each other, unless, that is, philosophy oversteps its bounds and pronounces on questions of theory derived from fact, which should be the prerogative of experimental science. But the social is both objective and subjective, and can therefore be open to scientific and philosophical explanation simultaneously, as Hobhouse would have had it. Quoting Husserl, Merleau-Ponty says that:

> Philosophy must accept the totality of what science has acquired, and thus historical relativism along with it, since science has the right to speak first in that which concerns knowledge. . . . But anthropology, like any positive science and like the totality of these sciences, if it has the first word in knowledge, has not the last. There would be an autonomy of knowledge after positive knowledge, not before it. It does not exempt the philosopher from collecting all that anthropology may offer. . . . It can remove nothing from the competence of the scientist that may be accessible to his research methods. It will simply establish itself in a dimension where no scientific knowledge can contest it.[26]

This seems to show that there can be a degree of certainty, based on proof, only so far as the experimental sciences are concerned, which does not extend to the world of ontology, the philosopher's world of being. Can the scientist, he asks, extend his empire to include this world, and in doing so attain the certainty in it which is an attribute of positive knowledge? That, he answers, is an impossibility; the sociologist cannot advance further than the philosopher if he puts himself in his place. Having done so, the knowledge of both is equally relative.

> The same historical dependence that prohibits the philosopher from claiming an immediate access to the universal or the eternal prohibits

the sociologist from substituting himself for the philosopher in this function, and from giving the scientific objectification of the social the value of an ontology. . . . It is just this presupposition that is discredited by our historical sense, namely, that we can liberate thought from our spatio-temporal restrictions. Simply to transfer to science the grand-mastery refused to systematic philosophy is out of the question. You believe you are thinking for all times and, for all men, the sociologist says to the philosopher, and in so doing you are merely expressing the prejudices or pretentions of your culture. True, but no less of the sociologist than of the philosopher. After all, where is the relativist himself located?

How then can the world of the philosopher be said to overlap with the world of the scientist, if it does so at all? Firstly, says Merleau-Ponty, the sociologist is already a philosopher because 'the sociologist does philosophy to the extent to which he is not merely charged with noting facts but with understanding them';[27] and secondly because the philosopher can reinterpret what the scientist says about the same world and the same experience which both share:

> Under the collective name of science there is nothing but systematic arrangement, a methodological exercise – narrower or wider, more or less insightful, of that same experience which begins with our first perception. . . . It may happen that science buys its exactitude at the price of schematisation. But the remedy is to confront it with an integral experience, and not oppose it to a philosophical knowledge arriving from no one knows where.'[28]

Merleau-Ponty's argument continues into a less hazardous area with the idea that what he calls 'inter-subjectivity', a state in which the subjective merges into the objective, or, in other words, crosses a line at which the personal becomes social. This, he argues, is the specific field of philosophy; it is embodied in the effort the philosopher makes to get outside himself, as it were, and to see himself as a figure encapsulated in history. The same can be said, no doubt, about one's personal life and experiences as a member of a group. This 'makes the understanding of the social an understanding of myself, calls for and authorises a *view of intersubjectivity as being my own*, which is *forgotten by science while utilised by it*'.[29] This is perhaps Merleau-Ponty's most suggestive contribution to the hitherto unsolved problem of defining the sense in which philosophy and science can be said to share the same world of fact and interpretation. This concerns the philosopher's ability to discuss with the social scientist the events in the world of shared experiences, experiences which are both personal and subjective on the one hand, and objective on the other, in the sense that personal events are, simultaneously and independently, individual and collective. In so far as they are the latter, they can be studied as objective phenomena, comparatively and analytically, free from the control of the individual will, and free also from the direct influence of desire. But the conception is a difficult one, and requires further explanation and clarification by illustration and experiment. It is still very much open to discussion.

Nevertheless, it is obvious that the first steps have been taken in this way to bring social science and philosophy together as equal partners in a common endeavour. Whilst, Merleau-Ponty says, if philosophy is 'always a breach with objectivism', it is also 'a returning from the *constructa* to the world of living experience, from the world to ourselves'; if this argument is followed, it can also be held that

> this indispensable step, that characterises philosophy, no longer transports it into the rarified atmosphere of introspection or into a domain numerically distinct from that of science. It does not pose philosophy as a rival to knowledge once we have recognised that the 'interior' to which it brings us is not a 'private life', but an intersubjectivity connecting us to an even greater extent, to all history.[30]

This argument, assuming the existence of a world of shared experiences, and a social reality that is both subjective and objective, reminds one of the core of the analysis of social living by empathy, which was largely common to thinkers as far apart in method as Dilthey and Planck, Sorokin and Redfield. The problem has been, hitherto, to distinguish empathy from the more simple and less sophisticated process of introspection; and the chief difficulty that has emerged has been the problem of distinguishing between personal feelings and emotions, and the common experiences that are contained in the group or society being studied. But there seems to be a profitable means of doing this. If this interpretation is accepted, social science can be regarded as far more than the application of ideas or generalisations to a society or social system; it is able to show how it can be more fully understood or explained as a result. This argument seeks to demonstrate that there is an objective or scientific component of a special kind which the philosophic approach can share. Moreover, scientific truth may be regarded as something essentially wider and deeper than it has been assumed to be hitherto, something that transcends the mere compiling of a series of generalisations arrived at by the analysis or manipulation statistically of crude data, assembled at random.

9. Conclusion

I

Value as a Necessary Component of Sociological Knowledge

The argument of the foregoing chapters leads to the conclusion that evaluation is a necessary part of the complex process of sociological discovery.

The reasons for this are both general, applying to science as a whole, and special, applying to social science as such. Miscellaneous facts regarded as raw data or mere information, cannot be accepted as the material out of which sociology, like any other science, can be constructed. The foundations of a science can only be laid if relevant data are available for their construction, and this implies the existence of a theory which makes it possible to establish the notion of significance itself. This is part of the prolegomena of every science, social and natural. Data or information that lack such support can only be regarded, at best, as a collection of amusing curiosities which might be of interest to a journalist compiling a 'book of records', 'wonders of the world', or the like, recalling to mind Robert Lynd's remark about 'the contents of the ditty bag of an idiot'; or they may serve a useful purpose, perhaps, as mental stimuli disturbing dogmatic slumbers, provoking one to more energetic thoughts, which may lead on to the ultimate production of the material of a philosophy or a science. But they are little more than this; they are not 'scientific' in themselves.[1]

There is also a more special argument, applying solely to the social sciences, which refers to the social conduct and interaction of responsible and rational men. If it is this to which sociological generalisations apply, they can only be valid if they are also relevant to evaluation, because evaluation is an important determinant of social conduct. Social conduct is an affair of judgment and discrimination or choice, rather than a mere type of behaviour which is occasioned by automatic responsiveness to stimuli, and nothing more. As has already been said, if the freedom that this implies does not exist, there can be no science, but the argument can now be taken further. For it is now clear that if the individual cannot be assumed to be able to behave according to his own values, there can be no social science; social behaviour can only be the subject of a social science if it is conditioned by values (which are the outcome of man's thought) in the same way that the scientific process itself can be seen to be conditioned by a very similar process of thought.

The logical complexities implied in the existence of the social sciences are therefore considerable. But the plain man has never encountered them. From the historical point of view the story of social administration is a simple one. The account that has been given of the work of Booth and his successors in the nineteenth century and beyond shows that the beginnings of the social sciences lay in new methods of dealing with the problems of urbanisation and industrialism that became urgent in the early nineteenth century. This story is in its essentials a straightforward and an optimistic one. It shows that an important contribution could be made to the welfare of mankind in a new way that had close associations with the processes of scientific discovery. Problems as to whether man's values were culturally determined never bothered the administrator who had a job to do. His freedom and autonomy were assumed as self-evident, rather than made the subject of laboured or sophisticated proof.

This account, particularly when the story gets near our own times, is also the history of a series of attempts on the part of social scientists to free themselves of the responsibility for man's own circumstances, that had been assumed without question by their Victorian ancestors. It is argued that it is non-human 'forces', rather than the human will, intention and foresight, or the sense of responsibility, that shapes human societies, and that human destiny is hardly under man's own control at all. To believe otherwise, it is argued, is mere self-delusion, and social institutions that incorporate a contrary assumption are only epiphenomena, mere appearances rather than a part of social realities. Although the sciences, especially the natural sciences, have achieved such wonders, so creatively and with such intellectual daring, attempts have been made to persuade us that we should abandon all our hopes that we may be able to promote human welfare by developing the social sciences, and the methods incorporated in them. The products of such hopes are written off as essentially 'unscientific' undertakings because the concept of 'welfare', and endeavours to promote it, imply and embody values. It is often argued, rather naïvely, that a scientific enterprise must be 'value-free', to use Weber's phrase.[2]

If one looks at things and events rather in the manner of a modern philosopher, however, one refrains from basing one's thinking on a refusal to face facts; man cannot be 'value-free', science or no science. One must accept the necessity to share the basic assumptions of the ordinary man when he seeks to bring as much intellectual order as he can into the world in which he lives. Values are part of his system of thought. It can be assumed without difficulty, therefore, that policy-makers and administrators will do their jobs better if they avail themselves of the world's wisdom in general, and in particular, of the intelligence the sociologist has contrived to collect. Paul Halmos' argument is that all sociological diagnosis has a demonstrable and empirically verifiable influence on society, if and when the diagnosis is communicated to society. He further maintains that a sociologist cannot disclaim an awareness of this influence when he communicates his findings or, indeed, already when he selects his field of enquiry. He must accept that he is not only communicating to society but also influencing it. But if he knows this and is still determined not to desist, it is fair to assume that he is also resolved to *influence* society: his communications are, therefore, both positive and normative at the same time. Whilst the scientists dealing with non-social subject-matter do not change the fundamental principles of their functioning, the very laws of the social process are susceptible to be repealed by sociological discussion of their nature. Also:

> 'To create social science is to influence society in its very method of making fundamental choices, and it is to expect society to manage itself in a scientific way .... The dicipline and rationality of the social sciences have understandably placed so much stress on calculability and determinism that they contributed to the weakening of man's faith in eschatological and non-scientific categories. In this way the influence of social science on society has been doctrinaire and ideological.'[3]

This has the consequence that the sociologist cannot help interesting himself in the study of values; for values lie at the centre of the process of choosing. Sociology provides much of the information on which policy-makers depend to make up their minds, and it also finds itself involved in the decision-making process itself. Sociological knowledge, then, cannot but be normative. It is, in the last analysis, just this that is the centre of the sociologist's interests.[4]

How sociology influences societies may be spelt out in terms of the scientific impact of a given research on the members of a society.[5] This is also evident in the influence of sociology on social policies and attitudes at large, particularly 'penal reform, our changing moral principles relating to responsibility, our consequent treatment of the poor, the criminal, the coward, the sexual pervert'. These have been so 'coloured by the discoveries of the social sciences',[6] that the latter have become part of the policy-making process itself. It is not the conditioning of social life by its physical circumstances which is of greatest interest to the social scientist, so much as the use man's societies make of their environment. The way in which men and communities achieve the purposes they make their own despite 'natural forces' lies at the heart of sociological thinking, and makes it possible for sociology to avoid the crudities of a belief that would be most akin to the theological predestination of a religious sect. For instance, the social scientist's reply to an assertion that a juvenile delinquent's criminal behaviour is due to the fact that he 'comes from a broken home' can only be that he must use this knowledge to some purpose. Knowledge does not excuse inaction; it makes it possible to act more intelligently, and, so far as misfortunes of this kind are concerned, 'do something about' them.

This answer is dynamic. It is directed to the realities of behaviour, rather than the static certainties of the physical world, and the same applies to sociological thought in general. The community with a high incidence of criminal behaviour endemic in it must be given the means of understanding why this is so, and the opportunity to its members to use their abilities and energies constructively rather than destructively. They must also be given incentives to do so. As Professor Robert K. Merton has put it, the social scientist must 'establish new goals and bench marks of the attainable'. This is, in effect, to introduce new values into a social situation. His conclusion was that if the conditions of a research do not permit this, the result will be

> a threat to the functions of a scientist *qua* scientist. So long as the scientist continues to accept a role in which he does not question policies, state problems and formulate alternatives, the more does he become routinised in the role of bureaucratic technician.[7]

The concern of the social scientist with the values which motivate behaviour is therefore inescapable, for it is impossible to understand the reasons which lie behind one pattern of behaviour or another without it, and it is equally impossible to influence the course that behaviour takes if one is ignorant about the purposes it incorporates.

II

'Pure' and 'Applied' Social Science

The only concern the social scientist has with the improvement of the lot of mankind, it may be argued, arises when he functions as an 'applied' scientist. As a 'pure' scientist, he is not concerned with the day-to-day troubles of individuals, or with the stimulation or direction of change. He is content to understand things as they are, rather than improve social welfare, or ameliorate the lot of his fellow-citizens in any way. This he leaves to his 'applied' colleagues, in the hope that they will learn enough 'pure' sociology to have something to apply. Sociological knowledge, he may feel, is 'knowledge for its own sake'. The desire to acquire knowledge with no more sense of purpose than this may completely satisfy its latent objective, which is to deal with the feelings provoked by the pursuit of a 'science' that is felt to be less than adequate to its task. But that is entirely irrational; the question whether there is any justification for the distinction between 'pure' and 'applied' social sciences is left entirely unanswered.

Nevertheless, the contrast that is drawn so freely between pure and applied social science has no better foundation than this. Many of the practical problems of developing sociological studies in universities would be solved if a division of interest of this kind were possible, but the logic of the social sciences prevents that from being done. An applied science cannot be developed without presupposing that there really is a 'pure' science to apply, namely that man's behaviour is entirely subject to the influence of identifiable and measurable impulses or attractions, social, psychological, and other. Or it must be assumed that he is a being who can and may be persuaded or cajoled to do this or that, in accordance with the values, intentions or whims of a capricious third party, whose behaviour cannot be so examined, and therefore must be taken for granted. In any event objective or 'pure' social science plus subjective values do not equal applied science, as this leaves the whole problem of conscious intention and motivation, and purposive action, out of account. If anything of the kind were adopted, as the basis for social action, it would be necessary to develop a third kind of social science dealing with social action, unless it were

N

assumed that man's fate is entirely determined, and then it would be hard to show how there comes to be consciously motivated conduct, and what its characteristics are; and the hunt for a means of explaining the world as it really is would start again.

Perhaps the best way of dealing with the pure versus applied controversy is that of the Heyworth Committee which, though inadequate, was designed to lay it to rest with a minimum of fuss. Time alone will show whether its treatment of the problem was at all successful. Advance in the social sciences, it was thought, will come in two ways, first, as a result of the free enquiries of researchers in universities and elsewhere; secondly 'through research in response to problems which clearly demand examination'.[8] If both these lines are pursued, then all will be well. These divisions are, of course, by no means co-terminous with the pure and applied divisions, if for no other reason than because what may be termed problem-centred work has been and no doubt will be carried out in universities. This is greatly to their profit, because, as Professor Robert K. Merton has pointed out, the process of empirical, as distinct from purely theoretical, research undoubtedly 'raises issues which may long go undetected in theoretic enquiry'.[9] Even if the conclusion of the Committee was briefly stated, it was forthright:

> As in all fields of study, basic and applied research are both essential if knowledge is to advance; and it would be an error to imagine that in the social sciences basic work proceeds in isolation and can be applied only when it has advanced far enough. Basic research and applied research both have to be carried out simultaneously; neither can advance without the other.

But if 'basic' work cannot proceed without 'applied' research, in what sense is 'basic' work basic, and 'applied' research applied? The distinction is evidently meaningless. Unfortunately, it is one thing to talk about 'pure' sociological work; it is another thing to carry any out, particularly so as to overcome the logical problems involved. The sociologist wishes to attain a knowledge of scientific propositions which can be propounded with complete certainty, but 'we all know how hard it is to discover important generalisations about society which are universal in their application. We are forced to be content with generalisations of more limited scope, say those applicable to a given time and region' and it is therefore a defeating task to attempt to develop a sociology of this kind that has any meaning or importance.[10]

The chief obstacle in the way of achieving this aim is, of course, the necessity to incorporate objectives, purposes, intentions and, in a word, values into sociological thinking. The usual way out of the practical difficulty for the researcher is to allow somebody else to decide one's values for one, and to devote one's time and energies to finding ways or means of carrying them into effect, but nevertheless to complain bitterly about being compelled to live in servitude. This may be called 'applied' sociology. It is true that this is a technically viable kind of activity, to some extent at least, but it is doubtful whether it can actually be pursued, on a broad front, save at the expense of one's moral responsibilities, and one's integrity as a scientist.

This argument leads to the conclusion that no attempt can or should be made to separate the study of a society from that of the values embodied in it. Two considerations must be borne in mind, firstly, one's sympathetic involvement with (and therefore moral responsibilities to) the subjects of one's studies,[11] and secondly, the need to understand the social significance of values, in which their logical validity and their social viability play so important a part. Both of these considerations lead to the final conclusion that the distinction between 'pure' and 'applied' sociology cannot be maintained, and that any social science which embodies anything like a substantial amount of the truth must be able to deal simultaneously with the analysis of fact and the appraisal of value.

III

The Attempted Abandonment of Values in the Social Sciences

It is obvious, therefore, that an attempt to abandon the study of values in the social sciences involves us in a fundamental contradiction. Social science, in its essentials, is not a 'value-free' process of discovering the fundamental principles according to which human behaviour operates. Neither is its objective to discover what the limitations are that are set by the nature of things to man's endeavours to improve his own lot. It seeks to find out, on the contrary, how the boundaries to knowledge can be pushed further back, and how human purposes can be given a better chance of fulfilment. The aeroplane, atomic power, and animal and plant breeding are examples from other fields; they are part of fundamental science rather than mere applications of more fundamental knowledge, discovered as the result of some process of enquiry not specifically directed to the immediate end in view, but to something more fundamental.

The history of the past century shows us, on the one hand, how proud the record of the social sciences has been, in so far as it can be fitted into the same frame of reference. Their contribution to the conquest of poverty and ignorance, and disease of body and mind have been striking. Civilisation has much to be grateful for to Booth and Beveridge, Seebohm Rowntree and Sir John Simon, for showing us how to achieve the victories of what has been called the welfare state in the development of the social services. These have had much to do with the improvement of the general level of living.

Yet, on the other hand, and even with all this before our eyes, many if not the majority of social scientists in the last generation have spent their energies in the search for what may be regarded as another version of the philosopher's stone, rejecting the successes and achievements of the past for what it is impossible to possess oneself of, namely, the secret of man's social being. They hope to reveal why exactly it is that men do what they do as social animals, and enable us to predict exactly what it is that they will do in the years that lie ahead. This is by no means a matter of social welfare or social purpose: what they seek is to discover how human nature can be made the basis of man's collective social disposition. As a result, what we are presented with amounts to a gigantic extension of scholasticism, or of natural law; those who attempt to bring this about are oblivious of the fact that they are making renewed attempts to overcome the failures of philosophers in past ages. What they seek is something that mankind rejected ages and centuries ago; the conditions of our 'discipline' would be much healthier if this were made clearer. As things are, they are trying to penetrate still further into an alley which has no outlet, and is blind in the truest sense.

The story starts at the point where, in the postwar world of the 1920s, American sociology turned its back on the prewar 'do-gooders' who were worried about 'problems' such as social irresponsibility or dependence, crime, class, or colour. Nothing could be allowed to have scientific meaning, the devotees of this new science thought, unless it was socially meaningless; the consequence is to be seen in *Knowledge for What?*, the appraisal of a decade or more of endeavour by an author who was particularly well fitted to evaluate and to judge. Then there came the 'Policy Sciences' period of the postwar era. With this, American scholarship advanced to a new position; not only were social scientists to be 'value-free' in their work, but they were to be prepared to accept other people's values in their own activities as men of affairs, when they took part in the application of policies to living societies, as, for instance, by government agencies.

Robert K. Merton stated what the illogicalities involved in this endeavour were, before any serious attempt to exploit the social sciences in this way had ever begun. The reaction of the world to the next attempt to put the business of policy-formation on a 'scientific' basis was even more startling. The Conference on the Future of Freedom which was intended to launch a new political era was based on the idea that science had taken over the functions that had been performed in human affairs down the ages by philosophers and political theorists. But this idea was frustrated by the newer and poorer nations of the world, who protested that this was at best a way of looking at things that was only possible for the rich nations by whom riches could be taken for granted, and that an idea of this kind could only sunder the poorer half of the world from the other, wealthier, half.

It was left to Rousseas and Farganis to show that it was equally unsound even for the more apparently rich countries to argue in this way. One of the failings of such countries was to tolerate gross inequality as between the wealth of their own citizens, and another was to condone the inequality of citizenship of their own coloured citizens; leaving aside international comparisons for the time being. The events that took place at the Conference, and the aftermath in the world of the social sciences, represented a third attempt to advance along lines that had been fully explored over the greater part of the previous half-century. On this occasion, the attempt was an international one, made on the broadest of fronts; the defeat that was experienced was even more complete and decisive than those that resulted from similar attempts made before on narrower fronts.

We have to recognise, when all this had been said and done, that the positivist belief that we can develop an all-embracing understanding of man's affairs based on scientific certainties is impossible. It is also undesirable. As a philosopher has recently said, in bringing his review of the attempts to understand social behaviour on this basis, and understanding in general, to a close:

> In the engineers' society, perhaps unwittingly promoted by the psychologists and sociologists bent on being scientists, we should have

to give up the concept of an open or civil society which, however inefficiently, serves as the prop for a social order based on respect for men as persons or autonomous agents.[12]

If we knock away the prop of the concept of the open society as a support for the modern polity, we must find another and a better one; we have surely advanced from the somewhat primitive and contradictory beliefs, sometimes embodied in the social sciences, that we can understand, analyse, and measure the totality of man's activities and thoughts, and plan his behaviour and the organisation of his societies. It is surely nothing more than an idle pipedream to believe that his life can be made to proceed with exactly the degrees of harmony or conflict that it is deemed by the supermen who are supposed to rule over him to be good. The actual achievements of social scientists are of a very different order. Far from producing a wide sweep of plans and proposals and really enlightening explanations of what actually does happen, the more 'scientifically' inclined of social scientists seem to spend their time pointing out one or another of a multitude of trivialities and glimpses of the obvious, in the manner to which such profound exception was taken by Robert S. Lynd. We do not seem, after all, to have advanced so very far since his day. Far from producing blueprints for a 'Brave New World' or a '1984' which really might have some chance of becoming effective to some extent at least, it appears from the philosophical point of view that

> To put it into a form acceptable to sociologists: methodological soundness is inversely proportional to factual significance. Triviality, redundancy and tautology are the epithets which I think can be properly applied to the behavioural scientist.[13]

We find social scientists often seem to be content to allow their work significance only in a random sense. At best, some parts of it are significant whilst others lack meaning. But the situation may be worse than this. The tendency is for it to lose significance altogether. There is a second or more advanced position, which is much more frightening. Social scientists seem to be beginning to make a practice of dealing with things that do not matter, or with things that matter, like wars and atom bombs, in a trivial way. The belief has become widespread that politics and social philosophy have become redundant, and that the discussion of values and morals by sociologists and philosophers is irrelevant to practical and important political and social issues. It may even be seriously argued that the scientific discoveries of social scientists have advanced so far that sociology itself, together with the other social sciences, could take the place of primitive 'nonsense' of this kind. In other words, it has even come to be held that the process of value-formation has died a natural death at the hands of science, and that man has profited greatly thereby. It is now our task to show how mistaken this is. It will be suggested, on the contrary, that not only can there be no social science without social values, but that the formulation of social policy must depend on the existence and identification of social values.

IV

Value Freedom in a New Sense

The sociologist could proceed much further in his work, of course, and be much more effective, in a way, if he could act as if he were 'value-free' entirely, or make explicit such values as he actually allows to enter into his work, discounting their influence for what he deems it to be, as Gunnar Myrdal suggested he should.

To think that the sociologist can achieve his ends if he merely sheds his responsibilities would be absurd, however. It is important to recognise that the motive for doing anything of the kind is at least as often escapist as it is genuine; its primary reason is to avoid the problem of evaluation rather than to make a calculated attempt to overcome it, openly and honestly. Attempts are not often made to identify and explain the values that have led to individual conclusions or recommendations. It is much more typical of our times to suggest that the problems of decision, which are commonly agreed to embody value judgments, can be overcome by entrusting them to machines, incorporating mechanisms capable of taking over from men what is now irksome to so many. Behaviourists have run riot with ideas about the functions of the brain, so as to make this plausible. As Professor Sir Cyril Burt has said, 'it is customary to talk of ... machines as "seeing", "perceiving", "thinking", and "deciding", concepts produced by behaviouristically-inclined psychologists' who interpret the world by expunging 'all words like "consciousness", "sensation", and "feeling"' from the scientist's vocabulary, 'on the ground that such things are incapable of experimental study or measurement, and in any case are mere meaningless by-products of the physiological processes in the brain'. With them, it may be noted, value judgments would be expunged too. One professor of experimental psychology has gone so far as to lay it down that:

> The forthcoming revolution is likely to have two facets. We shall come to treat information-processing machines in the same way that we treat people. And we shall treat people in the same way that we treat machines. The first process will be forced upon us as the ability of computers to process information comes to match and surpass that of man. The second process will result from our increased understanding of the way in which our own behaviour is determined by the atoms and molecules of which we are composed.[14]

Arguments of this kind have gone to quite extraordinary limits. Professor Sutherland, for instance, speaks of a computer as 'advising' a judge, as being potentially both more 'rational' and more 'intelligent' than he is, and as dispensing better 'justice', unaided; human judges are then to become redundant. Taking this line of reasoning to its extreme limits, it might even be thought that an 'ultra intelligent' machine might be built and that decisions could be reached more efficiently by computers. That would certainly be so, some people think, if such machines could be relied on to make decisions and the belief abandoned that the human mind is the instrument best fitted for the purpose. In other words, one would get from electronics not only the capacity to compute vast numbers of numerical data at speeds far beyond those that are possible for the brain, which is perfectly feasible, but the ability to execute all the functions of judgment and evaluation as well, which it is supposed would then be carried out in greater depth, and more efficiently.

There is, however, no reason to be overwhelmed by these possibilities, and talk of a machine as being able to make a kind of takeover bid for the whole array of man's intellectual powers. The same kind of process has already occurred whereby man has greatly extended the scope of his powers, by making and using many such artifacts, as the calculating machine, the counter-sorter, and business machines generally; and there is a host of other examples of the same kind. These are nothing more than complex tools, which enable man to accomplish limited (if complex) operations more perfectly, and at greater speed, than would otherwise be possible for the unaided brain, eyes, and fingers to achieve. Nobody has yet suggested that his autonomy has been undermined thereby. One of the tragedies of man's civilisations is that his purposes remain as primitive and his vision as restricted, as they are, whilst his use of machines becomes ever more elaborate and sophisticated. It is the animal in man that has to be tamed and domesticated, and this is not to be accomplished by a machine. One cannot ask a machine to write a programme for describing what the values of civilisation ought to be. As Professor Cyril Burt has also said, popular journalism has

> helped to drive home the crude materialistic outlook bequeathed to us by the out-of-date physics and physiology of the late nineteenth century – an outlook which seems all too plausible to a technological age.[15]

We are now beginning, in fact, to understand how the brain performs its tasks, and what its functions are. It is not

> a mere input-ouput mechanism, which in some miraculous but useless fashion converts physical processes into a concomitant consciousness, but . . . an 'organ of liaison', between the physical world and the conscious mind.

'Artificial mechanisms', Professor Cyril Burt concludes, 'which initiate or supplement the manifold abilities of the brain, may be a welcome aid to human intelligence: they can never supersede it.' It is the mind as a whole that is responsible for each man's life and his social relationships. Whether or not individual citizens should accept a share of the problems of formulating and executing a policy for the government of their nation and community is an issue that all communities and citizens must decide in their own way. But mankind has had to learn the hard way that, as no supermen are available, nothing but disaster is to be expected if we entrust men as we know them with uncontrolled authority over other men's lives. As intelligence is widely distributed in the community, power must be shared correspondingly widely. It is this necessity that is the substance of the case for democratic government.

It must be admitted that the idea that a social science might be developed to make efficient self-government more possible and effective is not generally or very willingly accepted. The more is the pity. This is partly because there is deep reluctance on the part of the social scientist to shoulder more than a minimum of the burden involved in making choices, or in studying the ways of making them, especially if this is done with a view to the improvement of social conditions. As has already been said, value-free sociology may from one angle be regarded as mere escapism. That is already becoming the reply of the twentieth century to the sociologists' argument. The range of choice open to modern man and the importance of the decisions he makes have increased, and will continue to increase at an alarming rate as the speed of change accelerates, and societies become more flexible. The burden involved in making up one's mind as to the rightness or the wrongness of any expedient becomes constantly greater; the same applied to the adoption or rejection of the values which determine the making of choices, which seems to have become too irksome for sociologists at large. Nevertheless, responsibility for coming to decisions has to be carried; an individual betrays his own nature if he tries to find some way of imposing it on other men or things. The same is true if men collectively try to shuffle it off altogether, and assert that there is some way which can be adopted of entrusting it to a minority, who can make decisions in the name of the masses of the people. This expedient can only end in disaster, as history has shown time and again.

At the same time, sociologists may well demand that they should be allowed to be free from the limitations or control of other people's values, personal or social. This is value freedom in a legitimate sense. The demand is justifiable because values no longer stem from social processes arising in small communities in whose affairs the common man is intimately involved: values are now a product of mass society, and the organs which create or control it. If sociology has become 'value-free' in this sense, one can only say that the fact is to be welcomed. Our times demand that this should be so, to enable sociologists to be free to participate in the process of value formation, for that is an essential requirement of liberty itself. They should be called upon to do so in order to resist the enslavement of man; they should seek to protect and maintain his liberties, rather than persuade him to accede to the tyranny of mass society, economic, social, or political. This is 'value freedom' with quite another meaning than that which the phrase usually carries with it. It requires sociologists to act responsibly, rather than submit themselves to the tyranny of 'social processes' or the unbridled will of others. 'Value freedom' then ceases to be the negative freedom to ignore the existence of values, and becomes the positive freedom to create and promote values which will provide the basis for the development of a purposive social science.

v

Social Science and Social Purpose

The outline of the argument of this book therefore runs as follows. Values possess a dual nature, and both philosopher and social scientist have made their own contributions to understanding this. Values embody components of reason, which is essentially an affair of the individual mind, and is therefore the philosopher's province. But they are also a living experience, and are also, for that reason, social. Values are social phenomena; they cannot be studied in the abstract. Their special nature arises from the fact that they are motives for action. Unless they are regarded as an essential part of action, they are meaningless. The roles of philosopher and sociologist must therefore be integrated and co-ordinated in this regard; better still, they must be fused, and that, one recalls, was Hobhouse's view.

Values, of course, often owe their origin to the socio-cultural context in which they come to life. Their connections with the material world and the influences to which they are subjected in specific societies and in the behaviour of given individuals are realities and can be studied as such. This is a social study, pure and simple. But it also has to be remembered that values are created by individuals, and their existence is to be seen in the behaviour of this or that member of a society, as well as in the customs and conventions which people accept generally. Values, therefore, though they may be social facts, are also moral in their nature they may act as individual motives as well as establish much of the social context within which social life is lived. It is as a stimulus to action that value is so important. As John Dewey argued in his day, merely to collect and perhaps to classify what exists is a parochial conception of science. When this unscientific limitation is removed, he wrote, larger social issues, and the moral values involved in them, necessarily and inevitably become an integral part of the subject-matter of enquiry. As he added:

> Anything that obscures the fundamentally moral nature of the social problem is harmful, no matter what proceeds from the side of physical or psychological theory. Any doctrine that eliminates or even obscures the function of choice of values and [the] enlistment of desire and emotions on behalf of those chosen, weakens personal responsibility for judgment and for action.[15a]

And it is 'responsibility for judgment and for action' that is one of the chief factors in man's social experience that actually motivates his conduct. If a social science is to have any substantial degree of viability and validity, it must take this into account. A substantial component in social science, therefore, is individual and moral. But that is from one point of view only. From another (which is that of the sociologist), the same phenomena and data are of the greatest significance to a science that is fundamentally and significantly social.

Values are therefore the link between the kind of social behaviour which can be studied at one and the same time from a truly objective point of view, and simultaneously from that of the world of purpose, which is primarily individual. On the one hand, attention can be directed to the phenomena connected with the life and organisation of communities. On the other, the aspirations and the social life of individuals are also relevant. When all is said and done, the end product is the analysis of the social behaviour of individuals, in the past, present and future. It may be thought that it is only the society and its organisation with which one is concerned; it is true that this is part of the subject-matter of our study, but unless the interaction between individuals and communities is understood, and the influence of individuals on communities attended to, as well as the reverse, then the study can have little significance or meaning. From this point of view, social conduct can be moral just as the essences of individual behaviour can be social.

The community can be legitimately studied as an entity, existing in its own right, if it is agreed or asserted that it is a part of a larger whole. This is because each community, in so far as it functions as such, establishes a system or style of life, and bases the way it functions on agreement of one kind or another. It incorporates in its life a system, of which values are an important and even essential part. It is the values that thus become incorporated in a way of life, which determine whether a society shall be dynamic or static in relation to other societies, and outward- or onward-looking. Or values may have a contrary effect on the society, making it static or decadent. The greater the degree of moral justification there is, for instance, for an action, the more effort it is reasonable to expect from the members of a society to carry it to a successful conclusion, when they take an active part in the world of action. Morals, even more than values in general, may then become relevant to sociology, in so far as morals are incorporated or implied in social processes, determining the actualities of conduct and effort. Still more important, they may awaken or inhibit potentialities for social action for the future. It is this that makes some things possible, others not; arousing some men to endurance and fortitude, giving others the inspiration to creative thought and action. Other societies, again, may be found to decline or stagnate in what amounts to decadence or decay; inhibiting the lives of those who might otherwise, in a more stimulating society or age, be prepared to question, to challenge, and create anew.

The essence of the story that has been told in the foregoing chapters is that our social relationships in the modern age have become dynamic rather than static; traditional forms of social life have lost their meaning and their effectiveness. The consciously learned wisdom of the present must be substituted for the accumulations of experience handed down from one generation to another, which was all that there was in the past to rely on in matters of social organisation, even in moments of trial and crisis. As the impact of higher education has increased on the community, the process of evaluating and criticising has become sharper and more powerful. So has the viability of invention and innovation. As the years go by, societies at large, and mankind in general, must therefore take the necessary social and political measures to make themselves increasingly responsible for their own political fate and their own social welfare. This is the typical style of social life of the twentieth century. It is a new style that must be shaped or reshaped to fulfil new demands on it. The present position of the social sciences cannot be regarded, however, as satisfactory in this regard, in so far as the notion that ideology has ended has inhibited their development as a means of restructuring the value-systems current in society, overtly and consciously, which give it direction and purpose.

These are, of course, gross oversimplifications. The foregoing argument is too abstract. Values can only be fully assessed in action. The way in which the history of Marxism (or much of democratic theorising too, for that matter) can be twisted to justify inhuman policies, is sufficient justification in itself for the conclusion that every theory, and the objectives associated with any theory, must be tested empirically, as well as by *a priori* analysis, by internal consistency and logical verification. What, one asks oneself, would have been the result, if the Russians had been allowed to ask themselves what the results of the expropriation of the kulaks in the name of the communist revolution actually were, and what steps could and should have been taken to put matters right? What, it should have been asked, was the precise effect of the uncontrolled expansion of American industry in the postwar period in terms of the living conditions of the masses of city-dwellers, and, again, what steps should have been taken to maintain and achieve civilised standards of urban living? What are the effects in human terms of closing mines or cotton mills or nationalising railways in this country, and moving urban populations wholesale from congested urban areas to New Towns? Modern civilisation demands constant watchfulness in the interests of mankind at large, if man is not to be exploited by his neighbours at home and overseas. The process steadily gets more complex as the years go by, and demands more and more skill and understanding, and correspondingly more complex institutions to facilitate it, locally, nationally, and internationally.

It is for this reason that one must hope that the sociology developed along the lines laid down in this book will be 'problem-centred', in the sense that its direction, purpose, and content will be devoted to the analysis of individual and actual problems that are significant in terms of the style of life of the modern community, and relevant to the solution of the difficulties that arise within it. Such questions as the colour-problem call for the most urgent attention. So do the problems of urban rehabilitation, and the poverty that is so oppressive at the lower levels of our industrial civilisation. Above all, the urgent and overwhelming crises of international tension, and our inabilities to cope with the conflicts that arise out of them, demand our attention.

Our final conclusion must be that every community, local or national, is based on a system and a style of life, in so far as it functions as one at all. Being reasonable in their nature, and therefore communicable, values are an essential part of any system. They can be discussed, examined and appraised, and improved; that has become the most important business of the social scientist today. It is the notion of intersubjectivity which provides the keystone of our work in the immediate future; it is this that will determine the content of social thinking, and establish the occasion for policy-making. It will now be for the social scientist to play a leading part in the clarification of values in their relation to situations and facts, from which will emerge the form as well as much of the content of all future policies.

VI
Values and Social Policy

The most important part of the argument of this book is in the section in which it is argued that experimental science on its own, cannot establish the ends or even the outline of any policy, economic or social.[16] Social science is much wider than an experimental science properly so-called, though experiment may make a vitally important and even an indispensable contribution to the totality of its activities. Values, in particular, cannot be prevented from intruding into sociological enquiries, and, much more important, assistance must often be sought by the social scientist from the philosopher. Values frequently play a leading part in the drama of social policy: they always constitute an essential factor in its formulation. The objectives of social administration must embody components, established by evaluation, with which it is impossible to dispense.

Barbara Wootton's *Social Science and Social Pathology*[17] may be regarded as representing a watershed in this argument. Whilst the conclusion of her book appears to demonstrate that she is on the side of the positivist social scientist, in the body of her text she shows that her awareness of realities runs too deeply in her mind to allow herself to identify with them as one of their allies. But she also shows that fact and value are confused in everyday life; she wishes to separate them, and she considers fact to be superior to value. The last words in her book are that science and values have amalgamated too easily and too freely; the doctor 'constitutes himself an authority not merely on health but also on morals', whilst 'current concepts of mental health and mental illness are heavily flavoured with "morals and ethics, religious fervour, personal investment, unvalidated psychological concepts", and are, in fact, largely composed of pure judgments of value'. This she utterly rejects:

> Such a confusion of medicine and morals, it could well be argued, does no service to science itself; for the success of scientific investigation always has depended, and always must depend, upon the complete exclusion of elements of value.

She continues the discussion by arguing that the struggle 'between the rival empires of medicine and morality seems to have become the contemporary equivalent of the nineteenth-century battle between scientific and religious explanations of cosmic events and terrestrial evolution'.

This she considers as regrettable as it is anachronistic. The final sentence in her book states

> the issues are akin, and the victory seems likely to go the same way. Psychiatrists since Freud have been busy doing for man's morals what Darwin and Huxley did for his pedigree, and with not much less success.[18]

This would seem at first sight to be plain enough. The argument is in favour, not of finding ways of justifying values, but of subordinating them to social requirements. The text itself must make us think that this is her aim. Barbara Wootton is in favour of re-focussing 'attention away from culpability and responsibility, and towards choice of treatment'. It is important to note, however, that she thinks that this 'in no way involves indifference to, or rejection of, moral considerations. . . . Choice itself must be conditioned by moral factors.' Science's 'morally neutral' task is to design

> the method of achieving a prescribed aim that is most likely to be effective; but whether this instrument be hydrogen bomb, hangman's noose, or analyst's couch, the demonstration of effectiveness is not, and cannot be, by itself a command to use.[19]

This is an indecisive end to an otherwise powerful argument. The conclusion is, therefore, that it is not the responsibility of the scientist to make the decision to use any given 'method of achieving a prescribed aim'. But somebody must do so, and it remains to discover whether the choice between methods can be made on reasonable and scientific lines, and how and by whom it can be made. It cannot be disputed that the decision as to whether an attempt should be made to attain a given end, and to use any specific means in the attempt, is as much one for social science as it is for social philosophy itself. Social functions of this kind are vitally important, and social science must take them into consideration. In this respect, the administration of the public social services is typical of all forms of public administration. These all embody ways of reasoning that are much wider than the experimental sciences. Government in its most basic form is directly concerned with questions of value, in so far as new understandings on objectives and methods have to be arrived at, and incorporated in policies, as well as in common social behaviour. These understandings represent, in fact, adaptations or extensions of the habits and cultures of individual societies, and are correspondingly hard to achieve. But the need to attempt something of the kind is overwhelming; the attempt has in fact been made on a multitude of occasions, and is evident in many public papers, most notably, perhaps, in the Atlantic Charter of 1941, the Universal Declaration of Human Rights of 1948, and the United Nations publication of 1950 entitled *These Rights and Freedoms*.

These declarations deal with social issues, racial and religious, and touch on the most intimate matters concerning everyday political behaviour. They also, of course, concern the widest questions such as the liberty of the subject and genocide, as well as their narrower aspects, such as social security measures.[20] They are fundamental to the existence of the polity of the world. Because their implications are far-reaching, they demand many fundamental changes, political, economic and social, in future social life. This leads us to conclude that all social reform must proceed on a basis that is equally wide. As Professor Donnison said, when commenting on Barbara Wootton's book,

> Social reform is a product, not merely of knowledge but of inventive thought and moral judgment. It demands a capacity for linking up known and unknown but hitherto unrelated facts . . . a capacity for inventing new social institutions . . . and a capacity for persuading, arguing and shaming people into accepting new aspirations and new concepts. . . .
>
> We must be clear about the relation between factual knowledge, and moral judgment and choice. I have said that choices cannot be derived from a knowledge of facts alone, but knowledge of the facts, and moral judgments are nevertheless related in two important ways. 'Facts' do not exist independently of human judgment. . . . Moreover, knowledge changes our attitude and hence our judgment and choices.[21]

This is unanswerable; the logic is impeccable. The only trouble hitherto, has been not that the problems arising out of positivism or scientism have left us in a dilemma, but the case for the incorporation of values in social science has been allowed to go by default. The literature of social work, in which the practical problems mentioned above have to be dealt with in one way or another, seems more or less invariably to avoid accepting the burden of responsibility, and to dispose of the situation that then arises under the heading of old-fashioned scientific determinism. This is entirely unreal, for social workers share to the full the worries of everybody in public life about the way one should respond to demands and opportunities. It is by no means sufficient for them to guide their actions only by getting to know what the consensus of opinion is on one issue or another. There are occasions on which they must lead rather than follow.

o

For all that, our dilemma, in so far as it is one, is simply solved. As Professor O'Doherty has put it:

> A society which rejects responsibility means totalitarianism: this is what value-free sociology leads to, for at least the person must be regarded as a value for which society is responsible, and not society as the value to which the person is instrumental. But irresponsible citizens mean anarchy. The two dimensions, the social and the personal, are as closely interlocked as time and space, as interdependent as freedom and restraint.[22]

There is no way back from that conclusion. There is only the one way forward to a better understanding of what the true meaning of social responsibility really is, and what it requires of us. This depends on the construction of a viable value system which establishes and defines valid purposes in terms of what should be done and what can be done, simultaneously. Sociology becomes a method of making a contribution to social life, regarded as a way of life lived by specific individuals. It is not a mere expedient which facilitates the abstract discovery of pre-existing truths. It does not pretend to be an encyclopaedia of what exists in the social world, for that is as impossible as it is undesirable. It is dynamic rather than static, forward- rather than backward-looking, creative rather than pre-determined. It is also in its essentials an exploration into the uncertainties of the future, rather than a firmly established and unadventurous account of the past, based on what has happened beyond recall. In the last analysis, as Professor Donnison has also said:

> If in time the student of Social Administration hammers out for himself some general system of social principles and priorities, that philosophy will not be his ultimate touchstone – the secure rock on which to build all his aims and aspirations. Rather it will be the provisional outcome of his exploration of the world in which he lives – an outcome liable to be modified for as long as he is capable of learning more.[23]

The conclusions of social science and the principles of social administration based on them must be formulated in an essentially tentative and provisional way; their very nature makes them always open to challenge, criticism, and improvement, even more so than those of any science. More than this, they are in our society the result of an elaborate process whereby opinions and experiences are sifted, and feelings of obligation, responsibility, and purpose are clarified. To this is added the results of administrative action, supplemented by researches, general and specific, carried out by social scientists. In total, this is a community activity; there is no specially qualified officer or official authority or agency entrusted with the formulation of policy. Professor Donnison and his colleagues have put the point beyond mistake:

> There is no cut-off point, in the administrative hierarchy, with people below it deliberating the facts, while people above exchange value judgments. There may indeed be levels of the hierarchy above which the decisions to be made become complex and important, each decision being unique and unrepeatable, and producing non-reversible results that take longer to appear. This is a useful distinction, sometimes employed to identify what are called 'policy decisions'. But the making of such decisions – or of any choice – calls for some understanding of the situation or context involved, *and* some selection of objectives; the two processes are part of the same experience.[24]

The formulation of public policy is therefore an exceedingly complicated process; it may be highly formal, as in the presentation of a Bill to Parliament, or be included in the intentions of the Government at large, as explained in a White Paper, or more generally in a Royal Commission's report. It may be less formal, as with conclusions based on a research scheme, for which a university department is responsible; it may verge on the quite informal, as with the publication of a book by a private author. One thing is plain throughout, which is that the field of social policy and administration is one in which values have come to occupy the important place which they demand and deserve. So far as social administration is concerned, intimately connected as it is with social policy, there has never been any sign that the subject should be 'value-free', as has so often been the case with sociology generally. In fact, Weber's own life has shown that, in matters of social policy, values must be given the most careful attention when programmes of action are being prepared and carried out. Any politician, civil servant, or local government officer would take this for granted, and recognise the importance of it.

Social policy, therefore, has always had incorporated in it its share of the burden of formulating social values, and carrying them into effect. The subject has grown over the generations; its foundations were laid in the nineteenth and early twentieth centuries in this country by such pioneers in administration as Sir John Simon, Sir Charles Trevelyan, and Sir Robert Morant, aided by more 'academically' inclined colleagues outside the civil service such as Charles Booth,

Seebohm Rowntree, and Sidney and Beatrice Webb. A book such as Lord Beveridge's early text, *Unemployment, A Problem of Industry*[25] is a classic of its kind. Starting from the assumption that there was a growing 'sense of responsibility in regard to unemployment' it used the social and economic analysis of English industry by Booth and the Webbs to the full, in making proposals whereby this responsibility might be efficiently discharged. The book was one of the first social science texts on which the social services of the twentieth century have been built. It was by no means the last. It is an early example of the literature of social policy that shows the way in which the social sciences in general will have to develop and can be developed in the future.

The point need not be laboured. The subject of social science has steadily grown over the years, and has only begun to reach full fruition. It has suffered from a lack of intellectual stimulus arising, perhaps, from the insistence of many sociologists that it is 'unscientific' in so far as it deals with matters of judgment and policy which cannot be made the subject of incontrovertible proof. It is hoped that the present book will put matters in a different light. Social science, it claims, occupies a firm position in the scientific and philosophic world which it is impossible to shake. Its foundation rests on a conception of science itself which may be novel to some, but it is much more revolutionary to sociologists than to natural scientists.

The social scientist's logic does not depend on the validity of the now old-fashioned concepts of Newtonian physics about permanent, continually operating, and unalterable forces. He accepts the conclusion that these concepts may be as valid as they ever were in the world of the stars and the tides, of astro-physics and navigation. Even so, the social scientist recognises that modifications have to be made in them, and more than this, that new worlds have now come to be recognised by the scientist, in which they have been superseded or abandoned outright. May not one of these new worlds be that of man's social behaviour, in which account has to be taken of purpose and planning as a form of conceptual thinking?

It is this that is a large part of the content of the social scientist's own world; a world that is permanently in process of creation and modification. It incorporates man's social relationships and the purposes which give them meaning, and occasion their existence. This certainly does not mean that the social scientist's function is entirely one of speculation, or is devoted exclusively to the forging of new ideas. He has to keep his feet firmly on the gound, start from actualities and end with possibilities. It is his function to see what can be made of things as they are at any given moment, or may become. Nevertheless, if he cannot allow himself to live in a world of dreams, neither can he allow himself to go to the other extreme, to be bound by events, or be dominated entirely by the rigidities incorporated in social situations. In any event, the philosopher in these days hardly ever starts by building some abstract or insubstantial Utopia. Moreover, the social scientist rarely restricts himself to examining possibilities or establishing facts, or the relevant facts which determine possibilities. Both philosopher and social scientist value the collaboration of the other too highly, and should be only too ready to go more than half way to meeting him.

Actualities, however, precede speculation; conversely, it is the understanding of the dynamic force of values that is so often a necessary prerequisite to the understanding of social facts. An alternative way ahead may be for social philosopher and scientist to fuse their functions, as Hobhouse would have wanted, and find out whether it is possible to live according to new patterns, or to deal with the fundamental problems of social life in new ways. Values, changes in values, and facts and changing facts, cannot be kept logically separate. The sociologist may therefore legitimately and properly seek to discover how current adaptations or innovations in our values emerge from the actualities of our social life day by day. He may also concern himself with finding out how these can be made the occasion and the opportunity for opening up new and viable ways into the future by or on behalf of any of the societies of the modern world. This is only possible, however, if values are not regarded as being solely or even mainly the product of the structure or tradition of a specific society, and conditioned by it for that reason. Their vitality is part of the conscious process of living and understanding which is essentially individual, yet takes place in a social context. It is also essential to the understanding and control of every society, and the life lived in it. That is the reason why evaluation is so essential an element in social policy, and is the indispensable foundation of social purpose. The sociologist cannot be 'value-free', if he is to cast any light on social policies or social facts alike. On the contrary, it is in his ability to understand the actualities of the experiences of living that he is best able to justify his claim to contribute to scientific study.

Notes and Sources

Notes to the Preface

1. A. D. Lindsay, *Religion, Science, and Society in the Modern World*, Oxford University Press 1943, pp. 32–3, 40.

2. *Julius Caesar*, I sc. ii, 1.134.

3. *The Times*, 18 December, 1967. The argument is included in a leading article.

4. Ibid.

Notes to Chapter 1

1. John Macmurray, *Religion, Art, and Science*, Liverpool University Press 1961, pp. 11, 19.

2. C. P. Snow, *The Two Cultures: and A Second Look*, Cambridge University Press 1964, pp. 3–5.

3. Ibid., pp. 14, 17.

4. Op. cit., p. 32. To which it has been added by Professor Edward Vogt: 'If one severs the factual content of a phenomenon from the values it embodies, one also severs it from reality.' 'Ueber das Probleme der Objectivitat in der religionssoziologische Forschung' in *Probleme der Religionssoziologie*, Westdeutsche Verlag 1962, p. 215.

5. Snow, op. cit., pp. 13, 63.

6. Macmurray, op. cit., p. 11.

7. *Science and the Modern World*, Cambridge University Press, edition of 1953 (first edition 1926), pp. 20, 63–4.

8. *Where is Science Going?* George Allen and Unwin, 1933, p. 73. Dr J. Bronowski has also written at length on this subject, in the same vein. See *The Commonsense of Science*, Heinemann 1951, particularly Ch. VIII, 'Truth and Value', and *Science and Human Values*, Hutchinson 1961, pp. 8, 72–80.

9. C. P. Snow, *Recent Thoughts on the Two Cultures*, Birkbeck Foundation Oration 1961.

10. C. Wright Mills, *The Sociological Imagination*. New York: Oxford University Press 1959, p. 13.

11. Snow, op. cit., pp. 79–80.

12. Robert S. Lynd, *Knowledge for What?*, Princeton University Press 1940, pp. 6–8.

13. Op. cit., pp. 19, 21.

14. Foreword in *Max Weber on The Methodology of the Social Sciences*, translated and edited by Edward A. Shils and Henry A. Finch, The Free Press 1949, p. vi.

15. Professor T. B. Bottomore, *Sociology*, Allen & Unwin 1962, pp. 314 et seq.

16. Snow, op. cit., p. 32.

17. *The Methodology of the Social Sciences*, pp. 6, 49–50.

18. See, in particular, Chapters V and VI of W. I. Beveridge's *The Art of Scientific Investigation*, Heinemann 1950.

19. *The Faith of the Counsellors*, Constable 1965, p. 6.

20. Shils, loc. cit., p. viii.

21. *The Methodology of the Social Sciences*, ibid.; *The Present State of American Sociology*, The Free Press 1948, pp. 57, 63.

22. Ibid., p. 62, 64.

23. Ibid., p. 63.

24. Joan Woodward, *Industrial Organisation, Theory and Practice*, Oxford University Press 1965, p. 257.

25. *The Martyrdom of Man*, edition of 1886, p. 513. (First edition, Trubner 1872.)

26. See Professor M. Postan's essay, 'History in the Social Sciences,' in *The Social Sciences: Their Relation in Theory and in Teaching*, Le Play House Press 1936, pp. 66–7.

27. The significance of the new concepts, particularly quantum theory and relativity, are dealt with at length by Werner Heisenberg in his *Philosophic Problems of Nuclear Science*, Faber & Faber 1952, especially pp. 12–14, 22–4, and 116–18.

NOTES TO CHAPTER 2

1. Sociological empiricism has been said to mean, as a theory of scientific method and of knowledge generally, either (a) 'the doctrine that whilst theory is essential and desirable, it ultimately depends for its validity on observation and experiment', or (b) 'a doctrine which asserts or recommends the absence of theory altogether.' It is used in the first rather than in the second of these two senses in this book. In the context of morals, experience may be opposed to principles; 'empiricism then becomes the doctrine which insists that those principles are, or should be, ultimately based on experience, or be absent altogether.' (It will be seen that a definition of 'empirical sociology' is arrived at in Ch. 7 below.) E. A. Gellner, 'Empiricism' in *A Dictionary of the Social Sciences*, (ed.) Julius Gould & William A. Kolb, Tavistock Publications 1964, pp. 238–9.

2. See T. S. and M. B. Simey, *Charles Booth: Social Scientist*, Oxford University Press 1960, pp. 244–6; also T. S. Simey, *Principles of Social Administration*, Oxford University Press 1937, Ch. 2. The collection of significant information on which policies could be based is dealt with at some length by O. R. Macgregor in 'Social Research and Social Policy in the Nineteenth Century', *The British Journal of Sociology* 1957, pp. 146–57.

3. For a description of Booth's work, and an appraisal of its scientific significance and practical importance, see T. S. and M. B. Simey, *Charles Booth*, Oxford University Press 1960, especially Chapters 5 and 12.

4. B. Seebohm Rowntree, *Poverty: A Study of Town Life*, Macmillan 1901, p. 300. Rowntree's position was in many respects similar to Booth's in this regard. He shared T. H. Huxley's distaste for *a priori* reasoning, but 'something more than intellectual distaste or preference was involved. . . . Like Charles Booth he believed that feeling and thinking were the same process.' Rowntree, again like Booth, had had his conscience stirred in his early years by contact with those less fortunately placed than himself, in his case through adult school work. Asa Briggs, *Seebohm Rowntree*, Longmans 1961, p. 24.

5. Charles Booth, *The Labour and Life of the People of London*, third edition, Macmillan 1903.

6. Ibid., Final Volume, pp. 136, 160, 190, 193, 248.

7. Sidney and Beatrice Webb, *Methods of Social Study*, Longmans 1932, p. 105.

8. Ibid., pp. 211–14, 223–4.

8a. See, for instance, Spencer's treatment of institutional analysis in *The Study of Society*. 'To what extent does it happen . . . that the multiplying and elaborating of institutions, and the perfecting of arrangements for gaining immediate ends, raises impediments to the development of better institutions and to the future gaining of higher ends? Socially, as well as individually, organisation is indispensable to growth: beyond a certain point their cannot be further growth without further organization'. Edition of 1873, reprinted 1888, p. 65.

9. Sidney and Beatrice Webb, *Our Partnership*, p. 43. It is interesting to note that Beatrice thought that the *History* was, in effect, a continuation of her own studies into co-operation which she had included in *The Co-operative Movement in Great Britain*, published in 1891. One of her 'discoveries' had been that democracies of consumers had to be complemented by trade unions and professional societies. 'Hence, when Our Partnership was set up, our first job was to turn the searchlight of investigation upon the associations of producers, in their most obvious form of trade unionism.' Ibid., p. 149.

10. Beatrice Webb, *My Apprenticeship*, p. 270.

11. See T. S. Simey, 'The Contribution of Sidney and Beatrice Webb to Sociology', *The British Journal of Sociology* 1961, pp. 106–23, for an account of the Webbs' methodology, and its significance in the social sciences.

12. *Methods of Social Study*, p. 126.

13. Ibid., p. 16.

14. Ibid., p. 219.

15. *Our Partnership*, p. 56.

16. Ibid., pp. 17–18.

17. *My Apprenticeship*, p. 216.

18. *Methods of Social Study*, p. 241.

19. Ibid., pp. 241–8.

20. Ibid., pp. 255–9.

21. Simey and Simey, op. cit., pp. 249–53.

22. The concluding passage of Hume's *Inquiry Concerning Human Understanding*, new (Edinburgh) edition 1804.

23. Dorothy Emmet, *The Nature of Metaphyiscal Thinking*, Macmillan 1949, p. 70.

24. R. G. Collingwood, *An Autobiography*, Pelican Books 1939, p. 17.

25. Macmillan, first edition 1899.

26. L. T. Hobhouse, *Metaphysical Theory of the State*, Allen & Unwin 1918.

27. See the Dedication, pp. 5–7.

28. Ibid., p. 136.

29. Ibid., p. 14–16.

30. Bernard Bosanquet, *The Philosophical Theory of the State* (third edition 1920), p. 42.

31. Ibid., pp. 44–5, 48.

32. Ibid., vi–vii, 254–6, 258. So also is his treatment of social groups.

33. See, for instance, *Social Purpose* by H. J. W. Hetherington and J. H. Muirhead, Allen & Unwin 1918, particularly the chapter on Neighbourhood, pp. 168–9, 172.

34. L. T. Hobhouse, *The Rational Good*, Allen & Unwin 1921.

35. See below, Chapter 8.

36. L. T. Hobhouse, *Development and Purpose*, Macmillan 1913, p. xxix. (Hobhouse returned to the same theme in Chapter III of *Democracy and Reaction*.) This passage may be compared with similar passages in the works of modern philosophers discussing the element of reason in what may now be termed 'normative discourse'. See also Chapter 1 of *Elements of Social Justice*, 'Ethics and Social Philosophy'; 'Reason as distinguished from feeling is not the basis of our social action, but the system of feeling at the basis of our social action is reasonable.' Allen & Unwin 1922, pp. 23–4.

37. Morris Ginsberg, 'The Work of L. T. Hobhouse', in J. A. Hobson

and Morris Ginsberg *L. T. Hobhouse: His Life and Work*, Allen & Unwin 1931, p. 124.

38. Ibid., pp. 124–5.

39. Ibid., p. 125.

40. Morris Ginsberg, Introduction to L. T. Hobhouse, *Sociology and Philosophy*, Bell 1966, p. xxi.

41. *Sociology and Philosophy*, pp. 29–30.

42. See R. H. Tawney, *Equality* (the Halley Stewart Lectures 1929), Allen & Unwin, fourth edition 1952.

43. *Sociology and Philosophy*, p. xxiv.

44. This is discussed in Chapter 8, below.

45. *Sociology and Philosophy*, pp. 14, 17.

46. 'The fundamental defect of the metaphysical treatment of society has been that in analysing the actual constitution of society it has seemed at the same time to determine what is and to lay down what ought to be'. Ibid., pp. 29–30.

47. *Metaphysical Theory of the State*, p. 17.

48. Ibid., p. 174. This idea was worked out in detail in *The Material Culture and Social Institutions of the Simpler Peoples* (with G. C. Wheeler and M. Ginsberg). London Monographs on Sociology No. 3 1915.

49. Ginsberg, op. cit., p. 171.

50. See his *The Material Culture and Social Institutions of the Simpler Peoples*.

51. A. D. Lindsay, *Religion, Science, and Society*, Oxford University Press 1943, pp. 38, 40.

52. Ibid., p. 40.

53. Ibid., p. 41.

54. Ibid., p. 43.

55. An example of this is his essay on 'The Historical Evolution of Property', *Sociology and Philosophy*, Chapter 4.

56. Ibid., Chapter 12.

NOTES TO CHAPTER 3

1. The first sociology textbooks, Prof. Myrdal points out, 'were almost exclusively concerned with the Negro problem': Fitzburgh, *Sociology for the South* (1854), Hughes, *Treatise on Sociology* (1854); *Value in Social Theory*, Routledge & Kegan Paul 1958, p. 90.

2. Edward A. Shils, *The Present State of American Sociology*, The Free Press 1948, pp. 2, 6–11. 'At the same time', Prof. Shils adds, 'their investigations have provided a body of knowledge of one large-scale society, such as exists for no other society in history.'

3. Ibid., p. 50.

4. The influence of German sociology was also exerted, at a very much earlier period, through American sociologists (such as Talcott Parsons) who undertook doctoral studies at German universities.

5. William L. Kolb, 'Values, Positivism, and the Functional Theory of Religion', *Social Forces* 1953, pp. 305–6. 'Philosophical positivism had a much greater effect than cultural relativism in bringing theoretically sophisticated sociologists to accept the view that value-judgments have no basis of validity in reality and are simply expressions of personal and group preference.'

6. Op. cit., pp. 58, 62–4.

7. Robert S. Lynd, *Knowledge for What?*, Princetown University Press 1940.

8. Ibid., pp. 120–3, 181–3. This statement only partially supports the argument of this book. In addition, it will be suggested that, though no value should be allowed to 'bias' a researcher's analysis of the evidence with which he is concerned, it is frequently necessary to be able to express genuine sympathy with a person's values in order to be able to understand their full significance. But this does not mean accepting them as valid in one's own life. Neither does it mean using the value-concept as explanatory, and assessing the validity of values, as some would say, 'objectively'. See below.

9. Ibid., pp. 140–1. C. Wright Mills' *The Power Elite* may be regarded as a first approach to this problem. It was not, of course, an attempt to solve it, any more than Weber attempted to solve the problem of bureaucracy in his day and age. Oxford University Press, New York, 1959.

10. *Knowledge for What?*, pp. 191–2, 200.

11. Ibid., pp. 201, 250.

12. The Bureau of Municipal Research carried out typical work of this kind. (Information supplied by Prof. I. L. Horowitz, who has kindly allowed the author to make use of an unpublished manuscript. This information has also been relied on below.)

13. Harold D. Lasswell, *Psychopathology and Politics* (1930); *Politics: Who Gets What, When, How?* (1936); *The Analysis of Political Behaviour* (reprinting articles published up to 1943), Kegan Paul 1948.

14. Harold D. Lasswell, *The Analysis of Political Behaviour*, Kegan Paul 1948. Part I. How to Integrate Science, Morals and Politics, Ch. 1; The Developing Science of Democracy (written 1942), pp. 1, 12.

15. Ibid., p. 9.

16. Ibid., pp. 46, 151, 196–7, 263, 265.

17. Ibid. The methods that this argument advocated had a decidedly psychoanalytic flavour. 'The trained psychologist', he wrote, 'watches the subject like a hawk for clues . . . [substitutive reactions]; the possibility of removing his "hunches" from the realm of art into the era of dependable knowledge depends on the objectification of his observations, and upon the development

of specifically experimental methods'. Ibid., p. 229.

18. G. H. Sabine, *A History of Political Thought*, Harrap, third edition 1961, pp. v–vi.

19. *The Policy Sciences*. Edited by Daniel Lerner and Harold D. Lasswell, Stanford University Press 1951. The introduction to this work defines the 'policy sciences' as 'improved methods of human relations'. Ibid., p. ix.

20. Ibid., pp. 7, 10, 14–15.

21. Ibid., p. ix.

22. Ibid., pp. 299–301.

23. Ibid., p. 306.

24. Ibid., pp. 306–7.

25. C. Wright Mills, *The Sociological Imagination*, Oxford University Press, New York 1959. Ch. 2, 'Grand Theory' and Ch. 3, 'Abstracted Empiricism'. It is this latter type of approach which Professor Shils has spoken of as one of flagrantly 'crude empiricism', from which all evaluations have been excised; it is thus exposed to a dangerous tendency towards becoming a merely 'descriptive inventory'. *The Present State of American Sociology*, pp. 2, 64.

26. I. L. Horowitz, *The New Sociology*, Oxford University Press, New York. The keynote of this book, as expressed by Prof. Horowitz in the Preface and Introduction, is contained in the following quotations: 'Wright Mills' "spear" was to understand the world better, and perhaps, towards the end of his life, to connect knowledge and action in a new way. . . . There can be little doubt that the prevailing tendency in American sociology during the past two decades between 1940 and 1960 has put this discipline into a *cul de sac.*' Ibid., pp. xi, 3.

27. 'No problem can be adequately formulated unless the values involved and the apparent threat in them are stated. These values and their imperilment constitute the terms of the problem itself. The values that have been the thread of classic social analysis . . . are freedom and reason.' *The Sociological Imagination*, pp. 129–30.

28. Attacks on the reputation of Charles Booth as a 'fact gatherer' or as what Wright Mills would have called an 'abstracted empiricist', have been particularly severe. See Simey and Simey, op. cit., pp. 254–5.

29. I. L. Horowitz, 'Social Science and Public Policy', in I. L. Horowitz, (ed.) *The Rise and Fall of Project Camelot*, The M.I.T. Press, 1967, pp. 342–3.

30. Professor Horowitz makes a fundamental distinction between a 'welfare system' which operates in this sense, and a 'command system', in which the services of social scientists are directed, but their freedom is suppressed. He contrasts these with a laissez-faire system which has led in America to accommodating social science to government needs, by employing social scientists on contract to help to satisfy them. In the welfare system,

policy and social sciences interact, but without any sense of tension or contradiction; in the laissez-faire system there is a decline in social science autonomy, and tension comes to prevail within the social sciences as to the role of the social scientist in the forging of public policy. In the command system the social scientists' autonomy disappears altogether. See ibid., pp. 341–2.

31. As to the somewhat disturbing events which arose from the administration of 'Project Camelot' in Chile by the Special Operations Research Organisation sponsored by the U.S. Department of Defence, see I. L. Horowitz, 'The Life and Death of Project Camelot', in *Trans-Action*, 1965, pp. 3–7, 44–7. This project dealt with revolution and counter-insurgency; its critics appear to have every reason for supposing that it embodied the assumption that 'revolutionary movements are dangerous to the interests of the United States, [which] must be prepared to assist, if not actually to participate in, measures to repress them'.

Criticism, particularly that based on the existence of repressive governments in Latin America, and the justification for opposing rather than aiding governments such as these, led to the abrupt ending of this project. In view of the opposition the project provoked locally, President Johnson finally stipulated that 'no government sponsorship of foreign area research should be undertaken which, in the judgment of the Secretary of State, would adversely affect United States relations'. See also *The Rise and Fall of Project Camelot*, op. cit., pp. 16–17.

32. Ibid., pp. 356–7. Professor Horowitz also adds that the involvement of the social sciences in the United States with the affairs of government 'policy organs' has 'made possible the corruption of social science on a scale hitherto unimagined; what the social scientist finds himself doing is providing justifications for other people's policies'. See also *The Rise and Fall of Project Camelot*, p. 375, and *The Life and Death of Project Camelot*, supra. The policy-maker is being confronted with the fact that he is not so much an applied social scientist as a representative of the State Department or a representative of Health, Education, and Welfare. There has been a general belief that the social scientists concerned were being employed within the terms of a policy science, which has protected them from the charge of peddling other people's values, but it has at length been realised that science can in no sense shield one from the charge of irresponsibility in such circumstances; one must always act according to one's values, and abide by the consequences.

33. On the other hand, rather less than half thought that 'one of the basic purposes of sociology is to help individuals cope with life in a complex society', though this exceeded the proportion of those who positively disagreed with the statement. Alvin W. Gouldner and J. Timothy Sprehe, 'The Study of Man' in *Trans-Action*, May–June 1966, pp. 42–4.

34. Just over half disagreed.
35. P. H. Furfey, 'Sociological Science and the Problem of Values', in Llewellyn Gross (ed.), *Symposium on Sociological Theory*, Harper & Row 1959, pp. 522–3.

NOTES TO CHAPTER 4

1. Published in *Max Weber on the Methodology of the Social Sciences*, translated and edited by Edward A. Shils and Henry A. Finch, The Free Press, Glencoe 1949, pp. 49–112. Referred to below as *Methodology*. It has to be read with 'The Fundamental Concepts of Sociology', published as Chapter 1 of Part I of *Wirtschaft und Gesellschaft*, translated by A. R. Henderson and Talcott Parsons, William Hodge 1947, pp. 79–144. The translation of the term *Wertfreiheit* as 'ethical neutrality' was, as will be seen, most misleading.

2. 'When moral judgments are applied, although they are given intellectual expression and presented in reasoned form, they are emotionally conceived. The common statement "I know what is right" would be more accurately put "I say what I feel to be right".' Raymond Firth, *Elements of Social Organisation*, Watts 1951, pp. 198–205, 213.

3. As Lord Snow has reminded us in *The Two Cultures and A Second Look*, Cambridge University Press 1964.

4. Dwight Waldo, *Political Science in the United States of America*, Unesco 1956, pp. 35–6.

5. Quoted Waldo, op. cit., p. 32.

6. Irving Louis Horowitz (ed.), Oxford University Press, New York 1964. Especially relevant are Horowitz's Introduction, and the Chapters by Fred H. Blum, ('C. Wright Mills: Social Conscience and Social Values'), Alvin W. Gouldner ('Anti-Minotaur: The Myth of a Value-Free Sociology'), and Abraham Edel ('Social Science and Values: A Study in Interrelations').

7. Ibid., p. 9.

8. Ibid., p. 13.

9. *Methodology*, pp. 19, 52.

10. Ibid., p. 83. See also p. 52.

11. H. S. Hughes: *Consciousness and Society*, MacGibbon & Kee 1959, p. 302.

12. Fred H. Blum, 'Max Weber's Postulate of "Freedom" ', *The American Journal of Sociology* 1944–5.

13. *Methodology*, p. 11.

14. Ibid., p. 60.

15. He made a special endeavour to overcome this difficulty. The concepts of 'understanding', 'meaning', and 'purpose' are fundamental to Weber's sociological treatment of human problems, and the use of them by

him laid the foundations of his *verstehende Soziologie*. See also ibid., pp. 79–80, 84.

16. *Methodology*, pp. 6, 9. There can be no doubt that it is sometimes correct to translate *Freiheit* as 'neutrality'. The two ideas were closely linked in Weber's mind. He used the word *Neutralität*, for instance, when he discussed the significance of an investigation in the field of industrial sociology from the point of view of social policy; it was, he said approvingly, not the intention in this research to make moral judgments, or to establish the existence of 'practical problems', but rather to discover the ways in which the situations of the moment had arisen. *Gesammelte Aufsätze zur Soziologie und Sozialpolitik*, Mohr, Tübingen 1924, pp. 1, 3.

17. *American Journal of Sociology*, loc. cit., p. 51, and see also the next chapter as to the origins of the dispute about values. It should be added that the strength of Weber's own passions left him with only too clear an understanding of the need for curbing them, and thus making it possible to attain the 'objectivity' in his studies which they endangered. See J. P. Mayer: *Max Weber and German Politics*, Faber & Faber 1944, pp. 26–7.

18. *Methodology*, p. 50. It was therefore not the value judgment made by the social scientist in choosing a subject of study that was a matter of concern to Weber, so much as his attitude of mind towards the study itself. See E. Baumgarten: *Max Weber: Werk und Person*; J. C. B. Mohr, Tübingen 1964, pp. 594–5.

19. 'Max Weber distinguishes between science as being "*Wertfrei*" and "*Wertlos*". *Wertfrei* is defined as being free from prevailing passion and prejudice; free, that is, to create its own values. *Wertlos*, on the other hand, is applied to the falsely objective or "scientistic" approach to social problems.' Horowitz, op. cit., p. 289.

20. *Methodology*, pp. 54, 57. Cf. R. Bendix: *Max Weber: An Intellectual Portrait*, Heinemann 1960, Ch. III, 'Ideas as Causes and Consequences', pp. 64–9.

21. *Methodology*, pp. 9, 63. See also pp. 53–4.

22. Fred H. Blum: 'Max Weber: The Man of Politics, and the Man Dedicated to Objectivity and Rationality', *Ethics* 1959, pp. 3, 16, quoting Marianne Weber: *Max Weber, ein Lebensbild*, Tübingen 1926, pp. 139–40. 'This', wrote Marianne Weber, 'was why he was against the *Kulturkampf*.'

23. This was anathema to Weber, because it contained an ethical component, and he thought that the mixing of findings of fact or logical analysis with subjective and practical value judgments was 'an affair of the Devil'. *Gesammelte Aufsätze zur Soziologie und Sozialpolitik*, pp. 416–18.

24. 'We want, so far as we can, to reshape man's social relationships, not to make them more comfortable, but so that, under the compulsion of the

unavoidable struggle for existence, the best in men may be preserved.'
Quoted Marianne Weber, ibid., p. 159.

25. *Methodology*, p. 40.

26. Blum, *Ethics*, loc. cit., p. 15.

27. *Methodology*, pp. 81–2.

28. Ibid., pp. 11, 112.

29. 'Sociologists tend to be relatively homogeneous in their social philosophy.' Content analysis of a series of sociological papers has shown that
they contain 'value postulates,' and that these postulates tend to be consistent
with one another. P. H. Furfey, 'Sociological Science and the Problem of
Values' in Llewelyn Gross (ed.), *Symposium on Sociological Theory*, Row
Peterson & Co. 1959, p. 522.

30. 'We are concerned with . . . values. . . . It is the political task of the
social scientist . . . continually to translate personal troubles into public
issues.' C. Wright Mills: *The Sociological Imagination*, Oxford University
Press, New York 1959, pp. 186–7.

31. 'In German, *Verstehen* has come to be applied to the situation where
a subjective motivational or symbolic reference is involved, while *Begreifen*
is employed for the "external" grasp of uniformities, where no such addi-
tional evidence is available.' Talcott Parsons: *The Structure of Social Action*,
The Free Press, second edition 1949, p. 584.

32. Hughes, op. cit., p. 335. Hughes' verdict on the concept of *Verstehen*
was more positive. 'This procedure I personally have found . . . the murkiest
of the many dark corners in the labyrinth of German social-science method.'
Ibid., p. 187. See also Thelma Z. Lavine, 'Concepts, Constructs, and Theory
Formulation', in Maurice Natanson (ed.), *Philosophy of the Social Sciences:
a Reader*, Random House 1963, pp. 256–61, and Ernst Nagel, 'On the Method
of *Verstehen* as the Sole Method of Philosophy', ibid., pp. 262–5.

33. See *Methodology*, pp. 52–4.

34. So far as problems of conscience were concerned, Weber's conclusion
was that 'here we reach the frontiers of human reason, and we enter a totally
new world, where a quite different part of our mind pronounces judgment
about things, and everyone knows that its judgments, though not based on
reason, are as clear and as certain as any logical conclusion at which reason
may arrive'. On which Mayer comments: 'It appears that Weber is steeped
in Plato's philosophy, but like Plato, he fails to explain how the idea of the
Good as distinct from the idea of the True can be applied to a world which
has *moral* and rational structure at the same time. If our moral laws are fundamentally enigmatic, enigmatic from the point of view of reason, the moral
universe becomes anarchic.' Mayer, op. cit., p. 27.

35. Loc. cit., p. 8.

36. Talcott Parsons, *Essays in Sociological Theory, Pure and Applied*,

P

The Free Press 1949, p. 65. Hughes' final conclusions are pessimistic. 'All that was sure was that human beings held to ethical and cultural values whose origin and ultimate meaning were veiled in mystery, and that the investigation of those values was alone made possible by the pursuit of certain frankly arbitrary methods that *in practice* gave comprehensible results.' Op. cit., p. 310.

37. Max Weber, *Fundamental Concepts*, p. 80.

38. See Bendix, op. cit., pp. 85–90.

39. Mayer, op. cit., p. 43.

40. Ibid., p. 44. He was, it has been said, 'never able to free himself from the "blood and iron" pattern of political thinking'. Ibid., p. 91.

41. Although he opposed proposals made during World War I that Germany should attempt to annex more territories, he nevertheless advocated the building and garrisoning of fortresses in Belgium and Poland, the occupation of Luxemburg, and the fortification of Ostend! (Ibid., p. 5.)

42. H. M. Gerth and C. Wright Mills, *From Max Weber*, Kegan Paul 1947, p. 35.

43. Blum, quoting Weber, loc. cit., p. 13.

44. Tr., Professor Talcott Parsons, Allen & Unwin, first edition 1930, pp. 182–3.

45. Op. cit., p. 89.

46. Quoted Bendix, from Troeltsch, 'The Ideas of Natural Law and Humanity in World Politics', in *Max Weber, an Intellectual Portrait*, p. 31.

47. 'I contend that Weber's thesis necessarily leads to nihilism, or to the view that every preference, however evil, base, or insane has to be judged before the tribunal of reason to be as legitimate as any other preference.' Leo Strauss, 'Natural Right and the Distinction between Facts and Values', in Maurice Natanson, op. cit., p. 425.

48. W. G. Runciman, *Social Science and Political Theory*, Cambridge University Press 1963.

49. Cf. Leo Strauss' alternative explanation of what Weber really meant by the 'rejection of value judgments'. Loc. cit., pp. 443 et seq.

NOTES TO CHAPTER 5

1. Reference may be made to Sigmund Neumann's 'The Institutional and Intellectual Background of [Alfred] Weber's Work', in H. E. Barnes (ed.), *An Introduction to the History of Sociology*, The University of Chicago Press 1948, pp. 353–7.

2. J. P. Mayer, *Max Weber and German Politics*, Faber & Faber, 1944, pp. 25–6.

3. H. M. Gerth and C. Wright Mills, *From Max Weber*, p. 4.

4. In 1891. Eduard Baumgarten, *Max Weber, Werk und Person*, J. C. B.

Mohr 1964, p. 341. See also *From Max Weber*, p. 33. As to the unwillingness of Bismarck to tolerate independence of mind amongst those around him, see Marianne Weber, *Max Weber, ein Lebensbild*, Verlag Lambert Schneider 1950, p. 135. A brief account of Bismarck's absolutism is contained in Reinhard Bendix, *Max Weber, an Intellectual Portrait*, Heinemann 1960, pp. 452 et seq.

5. Baumgarten, pp. 358–9.

6. Marianne Weber, *Max Weber, ein Lebensbild*, Lambert Schneider, Tübingen 1926, pp. 106–7, 164 et seq. See also Mayer, op. cit., p. 19, and *From Max Weber*, p. 3. A complete psychoanalytical account could be written of Weber's personality, based on the conflicting influence of his father, who was a nationalist and 'patriarchal and domineering', and his mother, who was liberal-minded. Particularly strong tensions came to exist between father and son: 'one may certainly infer an inordinately strong Oedipus situation'. *From Max Weber*, pp. 28–9.

7. *From Max Weber*, p. 41.

8. Ibid., pp. 25, 37.

9. Marianne Weber, op. cit., p. 149.

10. The history of the Association is outlined in Dr Franz Boese's *Geschichte des Vereins für Sozialpolitik*, Duncker & Humblot 1939. Dr Boese was its secretary when it was dissolved by the Nazis in 1936.

11. See 'Capitalism and Rural Society in Germany', in *From Max Weber*, pp. 363 et seq. See also Reinhard Bendix, op. cit., pp. 13–23, 30–48.

12. Boese, op. cit., pp. 108, 113, 119, 133, 135.

13. Ibid., pp. 135–7.

14. Ibid., p. 145. Little use appears to have been made of it. Only Max Weber's Continuation has been published.

15. These views were supported by the criticisms that had been made at the Vienna meeting.

16. Ibid., pp. 147–8. The paper that Weber circulated amongst the members of the Association's committee is reprinted in Baumgarten, op. cit., pp. 102–39. It was revised and republished by Weber in *Logos*, 1917–18, pp. 40–88.

17. *Gesammelte Aufsätze zur Soziologie und Sozialpolitik*, Mohr 1924, pp. 394–9.

18. Ibid., pp. 399–406. These passages are freely translated as it is impossible to follow Weber's colloquial German literally.

19. Ibid., pp. 407–12.

20. Ibid., pp. 412–16. A lively translation of the Vienna speech is printed as Appendix I to J. P. Mayer, op. cit., pp. 95–9. The following abstract is based on the latter.

21. Mayer, op. cit., pp. 96–9.

22. Ibid., pp. 416–20. This translation gives a very free outline of Weber's remarks. Extracts from several speeches have sometimes been conflated in the subsequent paragraphs.

23. See Julius Gould and William A. Kolb, *A Dictionary of the Social Sciences*, Tavistock Publications 1964, titles 'Sociology', pp. 676–7, and 'Ideal-Type Analysis', pp. 311–12. As to the relations between the ideas developed to explain the significance of the past and the thoughts of a man 'passionately involved in the events of his day', see Reinhard Bendix, *Max Weber: an Intellectual Portrait*, Anchor Books 1960, 1962, p. 266.

24. For him, the freedom of the intellect was the highest good. See Marianne Weber, op. cit., pp. 139, 145.

25. *From Max Weber*, p. 39.

26. Ibid., p. 213. 'In the future development of industrial society Weber saw the danger that socialism might result, not in the liberation of man, but in his enslavement to an all-powerful bureaucracy.' T. B. Bottomore, *Sociology*, Allen & Unwin 1962, p. 140.

27. J. P. Mayer, op. cit., p. 27.

28. Weber's complex position begins to become clear 'when we ask, if science cannot be the basis of value judgments, what then is to be their basis? . . . Weber certainly did not hold that personal values should derive from the existent culture, or from ancient tradition, nor again from formal ethical systems which he felt to be empty and lifeless. Unless men were to become inhuman robots, life, he insisted, must be guided by consciously made decisions. If men were to have dignity, they must choose their own fate.' Alvin W. Gouldner, 'Anti-Minotaur, the Myth of a Value-Free Sociology', in I. L. Horowitz (ed.) *The New Sociology*, Oxford University Press, New York 1964, p. 214.

29. *Gutachten zur Werturteilsdiscussion*, reprinted in Baumgarten, op. cit., pp. 102, 139.

30. Weber uses the word *'sachlich'* which can also mean 'objective'.

31. *Logos*, 1917–18, pp. 40–88.

32. Baumgarten, op. cit., p. 388. There can be no doubt that his mind was, in the end, clearly made up on this issue, and that this lasted to the end of his life. Baumgarten cites 'Science as a Vocation' (originally contained in a speech given in 1918) to establish this (pp. 401–2). See *From Max Weber*, pp. 147–9. 'What man will take upon himself to "refute scientifically" the ethic of the Sermon on the Mount? For instance, the sentence "Resist no evil" is extremely unpractical. And yet, it is clear, in mundane perspective, this is an ethic of undignified conduct. . . . The individual has to decide which is God for him and which is the devil. . . .'

33. Mayer, op. cit., pp. 62–3, 65, 67, 72.

34. *From Max Weber*, p. 334.

35. *The Theory of Social and Economic Organisation*, tr. Henderson and Talcott Parsons, William Hodge 1947, pp. 385–7.

36. Weber's voluminous political writings, reproduced in *Gesammelte Politische Schriften*, J. C. Mohr, Tübingen, third edition 1958, leaves his reputation much as it stood before the war. Familiar themes appear again: the inhibiting of the growth of German political education and political will, the emotional power of a mass democracy, the problem of the growth of bureaucracy in the modern state, and his own inability to allow himself to be identified with any political party. Although he was aware of the ways in which the English constitution had developed, he simply could not believe that any constitutional expedients could be adopted to bring a bureaucracy under successful control, or to arm a representative democracy with effective authority equipping it with responsible parliamentary institutions. His last writings were much of a rehash of his pre-war ideas (though lacking in the same liberality of outlook and adventurous thinking) and he died a man without ideals or illusions. See 'The legacy of Bismarck', pp. 299–308, and 'The mastery of officials and leadership', pp. 308–38.

37. Wolfgang Mommsen, 'Max Weber's Political Sociology and his Philosophy of World History', *The International Journal of Social Science* 1965, pp. 37–8. The quotations from Weber's writings are from *Religionsoziologie*, Vol. I, p. 204, and *Politische Schriften*, p. 60. It is important to note that the latter quotation dates from 1906.

38. Mommsen, loc. cit., p. 41.

39. Ibid., p. 45.

NOTES TO CHAPTER 6

1. Karl Mannheim, *Ideology and Utopia*, Kegan Paul 1940 (first published in 1936). This book was mainly based on writings published in Germany in 1929 and 1931.

2. This survey gave rise to the publication of *An American Dilemma*, Gunnar Myrdal, with the assistance of Richard Steiner and Arnold Rose, Harper 1944.

3. Karl Mannheim, *Man and Society in an Age of Reconstruction*, first published in Holland in 1935; English edition, Kegan Paul 1940.

4. Op. cit., pp. 114, 193.

5. Ibid., pp. 194 n. 1, 222.

6. *Preface*, to *Ideology and Utopia*, pp. xxvi–xxviii.

7. Ibid., p. xviii.

8. *Ideology and Utopia.*, p. 173.

9. Professor Donald G. Macrae, *Ideology and Society*, Heinemann 1961, pp. 64–5.

10. Ibid., pp. xxi, xxvii–viii.

11. Ibid., pp. xxix, 271–2.

12. Karl Mannheim, *Diagnosis of our Time*, Kegan Paul 1943.

13. Ibid., pp. 16–17, 22.

14. Ibid., pp. 23–5.

15. Ibid., pp. 28–9.

16. See the popular discussion, *Killers of the Dream*, Lillian Smith, Crescent Press 1950.

17. Gunnar Myrdal, *The Political Element in the Development of Economic Theory*, Routledge & Kegan Paul 1953, p. 193. (Published in Germany, 1932. Mannheim 'took the initiative in arranging an English version of the book'. Ibid., p. viii.)

18. Republished as Chapter 10 of Gunnar Myrdal's *Value in Social Theory*, Routledge & Kegan Paul 1958, pp. 206–30.

19. *Value in Social Theory*, pp. 214–15, 227, 229–30. Myrdal gave strong emphasis in his writings to the importance of discovering accurately the nature of the attitudes on which values and behaviour were based. 'A technology of economics', he wrote, 'should not be built upon social attitudes. "Attitude" means the emotive disposition of an individual or group to respond in a certain way to actual or potential situations. . . . Fortunately, there are many people whose attitudes are not identical with their interests. . . . We cannot always believe what people tell us.' *The Political Element*, p. 200.

20. *The Political Element*, p. 21; *Value in Social Theory*, p. 228.

21. *The Political Element*, p. vii.

22. As to the use of value-laden terms in economic theory, see *The Political Element*, pp. 20–1; as to the tendency in general, see *Value in Social Theory*, pp. 135–6, 138–9, 150–2.

23. Gunnar Myrdal, *An American Dilemma*. 2v., Harper & Brothers 1944. The whole of Part Two of *Value in Social Theory* was composed of extracts from the report, containing most of the relevant sections dealing with theoretical issues of fact and value.

24. *Value in Social Theory*, pp. 62–4, 153–4, 164. The source of the above quotations is ultimately from *An American Dilemma*.

25. Ibid., pp. 157–8, 160.

26. Ibid., pp. 134, 153–5, 161, 164.

27. Ibid., pp. 128–31.

28. *The Political Element*, pp. vii–viii, *Value in Social Theory*, pp. 51–2.

29. Ibid., p. 262.

30. 'The psychologists who, some forty to fifty years ago, set out to measure intelligence actually assumed that there were considerable innate differences between social groups. And it was to their surprise that their research carried them to conclusions very different from their hypotheses, a development which I therefore consider to be one of the great triumphs of

scientific endeavour. . . . The important changes in race relations now slowly taking place in America are to a considerable extent the result of the sociologists' exposure of the stereotyped superstitions present about the Negro in the popular mind; it is becoming more and more difficult for people to preserve their defensive rationalisations without appearing uneducated, which they are reluctant to do.' *Value in Social Theory*, pp. 12–13, 17.

31. Ibid., pp. 59, 258.

32. Ibid., Ch. 10, 'Ends and Means in Political Economy'. pp. 229 seq. (Originally published in German, 1933.)

NOTES TO CHAPTER 7

1. 'A basic premise of this book is that democracy is not only or even primarily a means through which different groups can attain their ends or seek the good society; it is the good society itself in operation.' S. M. Lipset, *Political Man*, Heinemann 1960, p. 403.

2. Except, of course, in South Africa and Rhodesia, where special difficulties have arisen.

3. The attitude of missionaries has often differed from that of the upper classes generally.

4. As to the meaning of the concept of 'race', see Gunnar Myrdal, *An American Dilemma*, Vol. 1, pp. 113–17.

5. E. C. Hughes, 'Race Relations and the Sociological Imagination', *American Sociological Review* 1963, p. 879.

6. See The International African Institute, *Social Implications of Industrialization and Urbanization South of the Sahara*, Unesco 1956; also *African Elites*, International Social Science Bulletin 1956.

7. *South of the Sahara*, op. cit., pp. 14–16.

8. Ibid., p. 47.

9. Ibid., p. 46.

10. Ibid., p. 691.

11. Ibid., p. 447. Some authors have been entirely blind to underlying trends and tensions. 'After forty-two years of the Belgian régime', writes Professor Jan-Albert Goris, 'it may well be said that from the technical as well as the administrative standpoint, the efforts of the Belgians in the Congo . . . have been crowned with sensational and complete success.' 'Belgian Action in Congo', *The Annals of the American Academy of Political and Social Science*, July 1950, p. 127. On the other hand, P. Mercier has remarked on the 'types and degee of tension between the African modernist élites and the European groups. . . . The conflict is fundamental, yet a balance, however temporary and precarious, may be discerned, though it varies enormously in degree.' 'Evolution of Senegalese Elites', in *African Elites* 1956, loc. cit., p. 449.

12. United Nations Publication No. 3. This report was largely based on the work of social scientists.

13. Ibid., p. 169.

14. *African Elites*, p. 458. This work is mainly composed of papers written by academic scholars; it was published as late as 1956.

15. Ibid., p. 476.

16. Melvin Conant, *Race Issues on the World Scene*, University of Hawaii Press 1955, pp. 4, 141–2. The expression of these views as late as 1954 is surprising when they are seen in the context of the careful and comprehensive treatment of the problem of morals and values given in Gunnar Myrdal's classic study.

17. Author's personal observation and conclusion, as a member of this conference.

18. Godfrey and Monica Wilson, *The Analysis of Social Change*, Cambridge University Press 1954, p. 155.

19. Ibid., p. 16.

20. Kenneth Little, 'The African Elite in British West Africa', *Race Relations in World Perspective*, ed. Andrew W. Lind, University of Hawaii Press 1955, p. 277.

21. Max Gluckman, *Custom and Conflict in Africa*, Basil Blackwell 1955, p. 165.

22. Hilda Kuper, *The Uniform of Colour*, Witwatersrand University Press. The argument contained in this book is also implicit (sometimes explicit) in Leo Kuper's *An African Bourgeoisie*, Yale 1965. What characterises these books most strikingly is the degree of involvement of their authors in the lives of the people studied. See also the survey for which Andrée Michel was responsible. This 'constitutes at once the most broad-minded and the most systematic attempt to define the factors entering into discrimination, and the effects it produces in psychological and human terms. One of these effects is violent revolt.' Jacques Berque, 'The North of Africa', in 'Recent Research on Racial Relations', *International Social Science Journal*, Unesco 1961, p. 187 and n. 47, p. 195.

23. Ibid., pp. 29–36, 156.

24. *Race Relations Handbook*, Cambridge University Press 1949, chapters XXII and XXIII, especially p. 685.

25. Cmd. 9475.

26. Chaps. 25 and 33. 'Initiative to try and bridge the gap [between European and African ideas as to land use] is being increasingly taken, and its value is very far from insignificant. Marked appreciation of individual settlers who have given a lead in this matter was made evident to us in parts of Kenya and Tanganyika; and how strongly the attitudes of individual personalities matter in the whole challenge of modernising African customary

agriculture was brought home to us in a number of instances. . . .' Examples to the contrary are also given.

27. Anthony Richmond, *The Colour Problem*, Penguin Books, section on Race Relations, pp. 150 et seq.

28. *The Listener* 1965, pp. 766, 814–15.

29. See Professor E. E. Evans-Pritchard, *Social Anthropology*, Cohen & West 1951, pp. 115 et seq.

30. Ibid., pp. 113–14.

31. The Conference was 'conceived' and guided by Professors Polanyi, Aron, and Hook, and M. Nabokov. The proceedings at it are briefly described by Prof. Shils in 'The End of Ideology', *Encounter* 1955, pp. 52–8.

The term 'ideology' was used in a broader sense than Mannheim would have understood it, meaning an abstract idea about what is justifiable politically or socially, and the grounds on which such a judgment is made.

As to the connection between the Congress for Cultural Freedom and the American Government's Central Intelligence Agency, see 'The Encounter Affair', *The Observer*, 14th May 1967. The Congress was financed by the C.I.A. from 1950 onwards, and *Encounter* was grant-aided by the latter up to 1963, though this has not been generally known until quite recently.

It was stated in *The Observer* article that the C.I.A. 'may have been intended as an instrument in the cold war', and *Encounter* was spoken of in it as a 'platform for cold warriors'. Social scientists thus became associated in the minds of many people with American policies when they took part in the activities of the C.I.A. in general, and the Milan Conference in particular; in so doing they identified themselves with an organisation that might be considered to be 'questionable'. Nevertheless, they often did so in good faith, in ignorance of the true facts and in the company of scholars of repute. Ultimately, the Ford Foundation assumed the responsibility for financing the C.I.A. For a long period, however, it was not generally known that the C.I.A.'s funds had come from the American Government, and much trouble arose when the fact became public knowledge.

The issues whether social scientists should participate in international affairs, and how they should do so, was much confused by these events; it became hard to establish their role in the troublesome conditions prevailing in the modern world, as their independent status as scientists had been so directly threatened.

32. Daniel Bell, *The End of Ideology: On the Exhaustion of Political Ideas*, The Free Press of Glencoe 1960. The following extract by no means does justice to the book as a whole, which contains a thoughtful discussion of values and the social sciences.

33. Op. cit., pp. 22, 371.

34. Ibid., pp. 372–3.

35. Ibid., p. 372.

36. For a suggested explanation, see Daniel Bell, op. cit., pp. 103, 116; also Myrdal, *Value in Social Theory*, Kegan Paul 1958, p. 67.

37. Shils, 'The End of Ideology', loc. cit. p. 52.

38. Ibid., p. 55.

39. Ibid., p. 54.

40. Ibid., p. 53.

41. One paper submitted to this Conference was 'remarkable for the fluent optimism with which [the author] looked on the economic future of India'. Ibid., p. 55.

42. Ibid., p. 55.

43. Ibid., p. 56.

44. Ibid., p. 57.

45. Mr A. D. Gorwala, stating an argument, apparently in reply to Mr Max Beloff's, leading to the conclusion that 'The time for gratefulness may be later, when foreign domination has ended, and the good that it did lives after it'. Ibid., p. 58.

46. It certainly led the Western delegates to accept ideology as a continuing fact in the underdeveloped countries: 'A few things are . . . very clear having recently freed ourselves from ideological radicalism, we must not be affronted to see it among our Asiatic and African friends who learned it in our own universities in the West; still ourselves penetrated by strong national identifications, we must not be repelled by the greater national sensitivities of the members of nations who have only recently become states. Condescension, resentment against resentment, insistence on gratitude will avail us nothing. It will only narrow our own minds. . . .' Ibid., p. 58.

47. S. M. Lipset, *Political Man*, Heinemann 1960.

48. Ibid., pp. 404–5.

49. Ibid., p. 416. 'Though passion and ideology are no longer needed in the affluent democracies of the West', Professor Lipset adds, 'they are very much needed in the less affluent countries of the world.'

50. Ibid., p. 417.

51. Stephen W. Rousseas and James Farganis, 'American Politics and the End of Ideology'. Republished as Chapter 17 in *The New Sociology* in 1964.

52. Ibid., pp. 276, 289.

53. *The New Sociology*, p. 272. The author quoted was Andrew Hacker.

54. Quoted, Rousseas and Farganis, ibid., p. 273.

55. 'The important point is that freedom, in the philosophical sense, and a social commitment which transcends the *status quo*, are inter-related and interdependent . . . and if modern democracy is predicated on the end of

ideology, that is, on the end of commitment, then it negates itself and becomes the very denial of freedom.' Ibid., pp. 274–5.

56. 'Humanising the Future' in *The Listener*, 13 March 1967. Dr Visser 'T Hooft adds that 'man's right to live a responsible life must be defended against the manipulators who want to give him the illusion of happiness; man's right to spiritual freedom must be defended against the pressures of mass propaganda; man's right to live meaningfully and therefore to play an active role in society must be defended against the tyranny of a purely technological planning'.

Notes to Chapter 8

1. Kingsley Davis, *Human Society*, The Macmillan Company 1948 and 1949, p. 13.

2. W. H. Werkmeister, 'Theory Construction and the Problem of Objectivity', in Llewellyn Gross (ed.), *Symposium on Sociological Theory*, Harper & Row 1959. p. 449.

3. Mr W. G. Runciman puts the argument the other way round in his *Social Science and Political Theory*, Cambridge University Press 1963, p. 11.

4. The argument of Emile Durkheim in *The Rules of Sociological Method* concerning 'What is a Social Fact?' may be borne in mind here.

5. See T. S. Simey, *The Concept of Love in Child Care*, National Children's Home 1964, pp. 35–9.

6. Pitirim Sorokin, *Fads and Foibles in Modern Sociology*, Regnery Co., Chicago 1956, pp. 159–60.

7. Gordon Allport, *Personality*, edition of 1938, p. 444. The same idea is contained in Professor Peter Winch's *The Idea of a Social Science* when he argues that a sociologist of religion must have some religious feeling if he is to make sense of the religious movement he is studying, and understand the considerations which govern the lives of its participants. And so on, so far as the historian of art is concerned. Kegan Paul, fourth impression 1965, p. 88. The difference between an account of religious activities, written with understanding sympathy (not necessarily agreement) and one written from a positivistic point of view by a 'pure scientist', is too obvious to require comment.

8. For an example of this, see T. S. Simey, *Social Purpose and Social Science*, Liverpool University Press 1964. This deals with the social example of the Rathbone family, embodied in a tradition which has had much influence in the modern world; it is in the blending of thought and action, theory and practice, that it has been most important.

9. H. S. Hodges, *Wilhelm Dilthey*, Kegan Paul 1944, pp. 15–16. Dilthey's work has left a deep mark on philosophy and the social sciences, but it is unfortunate that the term 'understanding' is used here in the sense of being

aware of the contents of someone else's mind, particularly so far as the play of emotion in it is concerned, and the connections between another's thoughts and feelings. 'Understanding', on the contrary, may be a limited apprehension of how something came to be, and it may be both wide in Dilthey's sense, and narrow in the sense of, for instance, a strictly limited process of statistical discovery of the decline of a population through a raising of the average age of childbirth. Nevertheless, a bridge may be built in this way between science and the arts, and, conversely, between the social and other sciences in so far as Dilthey's 'understanding' (that is typical of the social sciences) may be closely associated with the narrower understanding of the others.

10. Robert Redfield, *The Little Community*, Chicago University Press 1955, p. 82. See also *Human Nature and the Study of Society*, 1962, p. 73.

11. A. D. Lindsay, *Religion, Science, and Society in the Modern World*, Oxford University Press 1943, pp. 43–5.

12. Max Planck, *Where is Science Going?*, Allen & Unwin 1933, pp. 150–1.

13. Professor Dorothy Emmet, 'Philosophy in an Age of Science', *Impulse*, No. 28, 1966, p. 10. This point of view has been commonly held by social scientists with leanings towards positivism. 'When moral judgments are applied, although they are given intellectual expression and presented in reasoned form, they are emotionally conceived. The common statement "I know what is right" would be more accurately put "I say what I feel to be right".' Raymond Firth, *Elements of Social Organization* 1951, pp. 198–205, 213. It is necessary to give detailed consideration to morals, therefore, because the positivist theory would imply that social behaviour is merely a matter of influence, whereas it will be argued that it is a much more complex matter than this. Moral behaviour, again, can be regarded as examples of all evaluative behaviour, such as aesthetic and religious, in so far as it is more than a collection of epiphenomena arising out of the operation of influences, including the psychological and the social.

14. Peter Worsley, *The Third World*, Weidenfeld & Nicolson 1964, pp. 273–4. The problem of choice has proved exceedingly difficult from both the philosophical and psychological (or scientific) points of view. Richard Taylor, in the preface to his *Action and Purpose* (Prentice Hall 1966), explains how he came to conclude that the teaching of 'men of undoubted philosophical genius' about 'the idea of a man's having it within his power to do various alternative things', was 'basically false'.

The psychologists deliberately refrained from saying 'anything whatever about things so elementary as . . . a voluntary act of choice' unless they could be 'twisted' to fit natural science models. Psychological works, on the other hand, which dealt with practical problems of motivation, 'far from pretending that the questions that interested me did not exist, simply took them all for granted'. The philosophical problems with which Mr Taylor dealt in his book were therefore 'essentially original', and his purpose 'has been positive' (p. viii).

15. Stephen Toulmin, *Reason in Ethics*, Cambridge University Press, edition of 1964, Chapters 2 and 3, pp. 20–1, 38–9.

16. Ibid., p. 45. Similarly, R. M. Hare (in *Freedom and Reason*, Clarendon Press 1963, p. 2) comes to the conclusion that 'The answering of moral questions is, or ought to be, a rational activity. . . . [We] do not think that [it] is a quite arbitrary business, like the choice of one postage stamp from the sheet rather than another. [It] should engage our rational powers to the limit of their capacity.' And he makes it plain in his *The Language of Morals* (Clarendon Press 1961) that 'to become morally adult' one has to learn how 'to make decisions of principle' in accordance with 'a standard' we have made our own. 'That', he adds, 'is what our present generation is so painfully trying to do' (p. 77).

17. Paul W. Taylor, *Normative Discourse*, Prentice-Hall 1961, pp. 155–6.

18. Alasdair Macintyre, 'A Mistake About Causality in Social Science', in Peter Laslett and W. G. Runciman, *Philosophy, Politics, and Society*, Blackwell 1964, p. 62. See also Bernard J. F. Lonergan, *Insight*, Longmans 1958, p. 215: 'The individual is intelligent, and so he cannot enjoy peace of mind unless he subsumes his own feelings and actions under the general rules that he regards as intelligent.'

19. Peter Winch, *The Idea of a Social Science*, Routledge & Kegan Paul, fourth impression.

20. Louch's gloss on *The Idea of a Social Science*, op. cit., p. 164.

21. A. R. Louch, *Explanation and Human Action*, Blackwell 1966, pp. 173, 175. See also pp. vii, 4, 235.

22. Peter Winch, 'Understanding a Primitive Society', *The American Philosophical Quarterly*, Vol. 1, No. 4, October 1964, pp. 307–24.

23. Loc cit., pp. 308, 315.

24. The present author observed the dramatic change in the Jamaican peasant's belief in the magical practices of Obeah and the balm yard, on which the peasant relied traditionally to be healed of sicknesses. This was quickly abandoned in favour of a modern hospital when it became available to Jamaican country people. Science then overcame magic in their lives. Prof. Evans-Pritchard explains why, but not Prof. Winch.

25. Op. cit., p. 180.

26. Maurice Merleau-Ponty, 'The Philosopher and Sociology', in Maurice Natanson (ed.), *Philosophy of the Social Sciences: A Reader*, Random House, New York 1963, pp. 499–500.

27. 'Properly human acts – the act of speech, of work, the act of clothing oneself, for example – have no significance in their own right. They **are**

understood in reference to the aims of life.' Maurice Merleau-Ponty, *The Structure of Behaviour*, Methuen 1965 (first published in France 1942), p. 163.

28. Loc. cit., pp. 491–2.

29. Ibid., p. 501. Author's italics.

30. Ibid., p. 505.

Notes to Chapter 9

1. 'There is a myth of scientific knowledge which expects that from the mere notation of facts there should arise not only a science of worldly things, but in addition the science of that science, a sociology of knowledge (itself understood in an empirical manner), a knowledge having to constitute a closed universe of facts, and inserting therein everything down to the ideas we invent to interpret them, and to get rid, so to speak, of ourselves.' Maurice Merleau-Ponty, 'The Philosopher and Science', in Maurice Natanson, *Philosophy of the Social Sciences: A Reader*, Random House 1963, p. 488.

2. See Chapter 5.

3. Paul Halmos, 'Social Science and Social Change', *Ethics* 1959, pp. 109–10.

4. Compare the very important argument of Professor Paul Halmos in *Towards a Measure of Man*, Routledge and Kegan Paul 1957, pp. 214–29. One of the points in this argument is that 'the sociologist is a kind of architect who should not be expected to provide blueprints according to the whims of customers. The architect is not going to pander to the caprice of his clients if it meant that the house built according to the client's specifications would collapse in a few years' time. If he is an honest member of his profession the architect would try to enforce the basic principles of his speciality or abandon the commission. The code of the sociologist is no less exacting. The ends or values of reformers and administrators are socially realised; this process of "socially realising values" has its own norms; these the sociologist cannot disown without committing himself to a moral and philosophical scepticism which is incompatible with his scrupulousness and scientific honesty' (p. 224).

5. Halmos, loc. cit., pp. 109, 111–13. Professor Halmos discusses the influence of Professor W. M. Williams' *The Sociology of an English Village*, on the community about which it was written.

6. Halmos, loc. cit., p. 107.

7. 'Social Scientists and Research Policy', in *The Policy Sciences*, Daniel Lerner and Harold D. Lasswell (ed.), Stanford Univ. Press 1951, pp. 300, 306. See also Chapter III.

8. *Report of the Committee on Social Studies* 1965. Cmnd. 2660, paras. 88–9.

9. R. K. Merton, *Social Theory and Social Structure*, Free Press 1949, p. 111. It is noteworthy that 75% of American sociologists believe that 'some of the most powerful theories in sociology have emerged from the study of social problems'. Gouldner and Sprehe, loc. cit., p. 43.

10. In general, see Furfey, loc. cit., pp. 526–7.

11. On the whole problem of the responsibilities which interviewers must accept, especially when they stimulate emotional 'warmth' between those whom they interview and themselves, see Edward Shils, 'Social Enquiry and the Autonomy of the Individual' in *The Human Meaning of the Social Sciences*, (ed.) David Lerner, Meridian Books 1959, pp. 123–6.

12. A. R. Louch, *Explanation and Human Action*, Blackwell 1966, p. 239.

13. Ibid., p. 9. The whole passage is preceded by an assertion that methodological codes are formulated, but nobody applies them. This has 'led some sociologists and psychologists to design their studies in accordance with some conception of proper form, and almost wholly without reference to the subject-matter; in consequence, the putative laws are often thinly disguised tautologies. It has sometimes led eager theorists to embrace symbols, without a ghost of an idea as to the range of the variables or the function of the constants. . . .'

14. These extracts are from two articles published in *The Observer* on 9 and 16 April 1967. The second, by Professor Sir Cyril Burt, was a commentary on the first, by Professor N. S. Sutherland.

15. Loc. cit. 'When', he adds, 'one goes into the detailed facts, what is most striking are not the resemblances between computers and brains, but the very palpable differences.' The principles according to which the brain operates are entirely different from those of the computer; for one thing it is 'endowed with those elusive properties that we sum up in the vague word "life". . . . The problems, the purposes and the scale of values which such a machine embodies are merely those of its manufacturer or programmer. Nor can it ever initiate or originate action of its own.'

15a. Quoted, Daniel Bell, op. cit., p. 242. See also articles by Daniel Bell and Nathan Glazer, 'Adjusting Men to Machines', *Commentary*, July 1946 and January 1947. The point at issue here was whether a problem should be accepted for examination without criticism by the social scientist. This is fundamental to industrial sociology, because the acceptance of 'problems' without criticism tends to identify the social scientist with the point of view of the employer for whom he works. This concerns the supposed dispute about the 'cow' sociology, which is thought to have the objective of making workers into 'contented cows', irrespective of their conditions at work, and to extract the greatest amount of effort possible out of them, for the lowest possible pay.

16. Chapter 8.

17. Barbara Wootton, *Social Science and Social Pathology*, Allen & Unwin 1959.

18. Op. cit., p. 339.

19. Ibid., pp. 253–4.

20. The Declaration of the U.K. Government has given them a certain legal authority in this country. See the 'Declarations . . . recognising the competence of the European Commission of Human Rights to receive individual petitions and recognising as compulsory the jurisdiction of the European Court of Human Rights', 1966. Cmnd. 2894.

21. D. V. Donnison, 'Reform and Therapy', in Paul Halmos (ed.), *Moral Issues in the Training of Teachers and Social Workers*, The Sociological Review Monograph No. 3, University of Keele 1960, pp. 43–53.

22. Professor E. F. O'Doherty, 'Men, Criminals and Responsibility', *The Irish Jurist* 1966 (Winter), University College, Dublin.

23. D. V. Donnison, *The Development of Social Administration, An Inaugural Lecture*, London School of Economics 1962, p. 32.

24. D. V. Donnison and others, *Social Policy and Administration*, George Allen & Unwin 1965, p. 256.

25. Sir William Beveridge, *Unemployment, A Problem of Industry*, Longmans 1908. This may be compared with his report on *Social Insurance and Allied Services* 1942, Cmnd. 6404 (the 'Beveridge Plan').

Bibliography

Allport, Gordon, *Personality*, Constable, London edition of 1938.

Barnes, H. E. (ed.), *An Introduction to the History of Sociology*, University Press of Chicago 1948.

Baumgarten, E., *Max Weber, Werk und Person*, J. C. B. Mohr, Tübingen 1964.

Bell, Daniel, *The End of Ideology: On the Exhaustion of Political Ideas*, The Free Press of Glencoe 1960.

Bell, Daniel and Glazer, Nathan, 'Adjusting Men to Machines', *Commentary* (New York) July 1964 and January 1947.

Bendix, R., *Max Weber: an Intellectual Portrait*, Heinemann, London 1960.

Bergue, Jacques, 'The North of Africa', in *Recent Research on Race Relations*, *International Social Science Bulletin*, Unesco, Paris 1961.

Beveridge, Sir William (Lord), *Unemployment, A Problem of Industry*, Longmans, London 1908.

Beveridge, Sir William (Lord), *Report on Social Insurance and Allied Services*, Cmnd. 6404.

Beveridge, W. I., *The Art of Scientific Investigation*, Heinemann, London 1950.

Blum, Fred H., 'Max Weber's Portrait of "Freedom"', *The American Journal of Sociology* (Chicago) 1944–5.

Blum, Fred H., 'Max Weber, The Man of Politics and The Man Dedicated to Objectivity and Rationality', *Ethics*, (Chicago) 1959.

Blum, Fred H., C. Wright Mills, Social Conscience and Social Values' in I. L. Horowitz (ed.), *The New Sociology*, Oxford University Press, New York 1964.

Boese, Franz, *Geschichte des Vereins für Sozialpolitik*, Duncker & Humblot Berlin 1939.

Booth, Charles, *Life and Labour of the People in London*, third edition, 17 vols., Macmillan, London 1901.

Bosanquet, Bernard, *Philosophical Theory of the State*, Macmillan, London 1899.

Bottomore, T. B., *Sociology*, Allen & Unwin, London 1962.

Briggs, Asa, *Seebohm Rowntree*, Longmans, London 1961.

Bronowski, J., *The Commonsense of Science*, Heinemann, London 1951.

Bronowski, J., *Science and Human Values*, Hutchinson, London 1961.

Burt, Sir Cyril, 'Who'd Want a Computer for a Sweetheart?', *The Observer* (London) 16 April 1967.

Collingwood, R. G., *An Autobiography*, Pelican Books, London 1939.

Conant, Melville, *Race Relations on the World Scene*, University of Hawaii Press 1955.

Davies, Kingsley, *Human Society*, The Macmillan Company, New York 1948 and 1949.

Donnison, D. V., 'Reform and Therapy', in Paul Halmos (ed.), *Moral Issues in the Training of Teachers and Social Workers*, The Sociological Review Monograph No. 3, University of Keele 1960.

Donnison, D. V., *The Development of Social Administration*, An Inaugural Lecture, London School of Economics 1962.

Donnison, D. V. and others, *Social Policy and Administration*, Allen & Unwin, London 1965.

East Africa Royal Commission, *Report*, Cmd. 9475, 1955.

Edel, Abraham, 'Social Science and Values', in I. L. Horowitz (ed.), *The New Sociology*, Oxford University Press, New York 1964.

Emmet, Dorothy, *The Nature of Metaphysical Thinking*, Macmillan, London 1942.

Emmet, Dorothy, 'Philosophy in an Age of Science', *Impulse* (London), No. 201, 1966.

Evans-Pritchard, E. E., *Social Anthropology*, Cohen & West, London 1951.

Firth, Raymond, *Elements of Social Organization*, Watts, London 1951.

Furfey, P. H., 'Sociological Science and a Problem of Values', in Timothy Gross, *Symposium on Sociological Theory*, Harper & Row, New York 1959.

Gellner, E. A., 'Empiricism' in *A Dictionary of the Social Sciences*, Julius Gould and William A. Kolb (ed.), Tavistock Publications, London 1964.

Gerth, H. M., and Mills, C. Wright, *From Max Weber*, Kegan Paul, London 1947.

Gluckman, Max, *Custom and Conflict in Africa*, Basil Blackwell, Oxford 1955.

Goris, J. A., 'Belgian Action in the Congo', *The Annals*, American Academy of Political and Social Science (Philadelphia) July 1950.

Gould, Julius, and Kolb, William A., *A Dictionary of the Social Sciences*, Tavistock Publications, London 1964.

Gouldner, Alvin G., 'Anti-Minotaur: The Myth of a Value-Free Sociology', in I. L. Horowitz (ed.), *The New Sociology*, Oxford University Press, New York 1964.

Gouldner, Alvin G., and Sprehe, Timothy, 'The Study of Man', *Trans-Action* (St. Louis) May–June 1966.

Halmos, Paul, *The Faith of the Counsellors*, Constable, London 1965.

Hare, R. M., *The Language of Morals*, Clarendon Press, Oxford 1961.

Hare, R. M., *Freedom and Reason*, Clarendon Press, Oxford 1963.

Heisenberg, Werner, *Philosophic Problems of Nuclear Science*, Faber & Faber, London 1952.

Hobhouse, L. T., *Development and Purpose*, Macmillan, London 1913.

Hobhouse, L. T., *Metaphysical Theory of the State*, Allen & Unwin, London 1918.

Hobhouse, L. T., *Sociology and Philosophy*, introduction by Morris Ginsberg, Bell, London 1964.

Hobson, J. A., and Ginsberg, Morris, *L. T. Hobhouse: His Life and Work*, Allen & Unwin, London 1931.

Hodges, H. S., *Wilhelm Dilthey*, Kegan Paul, London 1944.

Horowitz, I. L., *The Rise and Fall of Project Camelot*, M. I. T. Press, St. Louis 1967.

Horowitz, I. L. (ed.), *The New Sociology*, Oxford University Press, New York 1964.

Hughes, H. S., *Consciousness and Society*, MacGibbon & Kee, London 1959.

Hume, David, *Inquiry Concerning Human Understanding*, New (Edinburgh) Edition 1804.

International African Institute, *Social Implications of Industrialisation and Urbanization South of the Sahara*, Unesco 1956.

Kolb, William L., 'Values, Positivism, and the Functional Theory of Religion', *Social Forces* (Chapel Hill) Vol. 31, 1952–3.

Kuper, Hilda, *The Uniform of Colour*, Witwatersrand University Press, Johannesburg 1947.

Kuper, Leo, *An African Bourgeoisie*, Yale University Press, New Haven 1965.

Laslett, Peter, and Runciman, W. G. (ed.), *Philosophy, Politics, and Society*, Blackwell, Oxford 1964.

Lasswell, Harold D., *Psychopathology and Politics*, Kegan Paul, London 1930.

Lasswell, Harold D., *Politics: Who Gets What, When, How?*, Kegan Paul, London 1936.

Lasswell, Harold D., *The Analysis of Political Behaviour*, Kegan Paul, London 1948.

Lerner, David, and Lasswell, Harold D. (ed.), *The Policy Sciences*, Stanford University Press, Stanford 1951.

Lerner, David (ed.), *The Human Meaning of the Social Sciences*, Meridian Books, New York 1959.

Levine, Thelma Z., 'Concepts, Constructs and Theory Formation', in Maurice Natanson (ed.), *The Philosophy of the Social Sciences: A Reader*, Random House, New York 1963.

Lindsay, A. D. (Lord), *Religion, Science, and Society*, Oxford University Press, London 1943.

Lipset, S. M., *Political Man*, Heinemann, London 1960.

Little, Kenneth, 'The African Elite in British West Africa', in Andrew W. Lynd (ed.), *Race Relations in World Perspective*, Hawaii University Press 1955.

Lonergan, Bernard J. F., *Insight*, Longmans, London 1958.

Louch, A. R., *Explanation and Human Action*, Blackwell, Oxford 1966.

Lynd, Robert S., *Knowledge for What?*, Princeton University Press 1940.

Macgregor, O. R., 'Social Research and Social Policy', *The British Journal of Sociology* (London) 1957.

MacIntyre, Alasdair, 'A Mistake About Causation in the Social Sciences' in Peter Laslett and W. G. Runciman (ed.), *Philosophy, Politics, and Society*, Blackwell, Oxford 1964.

Macmurray, J., *Religion, Art, and Science*, Liverpool University Press 1961.

Macrae, Donald, *Ideology and Society*, Heinemann, London 1961.

Mannheim, Karl, *Ideology and Utopia*, Kegan Paul, London 1940.

Mannheim, Karl, *Man and Society in an Age of Reconstruction*, Kegan Paul, London 1940.

Mannheim, Karl, *Diagnosis of Our Time*, Kegan Paul, London, 1943.

Mayer, P., *Max Weber and German Politics*, Faber & Faber, London 1944.

Mercier, P., 'Evolution of Senegalese Elites', in *African Elites, International Social Science Bulletin*, Unesco, Paris, Vol. VIII, No. 3, 1956.

Merleau-Ponty, Maurice, 'The Philosopher and Sociology' in Maurice Natanson (ed.), *Philosophy and the Social Sciences: A Reader*, Random House, New York 1963.

Merleau-Ponty, Maurice, *The Structure of Behaviour*, Methuen, London 1965.

Merton, Robert K., *Social Theory and Social Structure*, The Free Press, Glencoe 1949.

Mills, C. Wright, *The Sociological Imagination*, Oxford University Press, New York 1959.

Mills, C. Wright, *The Power Elite*, Oxford University Press, New York 1959.

Mommsen, Wolfgang, 'Max Weber's Political Sociology and his Philosophy in World History', *International Journal of Social Science*, Unesco 1965.

Myrdal, Gunnar, *An American Dilemma*, 2 vols., Harper, New York 1944.

Myrdal, Gunnar, *The Political Element in the Development of Economic Theory*, Routledge and Kegan Paul, London 1953.

Myrdal, Gunnar, *Value in Social Theory*, Routledge & Kegan Paul, London 1958.

Nagel, Ernst, 'On the Method of *Verstehen* as the Sole Method of Philosophy' in Maurice Natanson (ed.), *Philosophy of the Social Sciences: A Reader*, Random House, New York 1963.

Natanson, Maurice (ed.), *Philosophy of the Social Sciences: A Reader*, Random House, New York 1963.

Neumann, Sigmund, 'Alfred Weber's Conception of Historiocultural Sociology', in H. E. Barnes (ed.), *An Introduction to the History of Sociology*, University Press of Chicago 1948.

O'Doherty, E. F., 'Men, Criminals, and Responsibility', *The Irish Jurist*, University College, Dublin 1966.

Parsons, Talcott, tr., Max Weber, *The Protestant Ethic and the Spirit of Capitalism*, Allen & Unwin, London 1930.

Parsons, Talcott, *The Structure of Social Action*, The Free Press, Glencoe 1949.

Parsons, Talcott, *Essays in Sociological Theory, Pure and Applied*, The Free Press, Glencoe 1949.

Perham, Margery, 'Thinking Aloud About Africa', *The Listener* (London) 1965.

Planck, Max, *Where is Science Going?*, Allen & Unwin, London 1933.

Postan, M., 'History and the Social Sciences', in *The Social Sciences: Their Relation in Theory and in Teaching*, Le Play House Press, London 1936.

Reade, W. Windwood, *The Martyrdom of Man*, Trubner, London 1872.

Redfield, Robert, *The Little Community*, Chicago University Press 1955.

Redfield, Robert, *Human Nature and the Study of Society*, *The Papers of Robert Redfield*, Vol. I, Chicago University Press 1962.

Richmond, Anthony, *The Colour Problem*, Penguin Books, London 1955.

Rousseas, Stephen W., and Farganis, James, 'American Politics and the End of Ideology', in I. L. Horowitz (ed.), *The End of Ideology*, Oxford University Press, New York 1964.

Rowntree, Seebohm, *Poverty, A Study of Town Life*, Macmillan, London 1901.

Runciman, W. G., *Social Science and Political Theory*, Cambridge University Press 1963.

Sabine, G. H., *A History of Political Thought*, Harrap, London, third edition 1961.

Shils, Edward A., *The Present State of American Sociology*, The Free Press, Glencoe 1948.

Shils, Edward, A., 'The End of Ideology', *Encounter* (London) 1955.

Shils, Edward A., 'Social Enquiry and the Autonomy of the Individual', in David Lerner (ed.), *The Human Meaning of the Social Sciences*, Meridian Books, New York 1959.

Shils, Edward A., and Finch, Henry A., *Max Weber on the Methodology of the Social Sciences*, The Free Press, Glencoe 1949.

Simey, T. S. (Lord), *Principles of Social Administration*, Oxford University Press, London 1937.

Simey, T. S. (Lord), *The Concept of Love in Child Care*, National Children's Home, London 1964.

Simey, T. S., and M. B., *Charles Booth, Social Scientist*, Oxford University Press, London 1960.

Smith, Lilian, *Killers of the Dream*, Cresset Press, London 1950.

Snow, Sir Charles P., (Lord), *The Two Cultures: and a Second Look*, Cambridge University Press, London 1964.

Snow, Sir Charles P. (Lord), *Recent Thoughts on the Two Cultures*, Rocbuck Foundation Oration, Birkbeck College, London 1961.

Social Studies, Committee on, *Report*, Cmd. 2660 (London) 1965.

Sorokin, Pitirim A., *Fads and Foibles in the Social Sciences*, Regnery & Co., Chicago 1956.

Strauss, Leo, 'Natural Rights and the Distinction Between Fact and Values', in Maurice Natanson (ed.), *The Philosophy of the Social Sciences: A Reader*, Random House, New York 1963.

Sutherland, N. S., 'Revolution by Computer', *The Observer* (London) April 1967.

Tawney, R. H., *Equality*, Allen & Unwin, London, fourth edition 1952.

Taylor, Paul W., *Normative Discourse*, Prentice Hall, Englewood Cliffs 1961.

Taylor, Richard, *Action and Purpose*, Prentice Hall, Englewood Cliffs 1966.

'T Hooft, Visser, 'Humanising the Future', *The Listener* (London) 13 March 1967.

Toulmin, Stephen, *Reason in Ethics*, Cambridge University Press 1964.

Unesco, *African Elites, The International Social Science Bulletin* (Paris), Vol. VIII, No. 3 1956.

United Nations, *Report on the World Social Situation*, Publication No. 3 1957.

Vogt, Edward, 'Ueber das Problem der Objectivitat in der Religionsforschung', *Probleme der Religionssociologie*, Westdeutscher Verlag, Opladen 1962.

Waldo, Dwight, *Political Science in the United States of America*, Unesco 1956.

Webb, Beatrice, *My Apprenticeship*, Longmans, London 1926.

Webb (Potter, Beatrice), *The Co-operative Movement in Great Britain*, Swan, Sonnenscheim & Co., London 1891.

Webb, Sidney and Beatrice, *The History of Trade Unionism*, Longmans, London 1894.

Webb, Sidney and Beatrice, *Methods of Social Study*, Longmans, London 1932.

Webb, Sidney and Beatrice, *Our Partnership*, Longmans, London 1948.

Weber, Marianne, *Max Weber, ein Lebensbild*, Mohr, Tübingen 1926.

Weber, Max, *Gesammelte Aufsätze zur Soziologie und Soßialpolitik*, Mohr, Tübingen 1924.

Weber, Max, *From Max Weber*, C. M. Gerth and C. Wright Mills, Kegan Paul, London 1947.

Weber, Max, *The Theory of Social and Economic Organization*, tr. A. R. Henderson and T. Parsons, William Hodge, Edinburgh 1947.

Weber, Max, *Max Weber on the Methodology of the Social Sciences*, Edward A. Shils and Henry A. French, The Free Press, Glencoe 1949.

Werkmeister, W. H., 'Theory Construction and the Problem of Objectivity' in Llewellyn Gross (ed.), *Symposium on Sociological Theory*, Harper & Row, New York 1959.

Whitehead, A. N., *Science and the Modern World*, Cambridge University Press 1926 (edition of 1953).

Wilson, Godfrey and Monica, *The Analysis of Social Change*, Cambridge University Press 1954.

Winch, Peter, *The Idea of a Social Science*, Kegan Paul, London, fourth impression 1965.

Winch, Peter, 'Understanding a Primitive Society', *The American Philosophical Quarterly* (Philadelphia), Vol. I. No. 4, October 1964.

Wirth, Louis, Preface to Karl Mannheim, *Men and Society in an Age of Reconstruction*, Kegan Paul, London 1940.

Woodward, Joan, *Industrial Organisation, Theory and Practice*, Oxford University Press, London 1965.

Wootton, Barbara (Lady), *Social Science and Social Pathology*, Allen & Unwin, London 1959.

Worsley, Peter, *The Third World*, Weidenfeld & Nicolson, London 1964.

Yates, Ivor, 'The Encounter Affair', *The Observer* (London) 14 May 1967.

Index

Future of, *1955*, 138–44, 183;
see also determinism
Freud, Sigmund, 56, 57, 194
Fuchs, Carl Joh., 95
Furfey, P. H., 68 *35*, 81 *29*, 180 *10*

Geddes, Patrick, 33, 39
Gellner, E. A., 25 *1*
Germany; Hitler's régime in, 32,
111–12; political theories in, 36,
37, 84, 107; sociological develop-
ments in, 70, 74, 86, 89–91, 103;
influence of, 52 *and 4*; *see also*
Association for Social Policy
Gerth & Mills, 84 *42*, 91 *3*
Ginsberg, Morris, 41 *37*, 42 *40*, 45
Gluckman, Max, 135 *21*
Goris, Jan-Albert, 134 *11*
Gorwala, A. D., 143 *45*
Gould & Kolb, 104 *23*
Gouldner, Alvin W., 71 *6*, 72,
105 *28*; & Sprehe, J. T., 66 *33*
government, vii, 1, 104, 187, 194–5,
197; and social scientists, 64
and 30; *see also* administration,
bureaucracy, policy *and* state
Green, T. H., 36–7, 161
group adjustment, 115–16, 119;
community values, 165, 190–2
Grünberg, Karl, 97
Gumplowicz, Ludwig, 90

Hacker, Andrew, 146 *53*
Halmos, Paul, 18, 177, 178 *5 6*
Hare, R. M., 164 *16*
Hegel, Georg W. F., 35, 37, 38,
41, 90, 161, 162
Heisenberg, Werner, 24 *27*
Henderson & Parsons, 69 *1*
Hetherington & Muirhead, 39 *33*
Heyworth committee, the, 180
Hitler, Adolf, 32, 46, 111

Hobhouse, L. T., 33, 34, 37–9,
40–9, 73, 171, 189, 199
Hodges, H. S., 158 *9*
Honolulu conference, *1954*, 134–5
Hooft, Visser 'T, 147–8
Hoover, President Herbert, 55
Hoover Institute Studies, 58
Horowitz, Irving Louis, xi, 55 *12*,
63 *26*, 64 *29 30*, 65–6 *and 32*,
71–2 *6*, 76 *19*
Hughes, Everett C., 132–3
Hughes, H. S., 75 *11*, 82 *32 36*
humanitarianism, 45, 67–8
Hume, David, 35, 38
Huxley, T. H., 26 *4*

idealism; in Britain, 38–40, 44–6,
49, 161, 162; Weber and, 74–5,
76–7, 83, 104–5, 161
ideologies, 113, 138 *31*; end of,
138–41, 143, 144–8, 191
India, 142 *41*; *see also* underdeveloped countries
individual, the; Booth and, 26;
Weber and, 84, 92; and the
group, 115, 119; individualism,
27
industrial system, the, 2–3, 8, 26,
70; employees, 97–8, 151, 189,
15A; management, 22, 84, 100,
192, 198; revolution, 1, 11, 25, 50
institutional analysis, 29 *and 8A*
intelligence, distribution of, 126 *30*,
187; of machines, 186; *see also*
brain *and* reason
interests, 22; interest-groups, 76;
see also pure *and* applied
sociology
International Society for the
Scientific Study of Race
Relations, 134–5
inter-subjectivity, 172–3, 192